WHAT MAKES A  BOOK UNIQUE!

Maran Illustrated™ Windows XP 101 Hot Tips is jam-packed with exciting new topics and features that allow you to unleash the power of Windows XP! Completely updated to cover all the latest features of Windows XP SP2, this guide is sure to boost your knowledge and make you work smarter, not harder, in Windows XP.

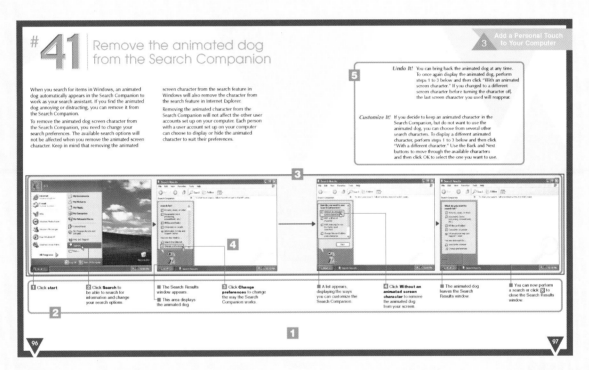

1 No page flipping! Topics are self-contained on two-page spreads.

2 Step-by-step instructions explain each topic using clear, easy-to-understand language.

3 Maran's Four Screens Across™ technology lets your eyes naturally follow the screens from left to right—just like traditional reading!

4 Maran's Red Line™ technology pinpoints the exact location to focus on in the screen.

5 Pump up your knowledge! Useful tips dig deeper into each topic.

Table of Contents

▼2 Maximize the Power of Your Files and Folders

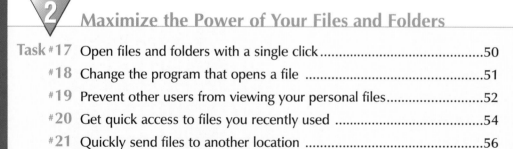

maran
illustrated™

Microsoft®
Windows® XP
101 HOT TIPS™

maranGraphics™

MARAN ILLUSTRATED™ Microsoft® Windows® XP 101 Hot Tips™

To purchase or find out more about maranGraphics' books, please contact:

maranGraphics Inc.
5755 Coopers Avenue
Mississauga, Ontario
L4Z 1R9

Phone: (905) 890-3300
       (800) 469-6616 (North America Only)
Fax: (905) 890-9434
E-mail: mail@maran.com
Web: www.maran.com

ISBN: 1-894182-27-8

Printed in Canada

10 9 8 7 6 5 4 3 2 1

Trademarks

Permissions

Google
Google Brand Features are trademarks of Google, Inc.

CBS SportsLine
Copyright © 2005 SportsLine USA, Inc.
http://www.sportsline.com All rights reserved.

Yahoo!
Reproduced with permission of Yahoo! Inc. 2005 by Yahoo! Inc. YAHOO! and the YAHOO! logo are trademarks of YAHOO! Inc.

Smithsonian Institution
www.si.edu
Copyright © 2005 Smithsonian Institution

Golf
www.golf.com
Copyright © 2005 golf.com LLC

Microsoft
© Microsoft Corporation. All rights reserved.

Other Permissions Granted:
Discovery Channel
Sunkist

Important

CREDITS

Authors:
Ruth Maran
Kelleigh Johnson

**Technical Consultant &
Post Production:**
Robert Maran

Project Manager:
Judy Maran

Editor:
Jill Maran Dutfield

Proofreader:
Jennifer March

Layout Artist & Screen Artist:
Richard Hung

Screen Artist:
Russ Marini

Indexer:
Kelleigh Johnson

ACKNOWLEDGEMENTS

Thanks to the dedicated staff of maranGraphics, including Richard Hung, Kelleigh Johnson, Wanda Lawrie, Jill Maran, Judy Maran, Robert Maran, Ruth Maran, Jennifer March, Russ Marini and Raquel Scott.

Finally, to Richard Maran who originated the easy-to-use graphic format of this guide. Thank you for your inspiration and guidance.

maranGraphics is a family-run business.

At **maranGraphics**, we believe in producing great computer books–one book at a time.

Each maranGraphics book uses the award-winning communication process that we have been developing over the last 30 years. Using this process, we organize screen shots and text in a way that makes it easy for you to learn new concepts and tasks.

We spend hours deciding the best way to perform each task, so you don't have to! Our clear, easy-to-follow screen shots and instructions walk you through each task from beginning to end.

We want to thank you for purchasing what we feel are the best books money can buy. We hope you enjoy using this book as much as we enjoyed creating it!

Sincerely,

The Maran Family

We would love to hear from you! Send your comments and feedback about our books to family@maran.com

To sign up for sneak peeks and news about our upcoming books, send an e-mail to newbooks@maran.com

Please visit us on the Web at:
www.maran.com

3 Add a Personal Touch to Your Computer

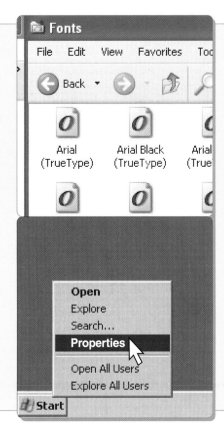

4 Boost Your Efficiency

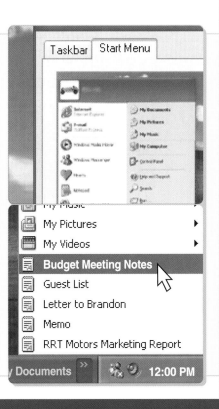

Table of Contents

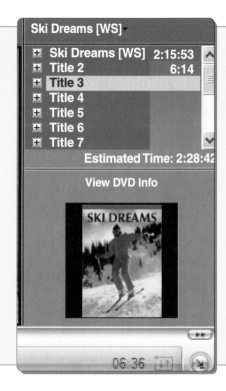

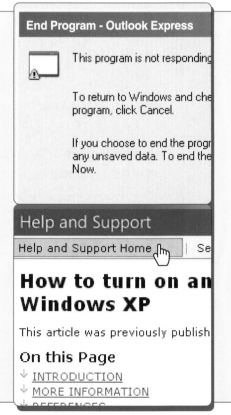

7 Smart Web Browsing

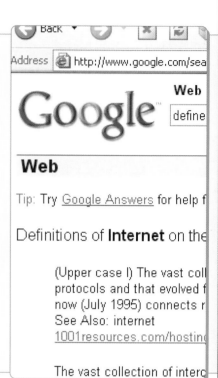

8 Tips and Tricks for E-mail, Instant Messages and Faxes

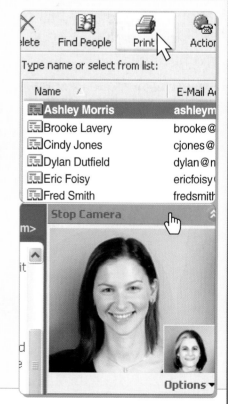

Unleash Your Computer's Potential

How often have you wondered if you are really getting the most out of your computer? After reviewing the tips and tricks for Windows XP that are discussed in this chapter, you'll be amazed at your computer's capabilities.

This chapter will introduce you to Windows XP Service Pack 2, including the top reasons why you should install it on your computer and how you can get it. You will learn how to use the new security features offered in Service Pack 2 to make sure your computer is secure and help keep your computer secure.

Read on to find out about all the ways that you can improve how you perform tasks and work with Windows XP. This chapter tells you how to set up your favorite programs to automatically start, make your computer more energy efficient and make your computer work while you play.

This chapter also shows you how to expand your desktop area by adding another monitor, as well as how to expand your horizons by setting up and connecting your computer to a wireless network.

If you are wondering how you can take advantage of Bluetooth wireless technology to reduce the cables and clutter on your desk, check out how to add a Bluetooth device in this chapter.

101 Hot Tips

#1 | What is Service Pack 2 for Windows XP?

Windows XP Service Pack 2 (SP2) is the newest update for Windows XP. About once a year, Microsoft provides a major update, called a Service Pack, for Windows XP. A Service Pack includes all the updates, corrections and tools that were made available during the previous year. The following list describes the top ten new features of Windows XP SP2.

1 Manage your computer's security settings

You can use the new Windows Security Center to view and manage the security settings that help protect your computer, all in one location.

2 Get Windows updates automatically

SP2 includes an enhanced version of the Automatic Updates feature, which makes it even easier to automatically install the latest important Windows updates for your computer from the Internet, free of charge.

3 Firewall protection

SP2 comes with firewall software that is turned on automatically. Firewall software helps protect your computer by preventing unauthorized people or unwanted programs, such as viruses, from accessing your computer through the Internet.

4 Check the status of your computer's antivirus software

SP2 regularly checks to see if your computer is using an antivirus program and whether the program is up to date. An antivirus program helps protect your computer against viruses and other security threats.

5 Reduce annoying pop-up windows

When you browse the Web, Internet Explorer blocks most pop-up windows from appearing. Pop-up windows are small windows that are often used to display advertisements.

6 Block Web content that could harm your computer

When you browse the Web, Internet Explorer prevents Web sites from downloading potentially harmful files and running software on your computer without your knowledge.

7 Reduce junk mail

With SP2, Outlook Express blocks pictures from displaying in e-mail messages. Pictures in junk mail can notify the sender that your e-mail address is valid, which can result in you receiving even more junk mail.

8 Avoid opening potentially harmful files

SP2 prevents you from opening potentially unsafe files you receive in e-mail and instant messages. Files attached to e-mail and instant messages can contain viruses that could harm your computer.

9 Set up and connect to a wireless network

SP2 helps you easily set up and connect to a wireless network at home, at the office or when traveling. A wireless network allows computers to share information on a network without cables.

10 Connect and use a Bluetooth device

SP2 allows you to easily connect and use the latest Bluetooth devices on your computer. Bluetooth wireless technology allows computers and devices, such as a mouse, keyboard, cell phone, printer or handheld device, to communicate without cables.

#2 How can I get Service Pack 2 for Windows XP?

Windows XP Service Pack 2 (SP2) is the newest update for Windows XP. If Windows XP SP2 is not already installed on your computer, you can download and install SP2 from the Microsoft Windows Update Web site.

If you have a slow connection to the Internet, such as a modem connection, downloading and installing SP2 may take a while. If you do not want to spend the time to download SP2, you can contact Microsoft to have them send you Service Pack 2 on a CD.

Before you download and install Service Pack 2, you should back up your important files and check your computer for spyware and other unwanted software that performs tasks on your computer, usually without your consent. You should also check your computer manufacturer's Web site to get the latest updates or instructions for your computer.

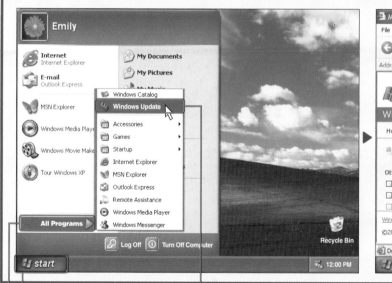
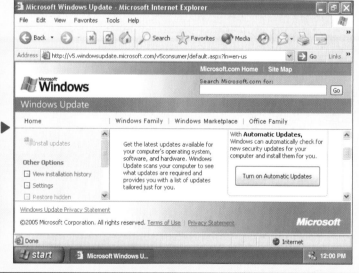

1 Click **start**.

2 Click **All Programs** to view a list of the programs on your computer.

3 Click **Windows Update** to obtain the latest updates for Windows XP.

■ The Microsoft Internet Explorer window appears, displaying the Microsoft Windows Update Web page.

4 Follow the instructions on the Web page to download and install the latest updates for your computer, including the updates for Service Pack 2.

Note: The Web page shown above may look different than the Web page shown on your computer screen. Web pages may change periodically to update and improve the pages.

#3 | Make sure your computer is secure

You can check the security settings that help protect your computer to make sure your computer is secure. You can check the status of the three most important security settings—Firewall, Automatic Updates and Virus Protection.

Windows comes with firewall software that is turned on automatically. The firewall software helps protect your computer by preventing unauthorized people or unwanted programs, such as viruses, from accessing your computer through the Internet or a network.

Windows is set up to automatically install the latest Windows updates from the Internet free of charge.

Windows regularly checks Microsoft's Web site for the latest important updates for your computer and downloads and installs the updates automatically.

Windows also checks to see if your computer is using an antivirus program and whether the program is up to date. A virus can cause a variety of problems, such as the appearance of annoying messages or the destruction of information. Windows does not come with an antivirus program and cannot detect some antivirus programs.

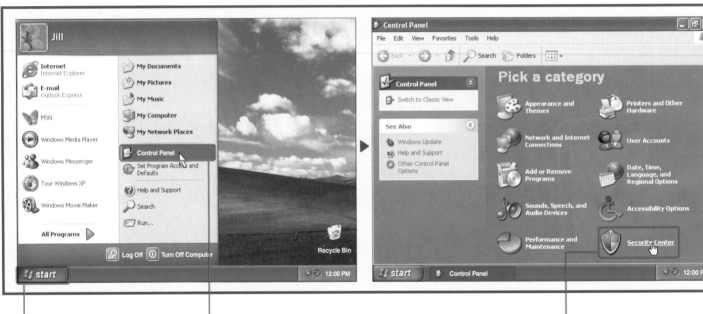

1 Click **start**.

2 Click **Control Panel** to view your computer's settings.

■ The Control Panel window appears.

3 Click **Security Center** to view and manage the security settings for your computer.

Alerts!   If Windows detects a problem with any of the three main security settings, including Firewall, Automatic Updates or Virus Protection, Windows displays an icon (🛡) in the taskbar and displays a message. You can click the icon to instantly display the Windows Security Center window to find information on how to fix the problem. If you do not want Windows to notify you of security problems, see task #5 to turn off the notifications.

Get an Antivirus Program!   To obtain an antivirus program, click the Virus Protection heading bar in the Windows Security Center window. Then click the Recommendations button that appears below the heading bar. In the Recommendation dialog box that appears, click How? to view a Microsoft Web page displaying a list of companies that offer antivirus programs. Select the company that provides the antivirus program you want to use and follow the instructions on your screen to install the program on your computer.

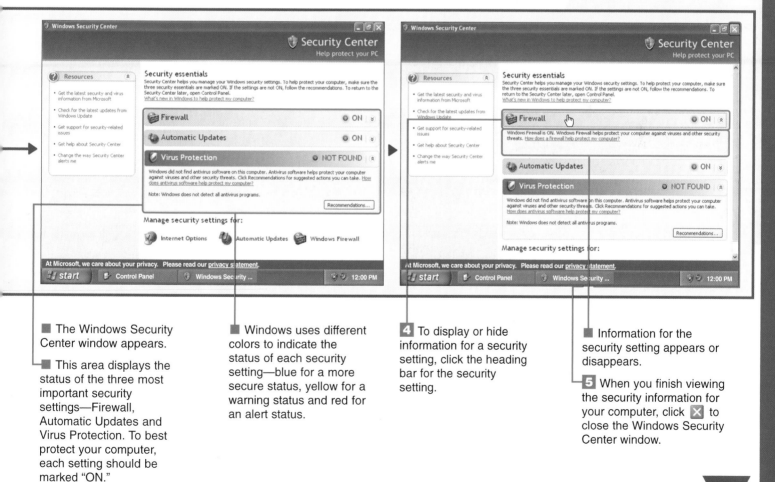

■ The Windows Security Center window appears.

■ This area displays the status of the three most important security settings—Firewall, Automatic Updates and Virus Protection. To best protect your computer, each setting should be marked "ON."

■ Windows uses different colors to indicate the status of each security setting—blue for a more secure status, yellow for a warning status and red for an alert status.

4 To display or hide information for a security setting, click the heading bar for the security setting.

■ Information for the security setting appears or disappears.

5 When you finish viewing the security information for your computer, click ☒ to close the Windows Security Center window.

Change when Windows installs important updates

The Automatic Updates feature is turned on automatically and is scheduled to download and install the latest important updates for your computer at 3:00 a.m. every night. You may want to set a more convenient time for installing the updates. For example, if you turn off your computer every night, you may want to set a time during the day when your computer will be turned on. You may also choose to update your computer once a week, such as every Sunday, rather than every day.

The Automatic Updates feature helps keep your computer safe by automatically installing the latest

important Windows updates from the Internet free of charge. Important updates can include critical updates and security updates to help protect your computer against viruses and other security threats.

On the day and time you specify, Windows will check Microsoft's Web site for the latest important updates for your computer and download and install the updates automatically.

You need an Internet connection for Windows to be able to update your computer automatically.

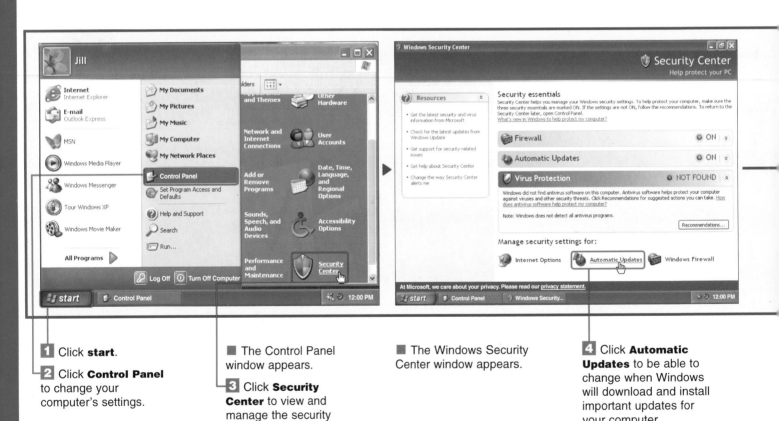

■ **1** Click **start**.

■ **2** Click **Control Panel** to change your computer's settings.

■ The Control Panel window appears.

■ **3** Click **Security Center** to view and manage the security settings for your computer.

■ The Windows Security Center window appears.

4 Click **Automatic Updates** to be able to change when Windows will download and install important updates for your computer.

Note: You may need to scroll down to view the Automatic Updates option.

See Installed Updates! To see a list of the updates that Windows has installed on your computer, click start, select All Programs and then click Windows Update. On the Microsoft Windows Update Web page that appears, click "View installation history" on the left side of the page to view a list of the updates installed on your computer.

Install Optional Updates! The Automatic Updates feature only installs high-priority updates that can help protect your computer. You can visit the Microsoft Windows Update Web page to immediately obtain high-priority updates as well as optional updates that can help improve the performance of your computer. Click start, select All Programs and then click Windows Update. On the Microsoft Windows Update Web page that appears, follow the instructions on your screen to install updates on your computer. You can return to the Web site on a regular basis to update your computer.

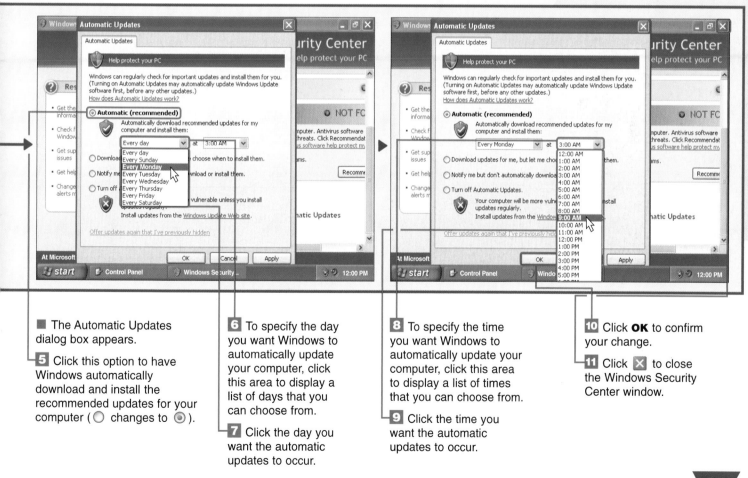

■ The Automatic Updates dialog box appears.

5 Click this option to have Windows automatically download and install the recommended updates for your computer (○ changes to ◉).

6 To specify the day you want Windows to automatically update your computer, click this area to display a list of days that you can choose from.

7 Click the day you want the automatic updates to occur.

8 To specify the time you want Windows to automatically update your computer, click this area to display a list of times that you can choose from.

9 Click the time you want the automatic updates to occur.

10 Click **OK** to confirm your change.

11 Click ☒ to close the Windows Security Center window.

#5 Stop Windows from notifying you of security problems

You can stop Windows from notifying you of security problems on your computer. Windows is set up to automatically notify you about potential problems that may put your computer at risk. For example, Windows will notify you if the firewall software included with Windows to prevent unauthorized access to your computer is turned off. Windows will also notify you if the Automatic Updates feature, which automatically installs the latest Windows updates on your computer, is turned off. If your computer is not using an

antivirus program, Windows will also notify you. You can have Windows stop notifying you of these types of problems.

If Windows detects a problem with any of the three main security settings, including Firewall, Automatic Updates or Virus Protection, Windows displays an icon (🛡) on the taskbar and displays a message on your screen. You can click the icon to instantly display the Windows Security Center window to find information on how to fix the problem.

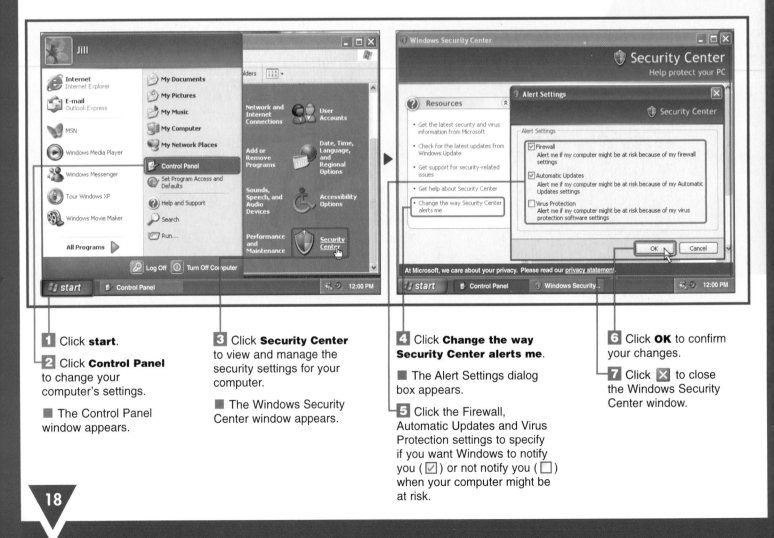

1 Click **start**.

2 Click **Control Panel** to change your computer's settings.

■ The Control Panel window appears.

3 Click **Security Center** to view and manage the security settings for your computer.

■ The Windows Security Center window appears.

4 Click **Change the way Security Center alerts me**.

■ The Alert Settings dialog box appears.

5 Click the Firewall, Automatic Updates and Virus Protection settings to specify if you want Windows to notify you (☑) or not notify you (☐) when your computer might be at risk.

6 Click **OK** to confirm your changes.

7 Click ✕ to close the Windows Security Center window.

#6 | Supercharge your computer with Microsoft PowerToys

You can add Microsoft PowerToys to your computer to enhance Windows. PowerToys are programs that help make Windows easier or more fun to use. You can obtain Microsoft PowerToys for Windows XP free of charge at www.microsoft.com/windowsxp/pro/downloads/powertoys.asp. You can download all or some of the PowerToy programs.

Only a user with a computer administrator account can install PowerToys on a computer.

ClearType Tuner

ClearType Tuner allows you to improve the readability of text on LCD (Liquid Crystal Display) screens, which are used on notebook computers and flat panel monitors. ClearType Tuner allows words on a computer screen to look almost as clear as text on a printed page. When you install ClearType Tuner, the PowerToy will appear as an item, under Appearance and Themes, in the Control Panel for easy access.

HTML Slide Show Wizard

You can use the HTML Slide Show Wizard to create a slide show of your pictures in HTML format. When you finish creating a slide show, you can place the slide show on the Web to share the pictures with your family and friends. When you install the HTML Slide Show Wizard, the PowerToy will appear on the Start menu.

Open Command Window Here

If you often use the Command Prompt window to type MS-DOS commands, you can use this PowerToy to easily access the Command Prompt window from any folder on your computer. When you right-click a folder on your computer, you will see the "Open Command Window Here" option on the menu that appears.

 #6 | Supercharge your computer with Microsoft PowerToys

Alt-Tab Replacement

The Alt-Tab Replacement PowerToy enhances the Windows feature that allows you to switch between programs running on your computer. When you hold down the Alt key and press the Tab key to switch between open windows, you will see an icon for each open window, as well as a preview of one window at a time.

Tweak UI

Tweak UI gives you access to computer settings that are unavailable or difficult to access in Windows, including settings that affect the mouse, Start menu and taskbar. When you install Tweak UI, the PowerToy will appear on the Start menu.

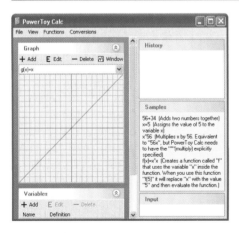

Power Calculator

Power Calculator provides features found on more powerful calculators. You can use Power Calculator to graph functions, convert units of measurement, display a history of your calculations and results, and more. When you install Power Calculator, the PowerToy will appear on the Start menu.

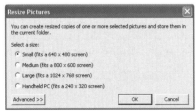

Image Resizer

Image Resizer allows you to quickly resize a picture based on the size of the screen that will display the picture. When you right-click a picture on your computer, you will see the "Resize Pictures" option on the menu that appears.

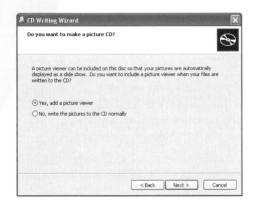

CD Slide Show Generator

When you burn pictures onto a blank CD, CD Slide Show Generator allows you to create a slide show of the pictures that will run automatically when the CD is inserted into a CD drive. When using the CD Writing Wizard to burn pictures onto a CD, select the "Yes, add a picture viewer" option to automatically display the pictures as a slide show.

Virtual Desktop Manager

Virtual Desktop Manager allows you to use up to four virtual desktops on your screen and run different programs on each desktop. To use the Virtual Desktop Manager, right-click the taskbar, click Toolbars and then click Desktop Manager.

Taskbar Magnifier

If you have difficulty seeing items on your screen, you can add Taskbar Magnifier to your computer. Taskbar Magnifier displays an enlarged picture of the area around the mouse pointer on the taskbar. To display Taskbar Magnifier, right-click the taskbar, click Toolbars and then click Taskbar Magnifier.

Webcam Timershot

Webcam Timershot allows you to set up a Webcam connected to your computer to take pictures at specific intervals and save the pictures on your computer. When you install Webcam Timershot, the PowerToy will appear on the Start menu.

Automatically launch your favorite program

If you use the same program every day, you can have the program start automatically each time you turn on your computer. Having a program start automatically is useful when you want to access the program immediately after your computer is turned on.

To have a program start automatically, you need to place a shortcut for the program in the Startup folder. A shortcut is a link to the program. The Start menu contains shortcuts for the programs on your computer. You can easily copy a program's shortcut from the Start menu to the Startup folder.

Each program in the Startup folder will start automatically each time you turn on your computer.

If the program you want to start automatically does not appear on the Start menu, you can find the program on your computer and then create a shortcut for the program. Once you locate the program on your computer, right-click the program's icon and choose Create Shortcut from the menu that appears. Then drag the shortcut you created to the Startup folder.

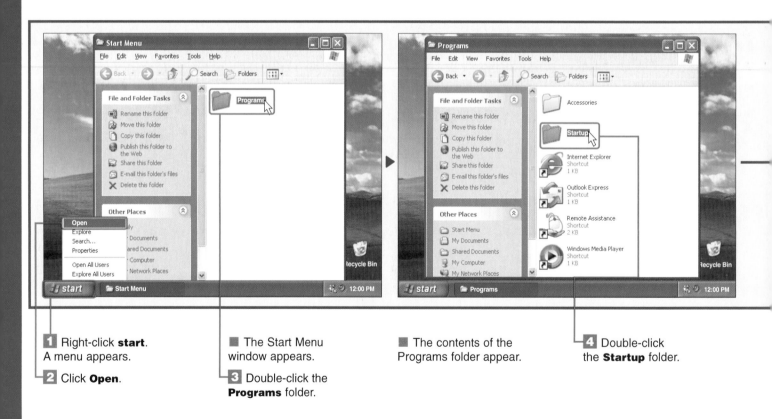

1 Right-click **start**. A menu appears.

2 Click **Open**.

■ The Start Menu window appears.

3 Double-click the **Programs** folder.

■ The contents of the Programs folder appear.

4 Double-click the **Startup** folder.

Stop It! To stop a program from starting automatically, you must remove the program's shortcut from the Startup folder. In the Startup folder, click the shortcut for the program you no longer want to start automatically and then press the Delete key. In the confirmation dialog box that appears, click Yes to delete the shortcut.

Customize It! You can have a button for a program appear minimized on the taskbar when the program starts automatically. In the Startup folder, right-click the shortcut for the program and then select Properties from the menu that appears. In the Properties dialog box, click the Shortcut tab, click the area beside Run and then choose the Minimized option. Then click OK.

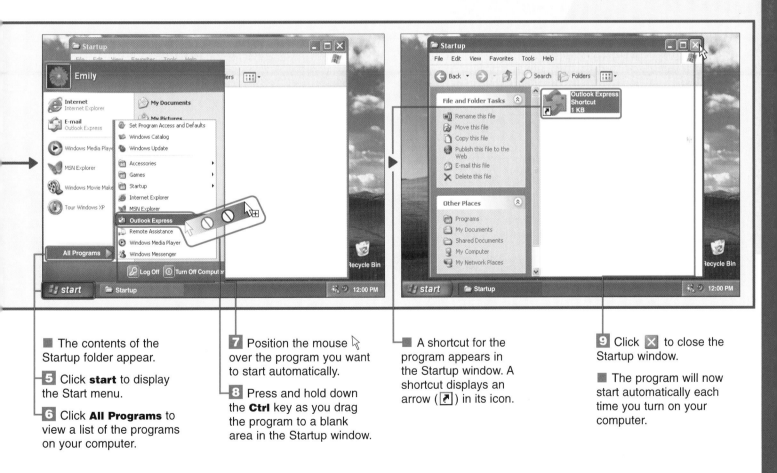

■ The contents of the Startup folder appear.

5 Click **start** to display the Start menu.

6 Click **All Programs** to view a list of the programs on your computer.

7 Position the mouse ⍾ over the program you want to start automatically.

8 Press and hold down the **Ctrl** key as you drag the program to a blank area in the Startup window.

■ A shortcut for the program appears in the Startup window. A shortcut displays an arrow (🡕) in its icon.

9 Click ☒ to close the Startup window.

■ The program will now start automatically each time you turn on your computer.

Make your computer more energy efficient

You can change the power settings on your computer to increase the battery life of your portable computer or reduce the energy consumption of your desktop computer. The available power settings depend on the hardware installed on your computer.

When changing power options, you can select a power scheme, which is a collection of settings that manage the power your computer uses.

Windows can conserve power by automatically turning off your monitor and hard disk when your computer is inactive for a specified time.

Windows can also place your computer on standby, which turns off items that use power when you do

not use the computer for a specified time. Since Windows does not save your documents before going on standby, you will lose unsaved work if a power outage occurs while your computer is on standby.

Many computers also support hibernation, which saves everything on your computer and then turns off the computer after a period of inactivity. When you bring your computer out of hibernation, any open programs and documents will appear as you left them on your computer.

You must be logged on to the computer as a computer administrator to change power options.

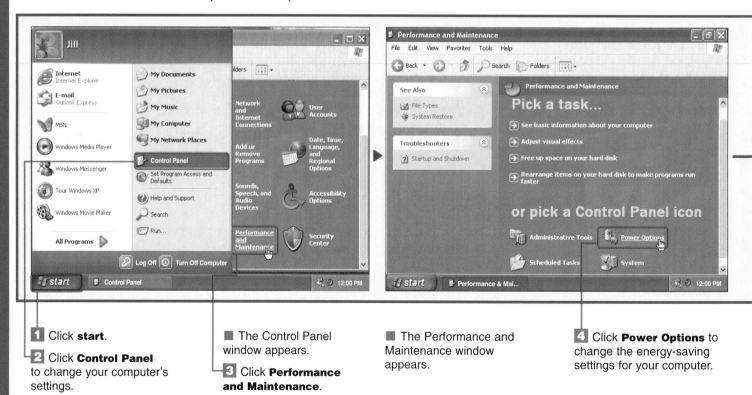

1 Click **start**.

2 Click **Control Panel** to change your computer's settings.

■ The Control Panel window appears.

3 Click **Performance and Maintenance**.

■ The Performance and Maintenance window appears.

4 Click **Power Options** to change the energy-saving settings for your computer.

Did You Know? You can immediately put your computer on standby or into hibernation. Click start and then select Turn Off Computer. To put the computer on standby, click Stand By. To put the computer into hibernation, press and hold down the Shift key until the Stand By option changes to Hibernate. Then click Hibernate.

Try This! You can specify what you want the computer to do when you press the power button. You can have the computer do nothing, ask what you want to do, go on standby, hibernate or shut down. In the Power Options Properties dialog box, click the Advanced tab. Then click the area below "When I press the power button on my computer" to select an option.

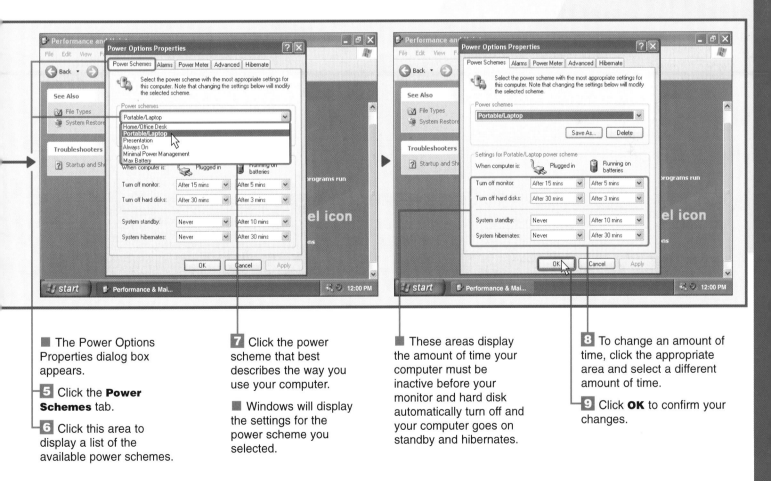

■ The Power Options Properties dialog box appears.

5 Click the **Power Schemes** tab.

6 Click this area to display a list of the available power schemes.

7 Click the power scheme that best describes the way you use your computer.

■ Windows will display the settings for the power scheme you selected.

■ These areas display the amount of time your computer must be inactive before your monitor and hard disk automatically turn off and your computer goes on standby and hibernates.

8 To change an amount of time, click the appropriate area and select a different amount of time.

9 Click **OK** to confirm your changes.

#9 Make your computer speak to you

If you have difficulty seeing the information displayed on your screen, you can have Narrator read aloud the items on the screen. To use Narrator, your computer must have sound capabilities.

Narrator will read aloud when you use Notepad, WordPad, Internet Explorer and items in the Control Panel or on the desktop. Narrator may not function properly with some programs and can speak only English.

You can customize Narrator to suit your needs. By default, Narrator will read aloud all the contents of active windows and dialog boxes. You can turn off this option to have Narrator only read aloud the items you select in windows, dialog boxes and menus.

Narrator can also read aloud each character you type, as well as any special keys you type, such as the Shift, Ctrl and Tab keys.

Narrator provides an option that automatically moves the mouse pointer to each item you select using the keyboard. This can help you select an option without having to move the mouse.

You can also have the Narrator window automatically open as a minimized button on the taskbar when you start Narrator.

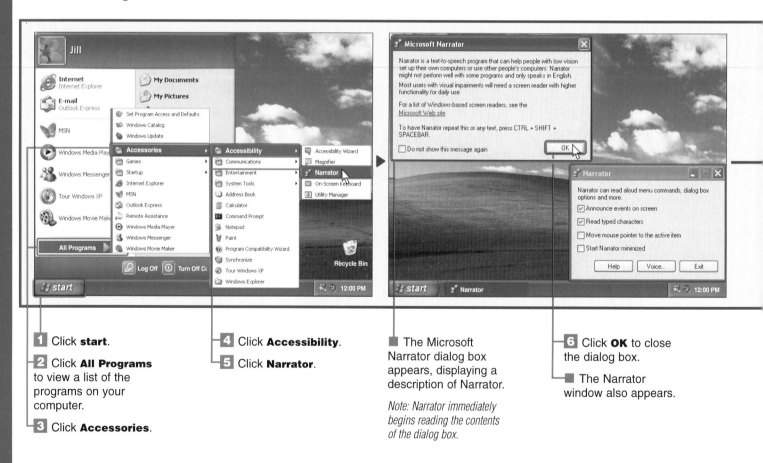

■1 Click **start**.

■2 Click **All Programs** to view a list of the programs on your computer.

■3 Click **Accessories**.

■4 Click **Accessibility**.

■5 Click **Narrator**.

■ The Microsoft Narrator dialog box appears, displaying a description of Narrator.

Note: Narrator immediately begins reading the contents of the dialog box.

■6 Click **OK** to close the dialog box.

■ The Narrator window also appears.

Use Keyboard Shortcuts! You can use keyboard shortcuts to control the information Narrator reads. To have Narrator repeat the contents of the active window or dialog box, press the Ctrl+Shift+Spacebar keys. To temporarily stop Narrator from speaking, press the Ctrl key.

Change It! To change the narrator's voice, click the Voice button in the Narrator window. The Voice Settings dialog box appears, allowing you to increase or decrease the speed, volume and pitch of the narrator's voice. Click ⌄ in the Speed, Volume or Pitch area to select a different setting. Click OK to confirm your changes.

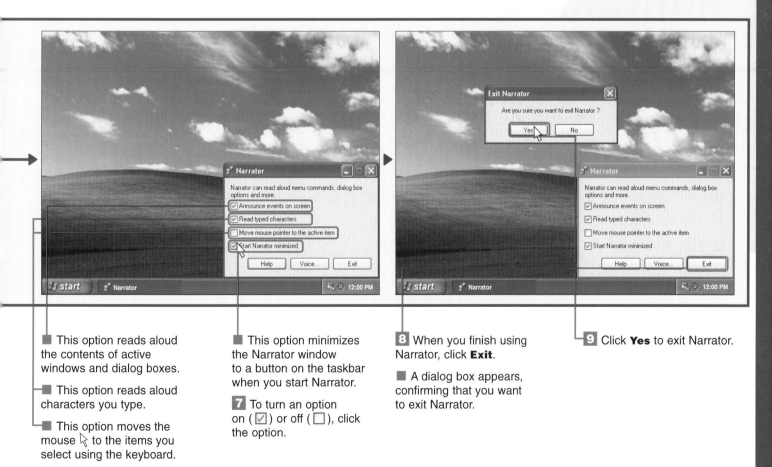

■ This option reads aloud the contents of active windows and dialog boxes.

■ This option reads aloud characters you type.

■ This option moves the mouse ⌖ to the items you select using the keyboard.

■ This option minimizes the Narrator window to a button on the taskbar when you start Narrator.

7 To turn an option on (☑) or off (☐), click the option.

8 When you finish using Narrator, click **Exit**.

■ A dialog box appears, confirming that you want to exit Narrator.

9 Click **Yes** to exit Narrator.

#10

Make your computer work while you play

You can schedule programs to run on your computer at times that are convenient for you. For example, you can set up your computer to perform time-consuming tasks, such as defragmenting the hard drive, while you are away from your computer.

The Scheduled Task wizard takes you step by step through the process of scheduling a new task. You can add any program on your computer to the list of programs that Scheduled Tasks will

start automatically. Scheduling a task is ideal for running computer maintenance programs, such as Disk Cleanup, on a regular basis.

Keep in mind that Scheduled Tasks uses the date and time set in your computer to determine when to run a scheduled program. You should make sure the date and time set in your computer are correct before you schedule a program.

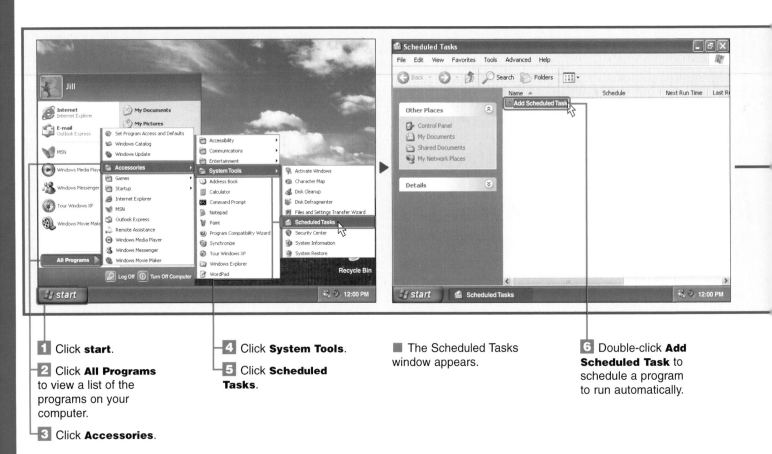

1 Click **start**.

2 Click **All Programs** to view a list of the programs on your computer.

3 Click **Accessories**.

4 Click **System Tools**.

5 Click **Scheduled Tasks**.

■ The Scheduled Tasks window appears.

6 Double-click **Add Scheduled Task** to schedule a program to run automatically.

28

Attention! Before scheduling a task to run automatically, you need to assign a password to your user account. To assign a password to your user account, click start, select Control Panel and choose User Accounts. Click your account, click the Create a password link and then follow the instructions on your screen to create the password.

Stop It! To stop Windows from running a program automatically, you must remove the program from the Scheduled Tasks window. Perform steps 1 to 5 below to display the Scheduled Tasks window. Click the program you no longer want to run automatically and then press the Delete key. In the confirmation dialog box that appears, click Yes to delete the program from the window.

CONTINUED ►

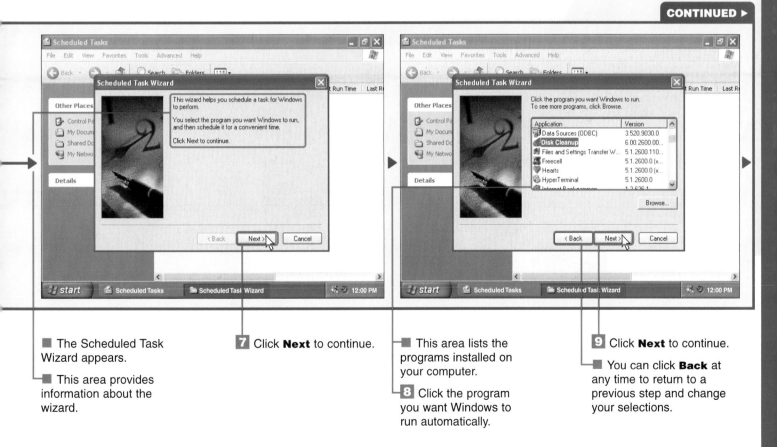

■ The Scheduled Task Wizard appears.

■ This area provides information about the wizard.

7 Click **Next** to continue.

■ This area lists the programs installed on your computer.

8 Click the program you want Windows to run automatically.

9 Click **Next** to continue.

■ You can click **Back** at any time to return to a previous step and change your selections.

You can specify the date and time you want Windows to run a program. You can select a daily, weekly or monthly schedule. Depending on the schedule you choose, additional options may be available. For example, if you select a weekly schedule, you can select which days of the week you want to run the program and at what time. You can also schedule a program to start only once, start each time you turn on the computer or start each time you log on to Windows.

Once you specify the date and time you want Windows to run a program, you should make sure the computer is turned on when you scheduled to run the task.

When scheduling a task, you will need to enter the password for your user account. You will need to enter your password twice to ensure you typed the password correctly. Entering your password helps ensure that the scheduled task will run properly.

After you set up a scheduled task, information about the task will appear in the Scheduled Tasks window. You can view information about a scheduled task in the window, such as when the task will run and the last time Windows ran the task.

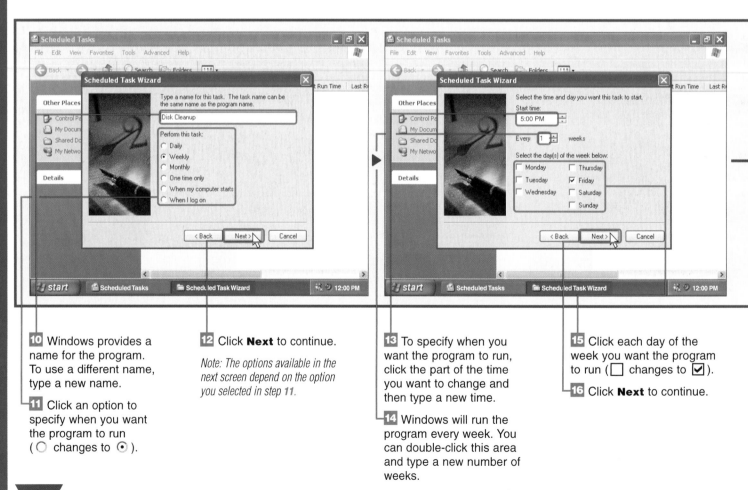

10 Windows provides a name for the program. To use a different name, type a new name.

11 Click an option to specify when you want the program to run (○ changes to ⊙).

12 Click **Next** to continue.

Note: The options available in the next screen depend on the option you selected in step 11.

13 To specify when you want the program to run, click the part of the time you want to change and then type a new time.

14 Windows will run the program every week. You can double-click this area and type a new number of weeks.

15 Click each day of the week you want the program to run (☐ changes to ☑).

16 Click **Next** to continue.

Did You Know? You can have Windows notify you of missed tasks. In the Scheduled Tasks window, select the Advanced menu and then click Notify Me of Missed Tasks. A check mark (✔) appears beside the option when the option is turned on. When a scheduled program is unable to run, a notification message will appear the next time Scheduled Tasks starts. For example, if your computer was turned off when a task was scheduled to run, Windows will notify you of the missed task the next time you turn on your computer. You must be logged on to the computer with a computer administrator account to be able to instruct Windows to notify you of missed tasks.

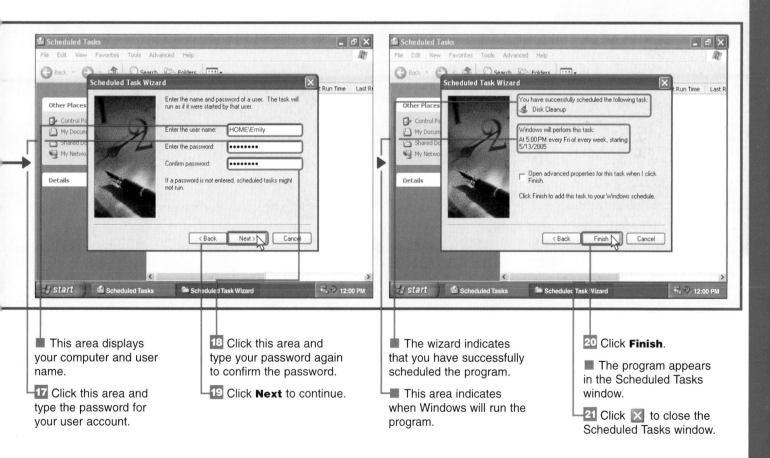

■ This area displays your computer and user name.

17 Click this area and type the password for your user account.

18 Click this area and type your password again to confirm the password.

19 Click **Next** to continue.

■ The wizard indicates that you have successfully scheduled the program.

■ This area indicates when Windows will run the program.

20 Click **Finish**.

■ The program appears in the Scheduled Tasks window.

21 Click ⊠ to close the Scheduled Tasks window.

Windows allows you to use more than one monitor to expand your desktop area. For example, graphic artists often use multiple monitors to display an image on one monitor and their software's tools on another monitor. You can also use multiple monitors to display several files at once or stretch a window across more than one monitor to view more of the window's contents without scrolling.

You can connect up to 10 separate monitors to your computer. When using multiple monitors, one monitor will be your primary monitor. The primary monitor

will display the taskbar and the Welcome screen that appears each time you start Windows. Most programs you open will also appear on the primary monitor.

You can change the arrangement of the monitor icons in the Display Properties dialog box to match the physical arrangement of your monitors. The position of the monitor icons determines how you will move items from one monitor to another.

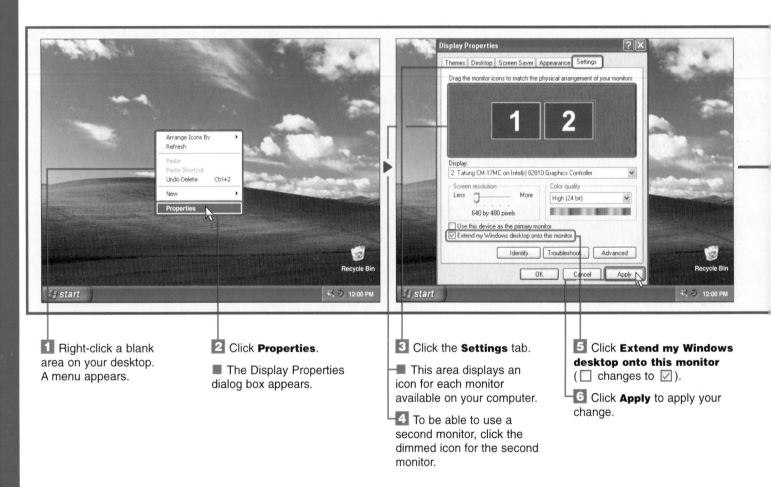

1 Right-click a blank area on your desktop. A menu appears.

2 Click **Properties**.

■ The Display Properties dialog box appears.

3 Click the **Settings** tab.

■ This area displays an icon for each monitor available on your computer.

4 To be able to use a second monitor, click the dimmed icon for the second monitor.

5 Click **Extend my Windows desktop onto this monitor** (☐ changes to ☑).

6 Click **Apply** to apply your change.

Add It!   To add a second monitor, you need to install a
video card for the second monitor. You can also
use a single video card that supports two monitors,
called a dual head video card. You can follow the
manufacturer's instructions to install a video card.
When you turn on your computer, Windows will
usually detect a new video card and automatically
install the appropriate software.

Check It Out!   You can easily determine which icon in the
Display Properties dialog box represents each
monitor. In the Display Properties dialog box,
click the Settings tab and select the Identify
button. Each monitor will display the number
of the icon that it corresponds to.

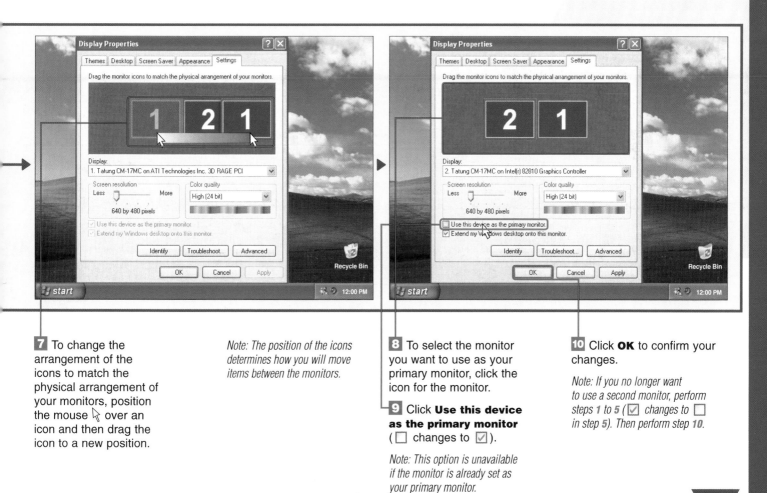

7 To change the
arrangement of the
icons to match the
physical arrangement of
your monitors, position
the mouse over an
icon and then drag the
icon to a new position.

*Note: The position of the icons
determines how you will move
items between the monitors.*

8 To select the monitor
you want to use as your
primary monitor, click the
icon for the monitor.

9 Click **Use this device
as the primary monitor**
(☐ changes to ☑).

*Note: This option is unavailable
if the monitor is already set as
your primary monitor.*

10 Click **OK** to confirm your
changes.

*Note: If you no longer want
to use a second monitor, perform
steps 1 to 5 (☑ changes to ☐
in step 5). Then perform step 10.*

Prevent other people from accessing your computer

You can increase the security of your computer by creating a password, called a startup key, to start your computer. You use the Syskey program to create the password that you will need to enter to start the computer. You must be logged on to Windows as a computer administrator to use the Syskey program.

Creating a password to start your computer makes it virtually impossible for an unauthorized user to log onto your computer. In addition, since the Welcome screen that prompts you to enter your Windows account password cannot be displayed without first entering the startup password, a hacker will not have the opportunity to try to determine your user account password.

After you create a startup password, a dialog box will appear when you start your computer, asking you to enter the password.

Passwords are case sensitive. When you enter your password, you will need to enter the characters in the password precisely. For example, if your password is abcdef123456, you cannot enter ABCDEF123456 to start your computer.

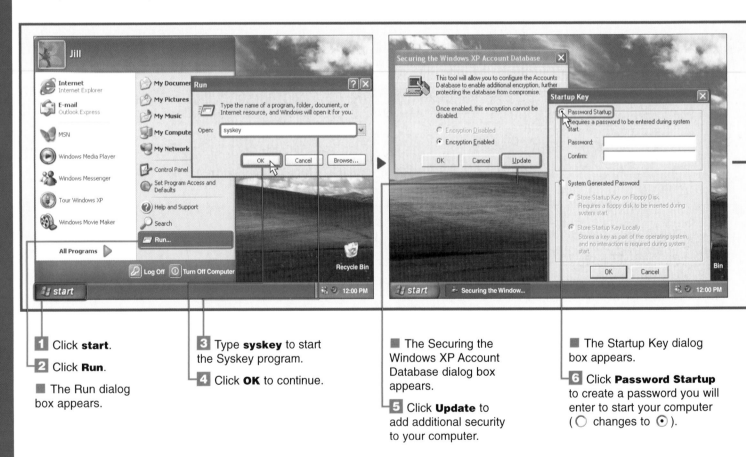

1 Click **start**.

2 Click **Run**.

■ The Run dialog box appears.

3 Type **syskey** to start the Syskey program.

4 Click **OK** to continue.

■ The Securing the Windows XP Account Database dialog box appears.

5 Click **Update** to add additional security to your computer.

■ The Startup Key dialog box appears.

6 Click **Password Startup** to create a password you will enter to start your computer (○ changes to ⊙).

Undo It! If you no longer want to enter a password to start
your computer, you can stop Windows from requesting
a password. Display the Startup Key dialog box by
performing steps 1 to 5 below. Click the "System
Generated Password" option and then choose the "Store
Startup Key Locally" option (○ changes to ⊙). Click OK
to confirm your changes. In the dialog box that appears,
type the password you enter to start your computer and
then press the Enter key twice.

Warning! Make sure you do not forget the password
required to start your computer. You may
want to write the password on a piece of
paper and store the paper in a secure
location. If you forget the password, you
will not be able to start your computer.

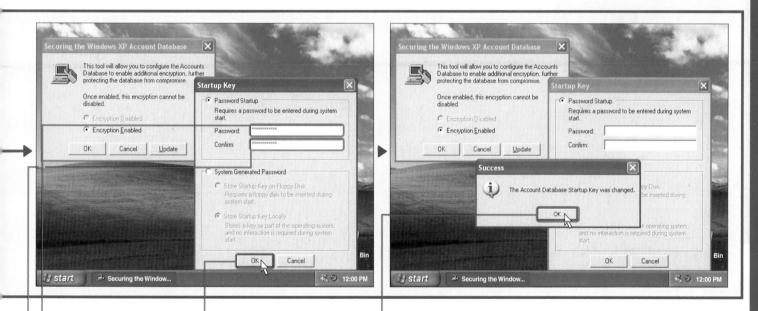

7 Click this area and
type a password you
want to use to start the
computer.

8 Click this area and
type the password again
to confirm the password.

*Note: For the best security, you
should choose a password that
is at least twelve characters long
and contains a combination of
letters, numbers and symbols.*

9 Click **OK** to continue.

■ The Success dialog box
appears, stating that the
Account Database Startup
Key was changed.

10 Click **OK** to close the
dialog box and the Syskey
program.

■ When you start your
computer, a Windows XP
Startup Password dialog
box will appear, asking you
to enter your password. To
start your computer, type the
password you created and
then press the **Enter** key.

#13 | Limit the hard disk space available for users

You can set quota limits to restrict the amount of hard disk space available for users to store files on your computer. Limiting the amount of disk space for users is useful when you have multiple users set up on your computer and limited hard disk space. For example, you may want to prevent your children from filling up space on the hard disk with music and video files.

You must be logged on to Windows as a computer administrator to limit hard disk space for users. In addition, your hard disk must use the NTFS file system. Most new computers use the NTFS file system.

The quota limit you set for users must be at least 2 MB. If you set a user's quota limit below 2 MB, the user may not be able to log on to Windows. You can set a quota limit for new users that you add to your computer. You cannot set a quota limit for users that are already set up on your computer.

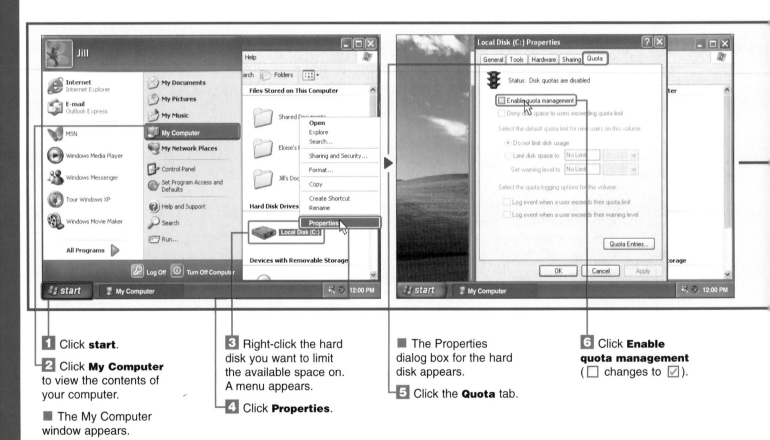

1 Click **start**.

2 Click **My Computer** to view the contents of your computer.

■ The My Computer window appears.

3 Right-click the hard disk you want to limit the available space on. A menu appears.

4 Click **Properties**.

■ The Properties dialog box for the hard disk appears.

5 Click the **Quota** tab.

6 Click **Enable quota management** (□ changes to ☑).

Give Warning! You should set the warning level an adequate amount below the quota limit so each user has sufficient notice before they run out of disk space. You should set the warning level to about 80 percent of the quota limit. For example, if you limit the amount of disk space available to each user to 10 GB, you should set the warning level to about 8 GB, so a warning message will appear when the amount of used hard disk space for a user reaches 8 GB.

More Space! If you have limited hard disk space, there are many ways you can free up space on your hard disk. You can start by removing files, such as documents, music and videos, you no longer need. You can also use a disk cleanup program to remove unnecessary files from your computer (see task #52). Removing programs you no longer use can also free up disk space (see task #53). If you have tried other ways of increasing the available storage space on a hard disk, you can also consider buying a second hard drive or buying a hard drive with a larger storage capacity.

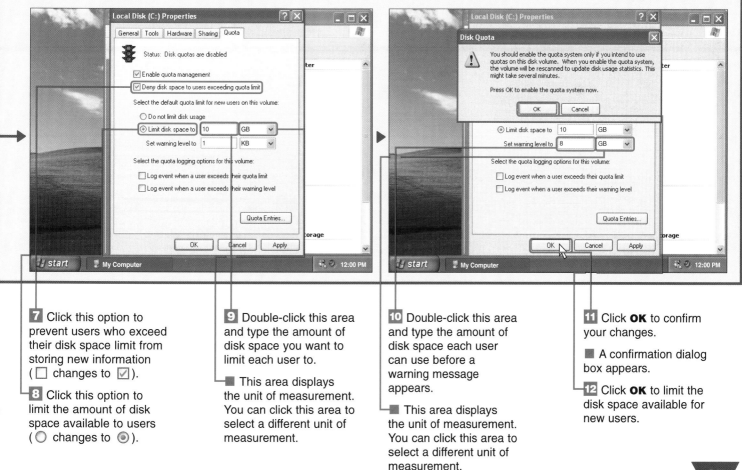

7 Click this option to prevent users who exceed their disk space limit from storing new information (☐ changes to ☑).

8 Click this option to limit the amount of disk space available to users (○ changes to ◉).

9 Double-click this area and type the amount of disk space you want to limit each user to.

■ This area displays the unit of measurement. You can click this area to select a different unit of measurement.

10 Double-click this area and type the amount of disk space each user can use before a warning message appears.

■ This area displays the unit of measurement. You can click this area to select a different unit of measurement.

11 Click **OK** to confirm your changes.

■ A confirmation dialog box appears.

12 Click **OK** to limit the disk space available for new users.

#14 | Set up a wireless network

Windows provides the Wireless Network Setup Wizard that will take you step by step through the process of setting up a wireless network. A wireless network allows computers to share information on a network using radio signals instead of cables to transmit information.

Wireless networks are useful when computers are located where cables are not practical or economical. Wireless networks also allow notebook computers to access a network from many locations in a home or office.

Wireless networks are much easier for unauthorized people to access compared to wired networks. When setting up a wireless network, Windows will automatically assign a network key, or password, to your network to help prevent outsiders from accessing your network. A network key encrypts, or scrambles, data transmitted over a network. You can use a Wired Equivalent Privacy (WEP) network key or choose a more secure network key, known as a Wireless Protected Access (WPA) key, that provides stronger network security. Some devices on a network do not support a WPA network key.

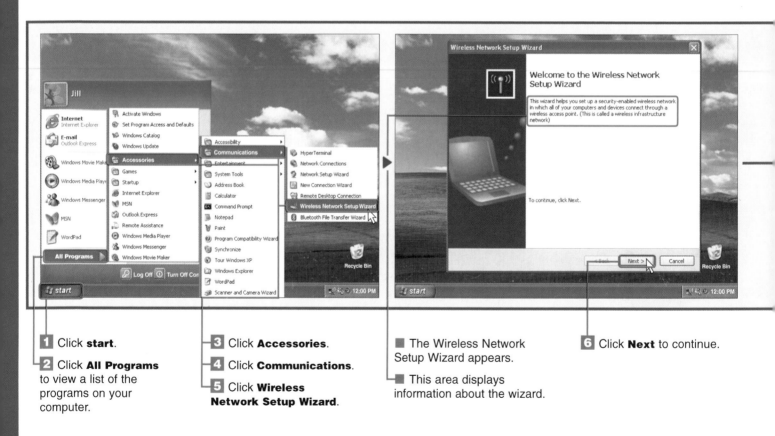

1 Click **start**.

2 Click **All Programs** to view a list of the programs on your computer.

3 Click **Accessories**.

4 Click **Communications**.

5 Click **Wireless Network Setup Wizard**.

■ The Wireless Network Setup Wizard appears.

■ This area displays information about the wizard.

6 Click **Next** to continue.

Equipment Needed! To set up a wireless network, each computer requires an internal wireless network card or an external wireless network adapter. A wireless network card or adapter allows computers on a wireless network to communicate using radio signals.

You will also need a wireless router or wireless access point, which is a device that uses radio signals to transmit and receive data between computers on a network. To set up a wireless network using the steps below, you need a wireless router or wireless access point that supports the Windows Connect Now feature.

You will also need a flash drive, which is a small, portable, lightweight storage device that plugs into a Universal Serial Bus (USB) port on a computer. You will use the flash drive to transfer your network settings to each computer and device on your network. A flash drive is also known as a USB key.

CONTINUED ►

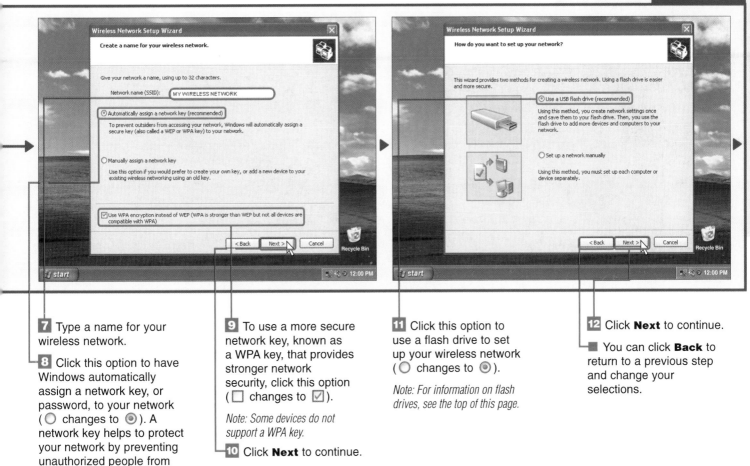

7 Type a name for your wireless network.

8 Click this option to have Windows automatically assign a network key, or password, to your network (○ changes to ◉). A network key helps to protect your network by preventing unauthorized people from accessing the network.

9 To use a more secure network key, known as a WPA key, that provides stronger network security, click this option (□ changes to ☑).

Note: Some devices do not support a WPA key.

10 Click **Next** to continue.

11 Click this option to use a flash drive to set up your wireless network (○ changes to ◉).

Note: For information on flash drives, see the top of this page.

12 Click **Next** to continue.

■ You can click **Back** to return to a previous step and change your selections.

#14 | Set up a wireless network

When setting up a wireless network, you can use a flash drive, or USB key, to transfer your network settings to all the other computers and devices on your network. Using a flash drive provides the easiest way to set up a wireless network.

You will need to plug your flash drive into a Universal Serial Bus (USB) port on your computer. Once plugged in, Windows can save the network settings on the flash drive. You then plug the flash drive into your wireless router or access point and then into each computer

and device that you want to add to your network. When you are done, you need to plug the flash drive back into your computer to finish setting up the network.

When you close the wizard, the wizard will remove the network settings from your flash drive for security reasons. If the network settings are not removed from the flash drive, unauthorized people could use the flash drive to add their computers to your network without your knowledge.

CONTINUED ►

13 Plug your flash drive into a USB port on your computer.

■ This area displays the drive letter for the flash drive. If the wizard does not show the correct drive letter, you can click this area to select a different drive letter.

14 Click **Next** to save the network settings to the flash drive.

■ This area displays the steps you need to perform to transfer the network settings to the other computers and devices on the network.

15 Unplug the flash drive from your computer.

16 Plug the flash drive into your wireless router or wireless access point. Wait about 30 seconds or until the device blinks its lights three times to indicate the data transfer is complete.

Did You Know? You can share an Internet connection on a wireless network. If you use a wireless router on your network, you can connect an Internet connection device, such as a cable modem or Digital Subscriber Line (DSL), directly to the router. Once connected, all the computers on the network will be able to use the device to connect to the Internet. If you use a wireless access point that does not have built-in router capabilities on your network, you can connect an Internet connection device directly to one computer on your network to share the Internet connection.

Attention! After you set up a wireless network, you should run the Network Setup Wizard on each computer on your network. The Network Setup Wizard allows you to turn on file and printer sharing for each computer on the network to enable the computers to share files and printers. To run the Network Setup Wizard, click start, All Programs, Accessories, Communications, Network Setup Wizard and then follow the steps on the screen.

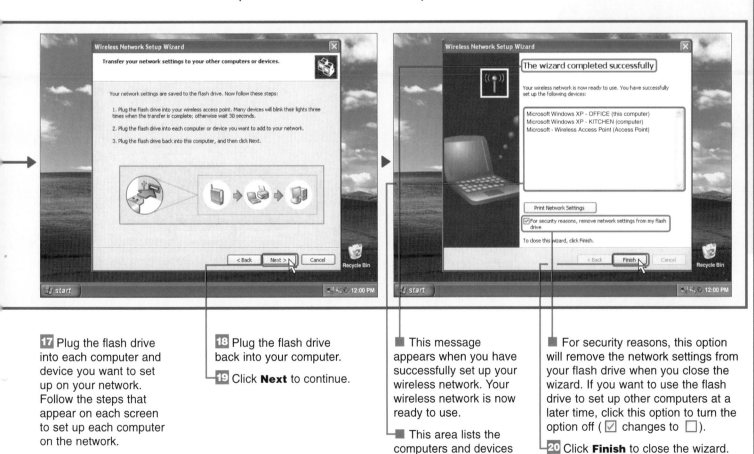

17 Plug the flash drive into each computer and device you want to set up on your network. Follow the steps that appear on each screen to set up each computer on the network.

18 Plug the flash drive back into your computer.

19 Click **Next** to continue.

■ This message appears when you have successfully set up your wireless network. Your wireless network is now ready to use.

■ This area lists the computers and devices that you have set up on your wireless network.

■ For security reasons, this option will remove the network settings from your flash drive when you close the wizard. If you want to use the flash drive to set up other computers at a later time, click this option to turn the option off (☑ changes to ☐).

20 Click **Finish** to close the wizard.

#15 | Connect to a wireless network

You can connect to a wireless network at home or at the office to access the information and equipment available on the network without using any cables. If a wireless network is connected to the Internet, connecting to the network will also allow you to access the Internet. Wireless networks are also known as wi-fi or wireless fidelity networks.

When you want to connect to a wireless network, Windows provides a list of all the wireless networks that are within range of your computer. Windows also indicates if each network is secure and the signal strength of each network.

When connecting to a wireless network, you may need to provide a network key, or password, that will help protect your connection from unauthorized access by encrypting the information transmitted on the network. If you are connecting to a network at work, ask your network administrator for the network key you need to type.

You only need to connect to a wireless network once. The next time you are within range of a wireless network you previously connected to, Windows will automatically connect you to the network.

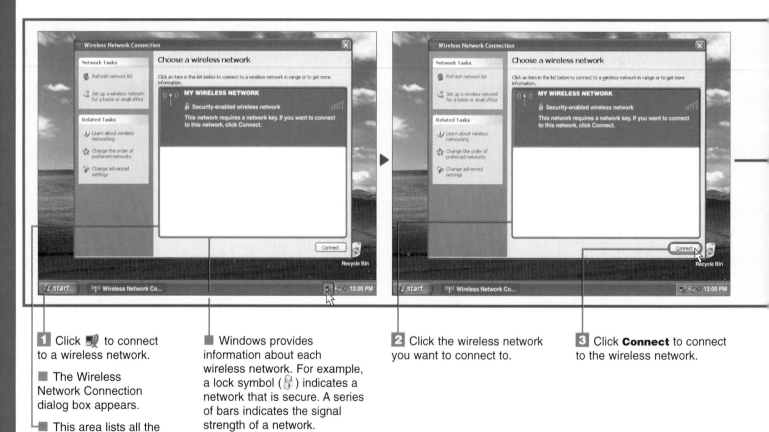

■1 Click 🕸 to connect to a wireless network.

■ The Wireless Network Connection dialog box appears.

■ This area lists all the wireless networks that are available to you.

■ Windows provides information about each wireless network. For example, a lock symbol (🔒) indicates a network that is secure. A series of bars indicates the signal strength of a network.

Note: You can position the mouse over the series of bars to display a brief description of the signal strength.

■2 Click the wireless network you want to connect to.

■3 Click **Connect** to connect to the wireless network.

Did You Know? When connecting to a wireless network, the strength of the radio signal used to connect to the network is very important. For the best signal, try to avoid obstacles between your computer and the wireless router or wireless access point, which is the device that allows computers on a network to exchange data using radio signals. Also try to avoid devices that use the same frequency as your wireless network, such as a cordless phone.

Hotspots! Increasing numbers of public places, such as coffee shops, hotels and airports, are allowing people to connect to the Internet through wireless networks set up on their premises. These locations are called wi-fi hotspots, or wireless hotspots, and provide a convenient way of accessing the Internet while you are away from home or the office.

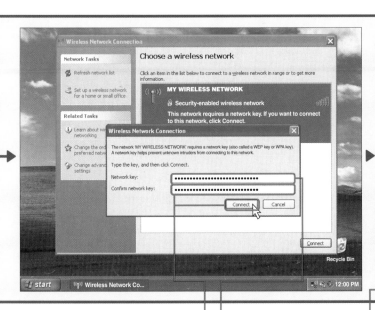
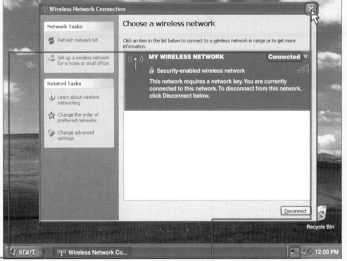

■ If the network requires you to enter a network key, or password, to gain access to the network, the Wireless Network Connection dialog box appears.

Note: A network key helps protect a network by preventing unauthorized people from accessing the network. If the Wireless Network Connection dialog box does not appear, skip to step 7.

4 Click this area and type the network key.

5 Click this area and type the network key again.

6 Click **Connect**.

■ This area indicates that you are connected to the wireless network. You can now access information on the network. If the network is connected to the Internet, you can also access the Internet.

■ The Wireless Network Connection icon indicates if you are connected (🖳) or not connected (🖳) to a wireless network.

7 To close the Wireless Network Connection dialog box, click ⊠.

Note: You only need to perform steps 1 to 7 once to connect to a wireless network. The next time you are within range of the wireless network, Windows will automatically connect you to the network.

#16 | Add a Bluetooth device to your computer

Bluetooth wireless technology allows computers and devices to communicate without cables. Bluetooth devices use radio signals to transmit information and operate over a distance of up to 30 feet. Bluetooth was named after a tenth-century Danish king named Harald Bluetooth.

You can obtain many types of Bluetooth devices, such as a mouse, keyboard, cell phone, printer and Personal Digital Assistant (PDA). Bluetooth devices run on batteries, which can be rechargeable, and can transmit information through barriers, such as a wall, desk or briefcase.

Before you can use a Bluetooth device with your computer, you need to add the device to your computer. You must also perform a few tasks to make sure that your computer can find the device. For example, you will need to turn the Bluetooth device on and make sure the device is discoverable, which means your computer can see the device.

Windows provides the Add Bluetooth Device Wizard that takes you step by step through the process of adding a Bluetooth device to your computer.

PREPARE A BLUETOOTH DEVICE

■ Before you can add a Bluetooth device to your computer, you must make sure the device is ready to be added.

1 Insert batteries into the Bluetooth device.

2 Turn the Bluetooth device on.

3 If you are adding a Bluetooth mouse or keyboard, make sure a mouse or keyboard with a cable is connected to your computer. You will need to use the mouse or keyboard to add the Bluetooth mouse or keyboard to your computer.

4 Make sure the Bluetooth device is "discoverable," which means that your computer can see the device.

■ If you are adding a Bluetooth mouse or keyboard, the device may have a button at the bottom of the device that you can press to make the device discoverable.

Note: To determine how to make your Bluetooth device discoverable, refer to the documentation that came with your device.

Why Use Bluetooth? You can use a Bluetooth wireless mouse, keyboard, printer or headset to prevent cables from cluttering your desk. Bluetooth technology also allows you to transfer information wirelessly between a computer and a Personal Digital Assistant (PDA). You can also use a Bluetooth cell phone to connect wirelessly to the Internet when traveling with a notebook computer.

Prepare Your Computer! Computers do not usually come with the capability to use Bluetooth devices. To add Bluetooth capabilities to a computer, you can plug in an external Bluetooth adapter, or transceiver, to a computer. Once you add Bluetooth capabilities to a computer, any Bluetooth device can communicate with the computer.

CONTINUED ▶

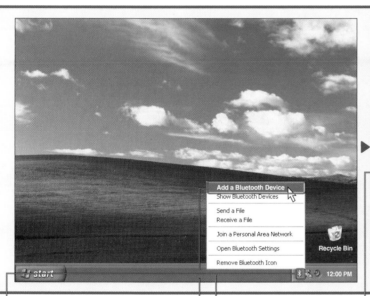

ADD A BLUETOOTH DEVICE

■ In this example, we are adding a Bluetooth mouse to a computer.

■ When Windows detects a Bluetooth device that is within range of your computer, the Bluetooth Devices icon (⟨Bluetooth⟩) appears on the taskbar.

1 To add a Bluetooth device to your computer, click the Bluetooth Devices icon (⟨Bluetooth⟩). A menu appears.

2 Click **Add a Bluetooth Device**.

■ The Add Bluetooth Device Wizard appears.

3 Click this option to specify that your Bluetooth device is ready to be found (☐ changes to ☑).

4 Click **Next** to continue.

#16 Add a Bluetooth device to your computer

When adding a Bluetooth device to your computer, the Add Bluetooth Device Wizard will search for a new Bluetooth device within range of your computer. The wizard will then display the device it found so you can add the device.

You may need to enter a passkey for the Bluetooth device you are adding. A passkey enables Windows to identify your Bluetooth device and helps to secure the data passing between your computer and the device. Some Bluetooth devices do not use a passkey.

If your device requires a passkey, you will need to specify how you want to enter a passkey for the device in the wizard. You will also need to enter the passkey on the device itself. You should refer to the documentation that came with your Bluetooth device to determine if your device requires a specific passkey.

Once you have successfully added the Bluetooth device to your computer, your computer and the device can communicate whenever the device is within range of your computer.

CONTINUED ▶

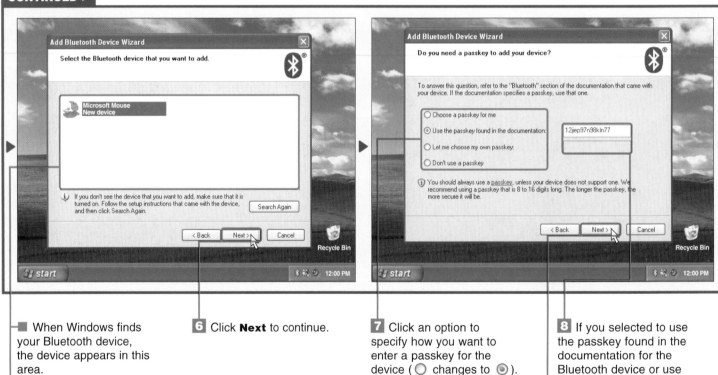

■ When Windows finds your Bluetooth device, the device appears in this area.

5 Click the Bluetooth device to add the device to your computer.

6 Click **Next** to continue.

7 Click an option to specify how you want to enter a passkey for the device (○ changes to ◉).

Note: For information on the available options, see the top of page 47.

8 If you selected to use the passkey found in the documentation for the Bluetooth device or use your own passkey, click the appropriate area and type the passkey.

9 Click **Next** to continue.

Passkey Options! When adding a Bluetooth device, you need to specify how you want to enter a passkey for the device.

- Select the "Choose a passkey for me" option if the documentation for the Bluetooth device does not specify a passkey, but the device can accept a passkey. Typically, Bluetooth devices such as keyboards, cell phones and Personal Digital Assistants (PDAs) can accept a passkey.

- Select the "Use the passkey found in the documentation" option if the documentation for the Bluetooth device specifies a passkey. Typically, devices such as Bluetooth headsets and mice specify a passkey in the documentation.

- Select the "Let me choose my own passkey" option if you want to create your own passkey. You should specify a passkey that is 8 to 16 characters long. Longer passkeys are more secure.

- Select the "Don't use a passkey" option if the documentation for the Bluetooth device does not specify a passkey and the device cannot accept a passkey.

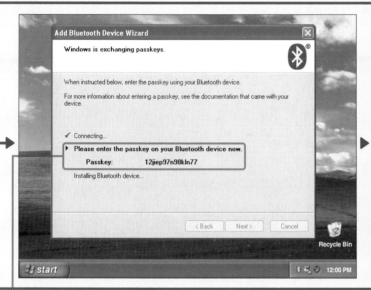

■ Windows starts adding the Bluetooth device to your computer.

■ If your Bluetooth device requires a passkey, the wizard indicates when you must enter the passkey on your device and displays the passkey you need to enter. The passkey will match the passkey you entered in step 8.

Note: You can refer to the documentation that came with your Bluetooth device to determine how to enter a passkey on the device.

■ This message appears when you have successfully added the Bluetooth device to your computer. Your computer and the device can now communicate whenever the device is within range of your computer.

10 Click **Finish** to close the wizard.

Note: Depending on the Bluetooth device you added, you may need to perform other steps to allow the device to communicate with your computer. You can refer to the documentation that came with your device to determine what steps, if any, you need to perform.

Maximize the Power of Your Files and Folders

You can use Windows XP's powerful tools for working with your files and folders to increase your efficiency and maximize your file management power.

Did you know that Windows XP allows you to compress folders so you can easily transfer a large number of files over the Internet at one time? Have you ever wished you could jazz up the appearance of folder icons? This chapter will discuss all of this, and more!

If you find that you often need to log off your computer while you are in the middle of a project, read on to find out how to have Windows automatically reopen your folders for you the next time you log on to the computer.

You can change the way you work with your files and folders by customizing Windows to allow you to open files and folders with a single click of your mouse or by specifying which program you want to use to open a file.

To speed up your work, you may want to learn how to quickly access recently used files from the Start menu and quickly send files to another location, such as to a memory card for storage.

If you are concerned about the security of your files, this chapter will show you how you can prevent other users from viewing your personal files and how to permanently delete a confidential file from your computer.

101 Hot Tips

You can choose to open files and folders on your computer using a single click. To open an item using a single click, you only need to position the mouse pointer over the item and then click to open the item. This saves you from constantly having to double-click to open items.

When you choose to open items using a single click, you can specify if you want icon titles to always appear underlined or appear underlined only when you position the mouse pointer over

the icon. Using a single click with underlined icon titles makes opening files on your computer seem more like clicking text links on a Web page.

To select an item when you have chosen to open items using a single click, simply position the mouse pointer over the item you want to select. To select more than one item, you can hold down the Ctrl key as you position the mouse pointer over each item you want to select.

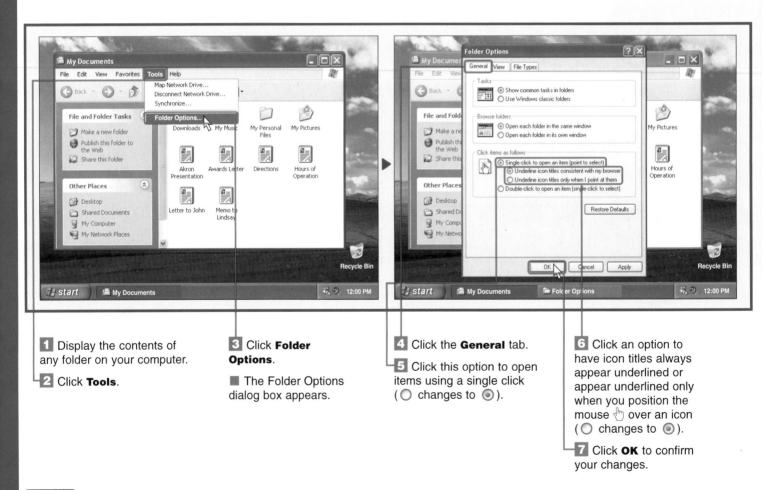

1 Display the contents of any folder on your computer.

2 Click **Tools**.

3 Click **Folder Options**.

■ The Folder Options dialog box appears.

4 Click the **General** tab.

5 Click this option to open items using a single click (○ changes to ◉).

6 Click an option to have icon titles always appear underlined or appear underlined only when you position the mouse 🖑 over an icon (○ changes to ◉).

7 Click **OK** to confirm your changes.

When you open a file on your computer, the program associated with the file starts automatically. Windows allows you to select a different program to open a file.

Changing the program that opens a file is beneficial when another program would prove more useful for working with the file. For example, when you open a text file, the Notepad program starts and opens the file. You may want to work with a text file in a word processor program instead of Notepad to have access to more advanced formatting options.

You can also specify that you want the program you select to always open the file and every other file of that type. Changing the default program for a file type is useful when you plan to regularly work with that type of file in a different program. For example, specifying that Bitmap images automatically open in Paint instead of Windows Picture and Fax Viewer is useful if you frequently edit images on your computer.

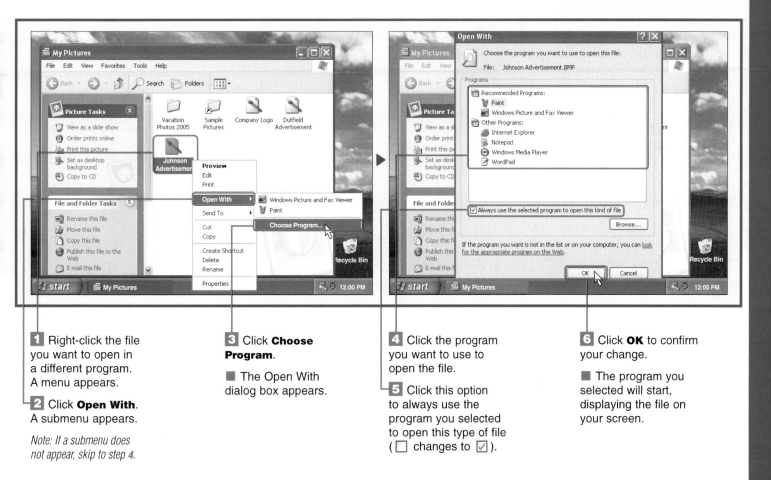

1 Right-click the file you want to open in a different program. A menu appears.

2 Click **Open With**. A submenu appears.

Note: If a submenu does not appear, skip to step 4.

3 Click **Choose Program**.

■ The Open With dialog box appears.

4 Click the program you want to use to open the file.

5 Click this option to always use the program you selected to open this type of file (☐ changes to ☑).

6 Click **OK** to confirm your change.

■ The program you selected will start, displaying the file on your screen.

#19 Prevent other users from viewing your personal files

You can make the contents of your personal folders private so that only you can access the files within the folders. Your computer must use the NTFS file system in order for you to make your personal folders private. Most new computers use the NTFS file system.

Your personal folders include the Cookies folder, which stores small text files created by Web pages you visit; the Desktop folder, which contains items you have placed on your desktop; and the Favorites folder, which stores shortcuts to Web pages you have added to your list of favorites. Your My Documents and Start Menu folders are also personal folders you can make private.

Your personal folders are initially available to every user with a computer administrator account set up on the computer.

You can make only the personal folders for the user account you are logged on to private. To make the folders of another user account private, you must first log on to their user account.

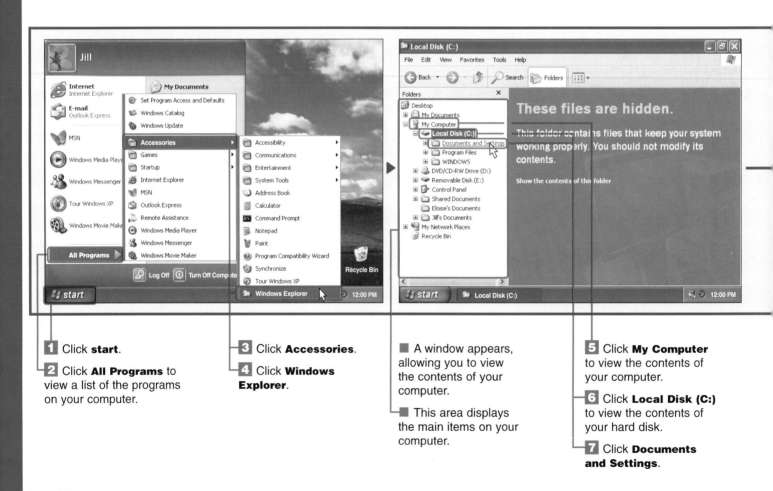

1 Click **start**.

2 Click **All Programs** to view a list of the programs on your computer.

3 Click **Accessories**.

4 Click **Windows Explorer**.

■ A window appears, allowing you to view the contents of your computer.

■ This area displays the main items on your computer.

5 Click **My Computer** to view the contents of your computer.

6 Click **Local Disk (C:)** to view the contents of your hard disk.

7 Click **Documents and Settings**.

Attention! You should assign a password to your user account to prevent other people from logging on to your account and viewing the contents of your folders. If you have not previously assigned a password to your user account, when you make a personal folder private, a dialog box will appear, asking if you want to create a password. Click Yes and follow the instructions on your screen to assign a password to your user account.

Did You Know? After making a personal folder private, you can share a file in the folder with every user set up on your computer by copying the file to the Shared Documents folder. To display the contents of the Shared Documents folder, click start, select My Computer and double-click the Shared Documents folder. Then hold down the Ctrl key as you drag each file you want to share to the Shared Documents folder.

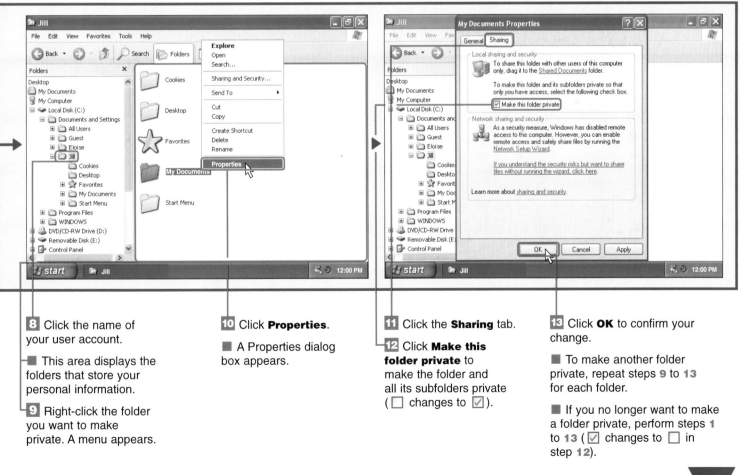

8 Click the name of your user account.

■ This area displays the folders that store your personal information.

9 Right-click the folder you want to make private. A menu appears.

10 Click **Properties**.

■ A Properties dialog box appears.

11 Click the **Sharing** tab.

12 Click **Make this folder private** to make the folder and all its subfolders private (☐ changes to ☑).

13 Click **OK** to confirm your change.

■ To make another folder private, repeat steps **9** to **13** for each folder.

■ If you no longer want to make a folder private, perform steps **1** to **13** (☑ changes to ☐ in step **12**).

20

Get quick access to files you recently used

You can have the Start menu display the My Recent Documents folder, which lists the 15 files you have most recently used. Displaying a list of the last files you worked with allows you to quickly open and work with the files again.

Windows makes it easy for you to find a file of interest in the My Recent Documents folder by listing the files in alphabetical order. Windows also displays an icon beside each file name to help you quickly see which program was used to create a file. For example, the 📄 icon indicates a WordPad file, while 🎨 indicates a Paint file.

If you have the Professional version of Windows XP installed on your computer, your Start menu will already display the My Recent Documents folder. Also, if you have changed the Start menu to the classic version (see task #31), your recently used files are already displayed on the Documents submenu of the Start menu.

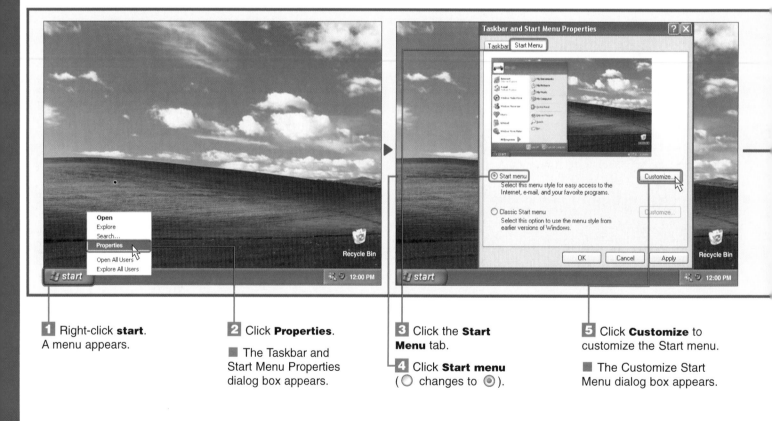

1 Right-click **start**. A menu appears.

2 Click **Properties**.

■ The Taskbar and Start Menu Properties dialog box appears.

3 Click the **Start Menu** tab.

4 Click **Start menu** (○ changes to ◉).

5 Click **Customize** to customize the Start menu.

■ The Customize Start Menu dialog box appears.

Clear It! If the list of recently used files on the Start menu contains files that you do not plan to use again any time soon, you can clear all the files from the list. Repeat steps 1 to 9 starting on page 54, except click Clear List in step 7 to remove all the files from the list. Clearing the list of recently used files on the Start menu does not delete the files from your computer. To completely remove the My Recent Documents folder from the Start menu, perform steps 1 to 9 starting on page 54 (☑ changes to ☐ in step 7).

Try This! You can add a shortcut to your desktop to provide a quick way of opening a file you regularly use. Right-click the file you want to create a shortcut to and then click Send To on the menu that appears. Then click Desktop (create shortcut). A shortcut icon for the file appears on your desktop, displaying an arrow (⬈).

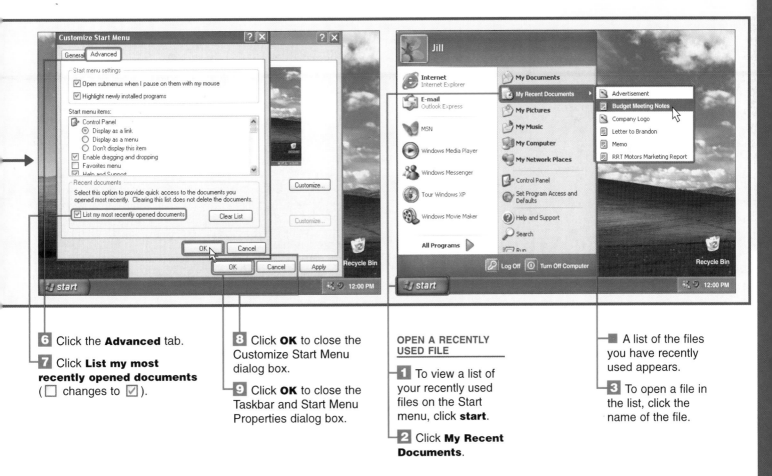

■6 Click the **Advanced** tab.

■7 Click **List my most recently opened documents** (☐ changes to ☑).

■8 Click **OK** to close the Customize Start Menu dialog box.

■9 Click **OK** to close the Taskbar and Start Menu Properties dialog box.

OPEN A RECENTLY USED FILE

■1 To view a list of your recently used files on the Start menu, click **start**.

■2 Click **My Recent Documents**.

■ A list of the files you have recently used appears.

■3 To open a file in the list, click the name of the file.

21

Quickly send files to another location

You can use the Send To menu to quickly send copies of files to another location. Using the Send To menu can save you time if you frequently send files to the same locations on your computer or network.

You can customize the Send To menu to include the folders and devices to which you most often send files. For example, if your company requires you to place daily copies of financial files in a folder on your network, you can place a shortcut for the folder on the Send To menu.

Windows automatically displays your floppy drive, the desktop and the My Documents folder on the Send To menu. The menu also displays the Mail Recipient item, which allows you to quickly send a file in an e-mail message. The Compressed (zipped) Folder item also appears, allowing you to create a compressed folder where you can store files using less space. If you have a CD, DVD or removable disk drive, these items will also appear on the menu.

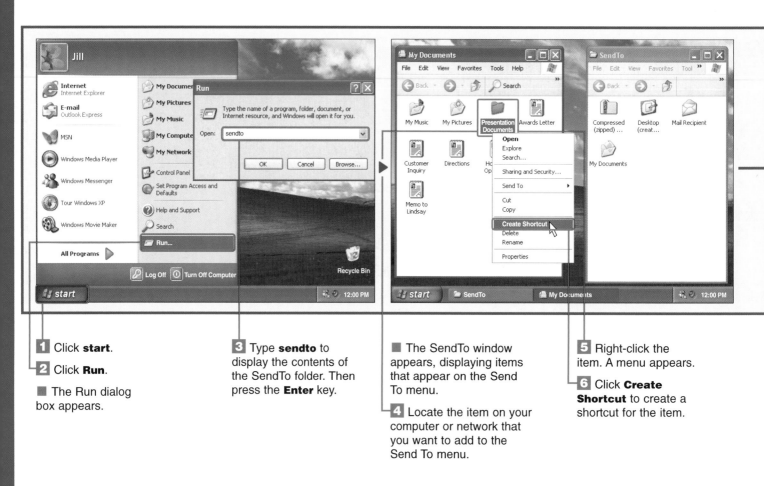

1 Click **start**.

2 Click **Run**.

■ The Run dialog box appears.

3 Type **sendto** to display the contents of the SendTo folder. Then press the **Enter** key.

■ The SendTo window appears, displaying items that appear on the Send To menu.

4 Locate the item on your computer or network that you want to add to the Send To menu.

5 Right-click the item. A menu appears.

6 Click **Create Shortcut** to create a shortcut for the item.

Keep It Organized! You can create folders to organize the items on the Send To menu. In the SendTo window, click the "Make a new folder" option to create a folder. Type a name for the new folder and then press the Enter key. You can then drag items to the new folder. The folder will appear on the Send To menu with an arrow (▶) indicating there are more choices. You can click the folder to display the choices.

Delete It! You can delete an item you no longer use from the Send To menu. In the SendTo window, click the item you want to delete and then press the Delete key. In the confirmation dialog box that appears, click Yes to delete the item.

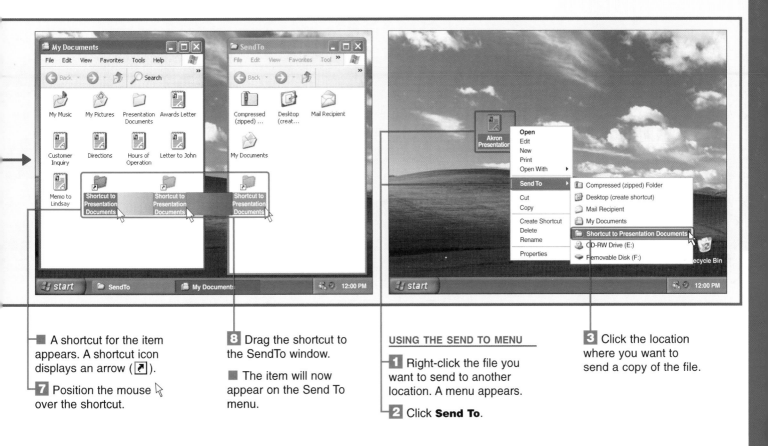

■ A shortcut for the item appears. A shortcut icon displays an arrow (↗).

7 Position the mouse over the shortcut.

8 Drag the shortcut to the SendTo window.

■ The item will now appear on the Send To menu.

USING THE SEND TO MENU

1 Right-click the file you want to send to another location. A menu appears.

2 Click **Send To**.

3 Click the location where you want to send a copy of the file.

If you frequently add the same information to files, you can place the information on your desktop by creating a file called a scrap.

Document scraps save you from having to constantly retype information. For example, you can create a scrap containing your name, address and telephone number, which you can then drag into a document when needed. You can also create a scrap for images, such as your company's logo.

When creating a scrap, make sure the window that contains the information does not fill the entire screen. Part of the desktop should be visible so you can drag the information to the desktop.

Scraps are available only for programs that allow you to drag and drop information to other programs. For example, you cannot create scraps using a Notepad document. You can work with a scrap the same way you would work with any file.

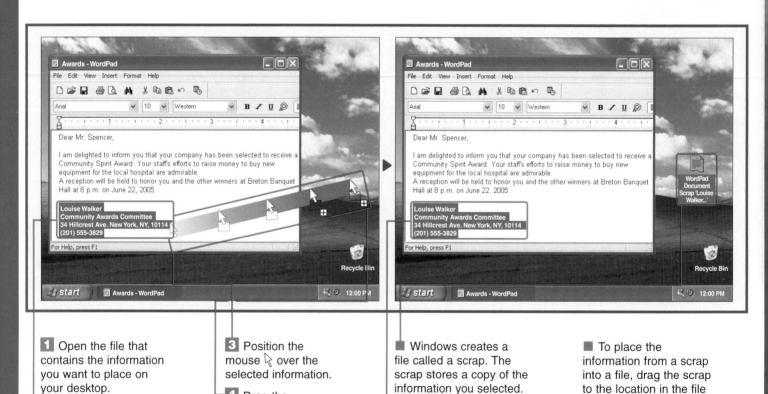

1 Open the file that contains the information you want to place on your desktop.

2 Select the information in the file.

3 Position the mouse ⬚ over the selected information.

4 Drag the information to a blank area on your desktop.

■ Windows creates a file called a scrap. The scrap stores a copy of the information you selected.

■ The information remains in the original file.

■ To place the information from a scrap into a file, drag the scrap to the location in the file where you want to place the information. You can place the information from a scrap in as many files as you want.

You can permanently delete a confidential file from your computer so the file cannot be recovered.

Windows usually places a file you delete in the Recycle Bin in case you want to restore the file later. When you use the method shown below to delete a file, Windows deletes the file permanently from your computer without placing the file in the Recycle Bin. Before deleting a file, make completely sure you no longer need the file.

Did You Know?

If you want to be absolutely certain that confidential files are permanently erased from your computer, you can use a program that wipes your hard drive clean of all traces of the files. There are many programs available on the Web, such as East-Tec Eraser (www.east-tec.com) and Evidence Cleaner (www.evidence-cleaner.net).

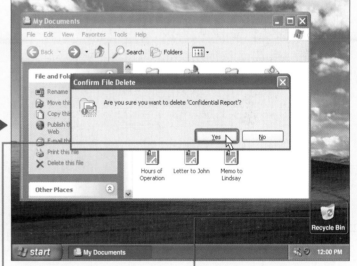

1 Click the file you want to permanently delete from your computer.

■ To permanently delete more than one file, press and hold down the **Ctrl** key as you click each additional file you want to permanently delete.

2 Press and hold down the **Shift** key as you press the **Delete** key.

■ The Confirm File Delete dialog box appears.

3 Click **Yes** to permanently delete the file.

■ The file is permanently deleted from your computer.

■ Windows will not place the file in the Recycle Bin.

#24 Find lost files

If you cannot remember the name or location of a file you want to work with, you can have Windows search for the file. For example, you may have trouble finding a file if you did not give it a very specific name. You may also require Windows' help if you accidentally saved a file in the wrong folder.

You can search specifically for media files, such as pictures, music or videos, or search for documents, such as spreadsheets and word processing documents. You can also have Windows perform a more extensive search through all the files and folders on your computer.

Searching for a file by name is an effective way of finding a file when you know all or part of the file name. For example, searching for a file named "Report" will find every file or folder with a name that contains the word "report."

If you know a word or phrase that a file contains, you can have Windows search for the file using this information. Searching by file content will slow down your search.

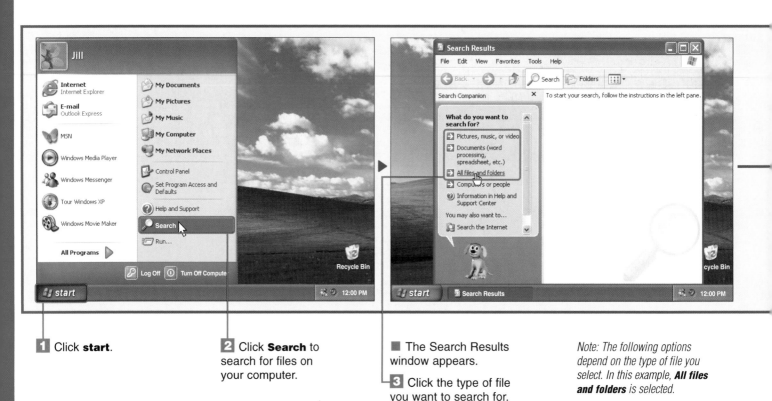

1 Click **start**.

2 Click **Search** to search for files on your computer.

■ The Search Results window appears.

3 Click the type of file you want to search for.

*Note: The following options depend on the type of file you select. In this example, **All files and folders** is selected.*

Did You Know? You can search for a file according to when it was last modified. Perform steps 1 to 3 below, selecting All files and folders in step 3, then click When was it modified? Click an option to specify whether the file was modified within the last week, month or year. You can also click Specify dates and then enter a range of dates indicating when the file was last modified.

Try This! You can also specify the exact type of file you are looking for, such as an MP3 file. Perform steps 1 to 3 below, selecting All files and folders in step 3, then click More advanced options. Click the area below "Type of file" and then select the type of file you want to search for.

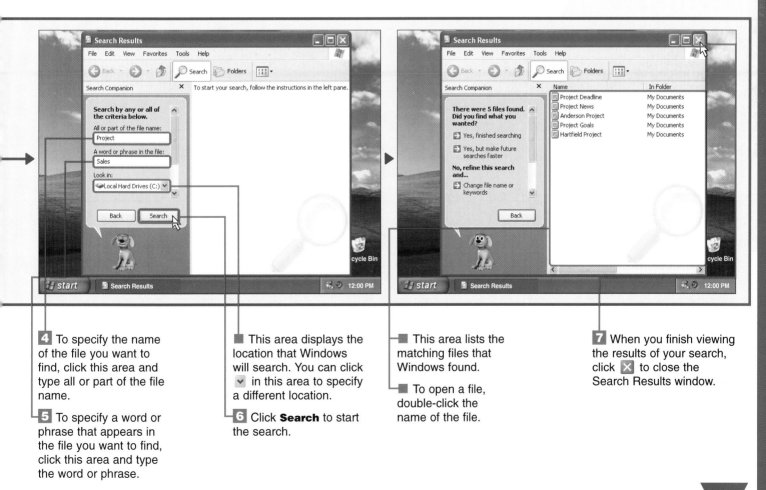

4 To specify the name of the file you want to find, click this area and type all or part of the file name.

5 To specify a word or phrase that appears in the file you want to find, click this area and type the word or phrase.

■ This area displays the location that Windows will search. You can click ✓ in this area to specify a different location.

6 Click **Search** to start the search.

■ This area lists the matching files that Windows found.

■ To open a file, double-click the name of the file.

7 When you finish viewing the results of your search, click ☒ to close the Search Results window.

Jazz up the appearance of your folder icons

You can add a picture to a folder's icon when the folder is displayed in the Thumbnails view. Displaying a picture on a folder's icon enhances the appearance of the icon and can help you quickly identify the contents of the folder.

When a folder contains pictures, the folder's icon automatically displays up to four of the pictures in the folder. You can specify which picture stored in the folder you want to display on the folder's icon. You can also choose a picture stored in any other folder on your computer.

Windows cannot display a picture on a folder's icon on the desktop or on the My Documents, My Pictures or My Music folder icons. Windows can, however, display pictures on the folder icons within these folders.

You may notice that the folder icons in your My Music folder display pictures of album covers. When you copy songs from a music CD to your computer while you are connected to the Internet, Windows attempts to download the album cover for the CD. For information on copying songs from a music CD, see task #59.

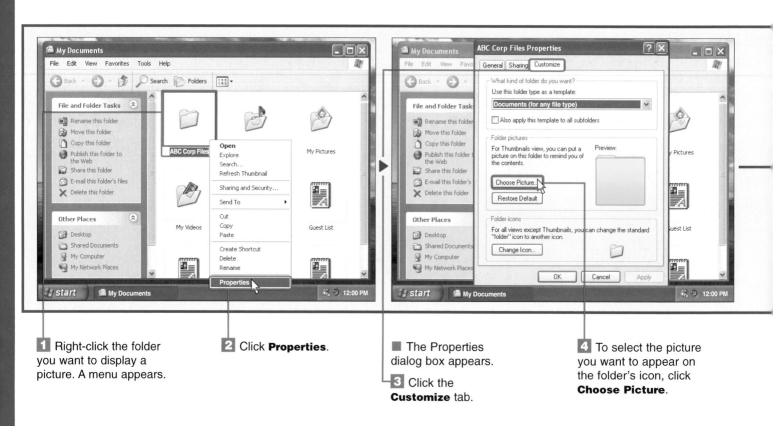

1 Right-click the folder you want to display a picture. A menu appears.

2 Click **Properties**.

■ The Properties dialog box appears.

3 Click the **Customize** tab.

4 To select the picture you want to appear on the folder's icon, click **Choose Picture**.

See It! To be able to see the picture you added to a folder's icon, the folder must be displayed in the Thumbnails view. To display the items in a folder in the Thumbnails view, select the View menu and then click Thumbnails.

Back To Default! To return a folder's icon to its original appearance, perform steps 1 to 3 below and then click the Restore Default button. If the folder does not contain any pictures, the folder's icon will be blank. If the folder contains pictures, the folder's icon will display up to four of the pictures.

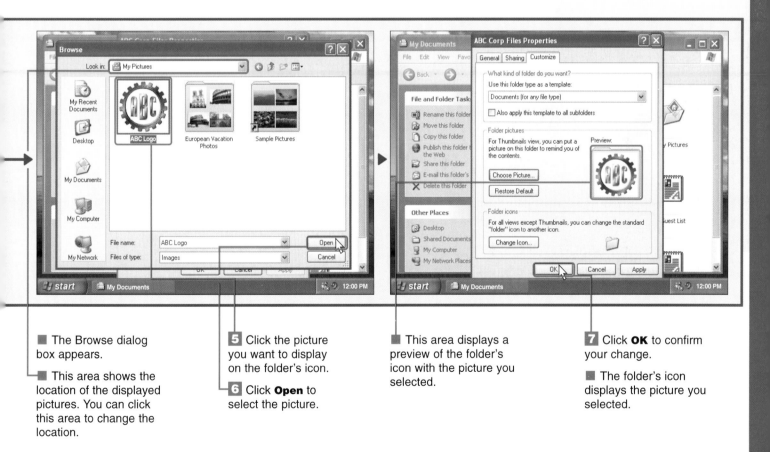

■ The Browse dialog box appears.

■ This area shows the location of the displayed pictures. You can click this area to change the location.

5 Click the picture you want to display on the folder's icon.

6 Click **Open** to select the picture.

■ This area displays a preview of the folder's icon with the picture you selected.

7 Click **OK** to confirm your change.

■ The folder's icon displays the picture you selected.

#26 Have each folder open in its own window

By default, Windows has each folder you open appear in the same window to help reduce clutter on your desktop. You can change this setting to have each folder you open appear in its own window.

Having each folder open in its own window is useful because it allows you to view the contents of several folders at once, which can help make copying and moving files between windows easier.

You can easily switch between the windows you have open by clicking anywhere in a window containing the items you want to view.

Changing this setting in the Folder Options dialog box will affect all the folders on your computer. You can access the Folder Options dialog box from any folder you have open.

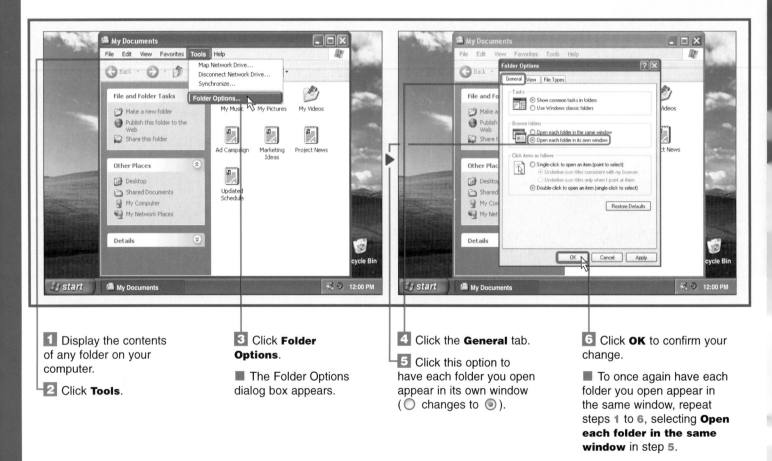

1 Display the contents of any folder on your computer.

2 Click **Tools**.

3 Click **Folder Options**.

■ The Folder Options dialog box appears.

4 Click the **General** tab.

5 Click this option to have each folder you open appear in its own window (○ changes to ◉).

6 Click **OK** to confirm your change.

■ To once again have each folder you open appear in the same window, repeat steps **1** to **6**, selecting **Open each folder in the same window** in step **5**.

Windows can remember which folders were left open when you logged off your computer and reopen those folders when you log on again. This helps you keep track of the tasks you were performing before you logged off and allows you to quickly start working where you left off the last time.

Although you perform the steps below using one folder on your computer, the changes will affect all folders that are open when you log off your computer.

You should be aware that turning on this feature may increase the time your computer takes to log on. If you no longer want Windows to automatically reopen your folders when you log on, you can repeat the steps below to turn off the option (☑ changes to ☐ in step 5).

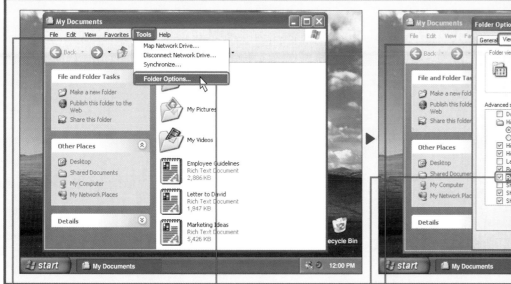

1 Open a folder on your computer.

Note: In this example, we open the My Documents folder.

2 Click **Tools**.

3 Click **Folder Options** to change your folder settings.

■ The Folder Options dialog box appears.

4 Click the **View** tab.

5 Click **Restore previous folder windows at logon** (☐ changes to ☑).

■ You may have to drag the scroll bar down to display the option on your screen.

6 Click **OK** to confirm your changes.

■ Windows will now remember which folders are open when you log off your computer and reopen those folders when you log on.

After you customize the way Windows displays items in a folder, you can quickly make the items in all your folders look the same. For example, if you have customized a folder to show items in the Details view and sorted the items by name, you can quickly make all your folders display items in the Details view and sorted by name. Once you apply this setting, the changes will take effect immediately.

Return To Default!

You can return all the folders on your computer to their default views. The default view is the view of each folder when Windows was installed on your computer. Perform steps 1 to 7 below, except click the Reset All Folders button in step 5.

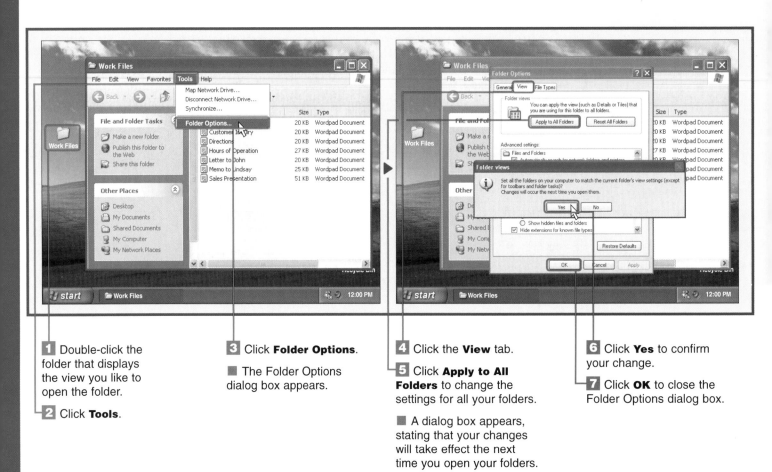

1 Double-click the folder that displays the view you like to open the folder.

2 Click **Tools**.

3 Click **Folder Options**.

■ The Folder Options dialog box appears.

4 Click the **View** tab.

5 Click **Apply to All Folders** to change the settings for all your folders.

■ A dialog box appears, stating that your changes will take effect the next time you open your folders.

6 Click **Yes** to confirm your change.

7 Click **OK** to close the Folder Options dialog box.

You can change the information that appears when the contents of a window are displayed in the Details view. The Details view displays columns of information about each item, such as the name, size and type of item. Changing the information allows you to display only the columns that you find most useful. The changes you make will affect only the window you currently have open. Each time you open that window, the details you specified will appear.

Rearrange It!

You can rearrange the columns of information shown in the Details view. In the Choose Details dialog box, click the name of the column you want to move to a new location and then click the Move Up or Move Down button until the column appears in the location you want. Then click OK.

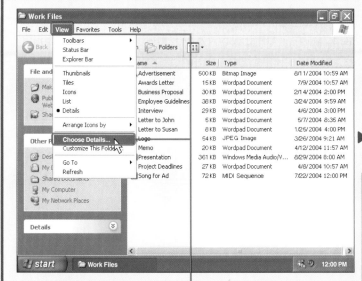

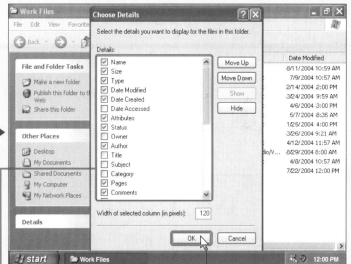

■ By default, the Details view displays the name, size, type and date each file and folder in a window was last changed.

*Note: To display files and folders in the Details view, click **View** and then select **Details**.*

1 To change which columns of information appear in a window, click **View**.

2 Click **Choose Details**.

■ The Choose Details dialog box appears.

■ This area displays the details you can show in the window. A check mark (☑) appears beside each detail that currently appears in the window.

3 To add (☑) or remove (☐) a detail from the window, click the box beside the detail.

4 Click **OK** to confirm your changes.

■ The details you specified will appear in the window.

#30 Save storage space using compressed folders

You can create zipped compressed folders that take up less storage space than regular folders on your computer. Zipped compressed folders compress, or squeeze, the files stored in the folders so the files take up less room. Zipped compressed folders are often simply called compressed folders.

Creating a compressed folder is especially useful when you want to send a group of files in an e-mail message. A compressed folder containing several files is smaller and transfers more quickly over the Internet than individual, uncompressed files. Since many companies that provide e-mail accounts do

not allow you to send messages larger than 10 MB, compressed folders can help reduce the size of your messages.

You can also create compressed folders to save storage space on removable storage media, such as memory cards and recordable CDs.

The amount of space a compressed folder saves depends on the types of files you add to the folder. Some files, such as video, sound and graphic files, will not save any storage space when they are compressed. Other files, such as text documents, will compress significantly.

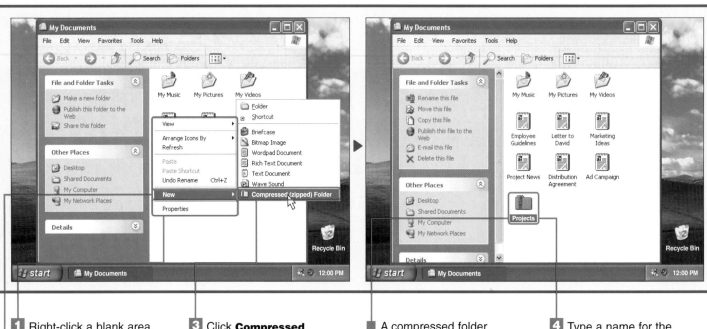

1 Right-click a blank area on the desktop or in the window where you want to place a compressed folder. A menu appears.

2 Click **New**.

3 Click **Compressed (zipped) Folder** to create a compressed folder.

■ A compressed folder appears with a temporary name. A compressed folder displays a zipper in its icon (📁).

4 Type a name for the compressed folder and then press the **Enter** key.

*Note: A compressed folder name cannot contain the \ / : * ? " < > or | characters.*

E-mail It!   To quickly e-mail a compressed folder, right-click the folder. In the menu that appears, select Send To and then select Mail Recipient. In the window that appears, type the recipient's e-mail address in the To area. You can replace the subject text provided with your own text and type your own message. Then click the Send button.

Decompress It!   You need to extract files from a compressed folder before you can make changes to the files. To extract a file from a compressed folder, double-click the compressed folder to display its contents. Drag the file you want to extract to a new location outside the compressed folder. Windows will create a decompressed copy of the file in the new location.

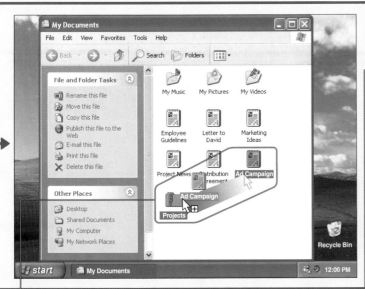

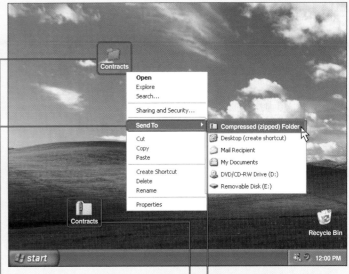

5 To add a file to the compressed folder, position the mouse ⊳ over the file and then drag the file to the folder.

■ Windows will add a compressed copy of the file to the folder.

■ The original file will remain in its original location.

Note: You can open the files in a compressed folder as you would open any file on your computer. You cannot make changes to the files in a compressed folder.

COMPRESS AN EXISTING FOLDER

1 Right-click the folder you want to compress. A menu appears.

2 Click **Send To**.

3 Click **Compressed (zipped) Folder**.

■ A compressed version of the folder appears. Compressed folders display the 🗐 icon.

Add a Personal Touch to Your Computer

Have you been wondering how to make Windows XP look and act more like you want it to? Do you want to give your desktop a makeover to reflect some of your own personality and pizzazz? The tasks in this chapter will help you find the ways to do just that!

You can make your desktop look more like an older version of Windows with just a few clicks of your mouse. Or, if you want to personalize your desktop, you can display a favorite picture or interesting Web content on the desktop.

To help add personality to the Start menu, you can change the picture that appears beside your user name to a picture provided by Windows that better

suits your tastes, or even a picture of yourself! Windows can even help you personalize the documents you create by allowing you to add extra fonts to your computer. You'll always be sure to have just the font you need for any occasion.

When you are taking a break away from your desk, you can set up a screen saver slide show that uses the contents of your My Pictures folder to hide your screen.

Does the animated dog in the Search Companion distract you while you are searching for files? Read on to learn how to customize the Search Companion by removing the dog so you can focus on your search.

101 Hot Tips

#31 Give Windows a retro look

You can use the Windows Classic desktop theme to make Windows XP look like an older version of Windows. A desktop theme is a collection of coordinated items, such as a background picture, screen saver, colors, sounds, mouse pointers, icons and fonts.

The Windows Classic theme changes the overall appearance of Windows XP so your computer looks like a previous Windows version, but the features of Windows XP are not affected.

If there are multiple user accounts set up on your computer, each person can choose a different desktop theme for his or her own user account. Changing the desktop theme for one user account will not affect the themes used by other user accounts.

You can also change the Start menu to the style used in a previous version of Windows. Using the Classic Start menu will change which items appear on the Start menu, as well as how the items are displayed.

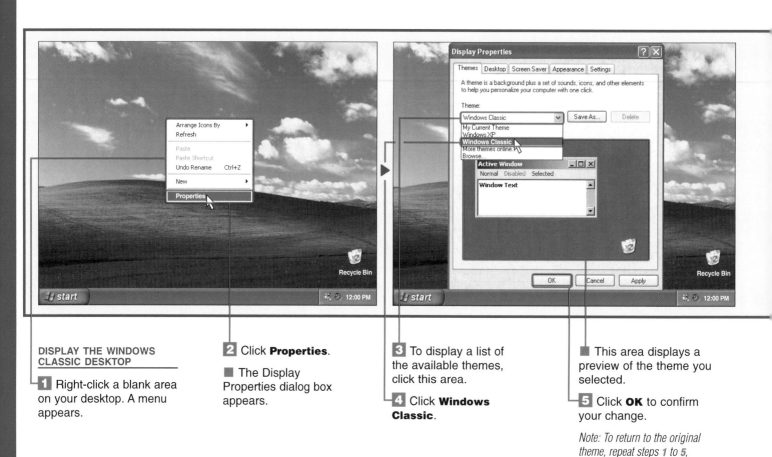

DISPLAY THE WINDOWS CLASSIC DESKTOP

1 Right-click a blank area on your desktop. A menu appears.

2 Click **Properties**.

■ The Display Properties dialog box appears.

3 To display a list of the available themes, click this area.

4 Click **Windows Classic**.

■ This area displays a preview of the theme you selected.

5 Click **OK** to confirm your change.

Note: To return to the original theme, repeat steps 1 to 5, selecting Windows XP in step 4.

Retro Folders! You can have all your open folders look like folders from an older version of Windows. Display the contents of any folder on your computer. Click Tools and then select Folder Options. In the Folder Options dialog box, click Use Windows classic folders and then click OK.

Retro Control Panel! If you have trouble finding items in the Control Panel, you can have the Control Panel window look like the Control Panel from an older version of Windows. Click start and select Control Panel or click start, Settings and then select Control Panel. On the left side of the Control Panel window, click the Switch to Classic View option. The Classic View displays all the Control Panel items. To return to the original view, click the Switch to Category View option in the Control Panel window.

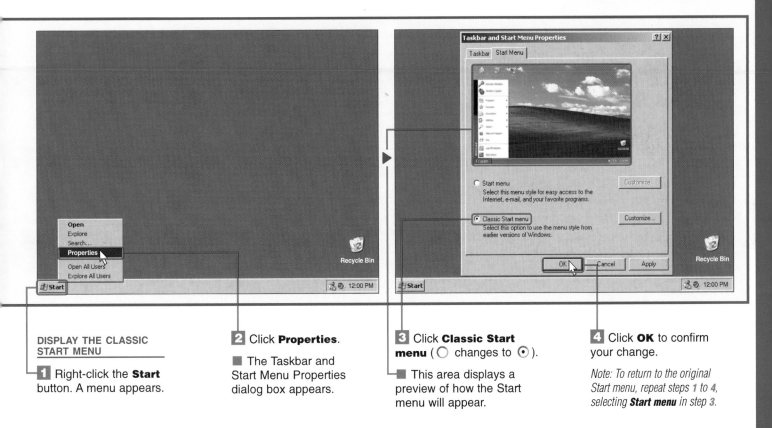

DISPLAY THE CLASSIC START MENU

1 Right-click the **Start** button. A menu appears.

2 Click **Properties**.

■ The Taskbar and Start Menu Properties dialog box appears.

3 Click **Classic Start menu** (○ changes to ⊙).

■ This area displays a preview of how the Start menu will appear.

4 Click **OK** to confirm your change.

*Note: To return to the original Start menu, repeat steps 1 to 4, selecting **Start menu** in step 3.*

Like hanging posters on your wall or placing photographs on your desk, you can customize the Windows desktop to create a friendly, personalized work environment. Windows allows you to use your favorite picture, such as a scenic picture taken on vacation or a picture of your child, as your desktop background.

Using a scanner or a digital camera, you can copy your own photographs or artwork onto your computer so you can use the pictures as desktop backgrounds. Windows automatically adds any image stored in your My Pictures folder to the list of available backgrounds.

You can also choose a picture from the background pictures Windows provides or you can search the Internet for images to use as desktop backgrounds. Alternatively, you may want to go to a computer store and purchase collections of clip art and photographs you can use as desktop backgrounds.

When using a picture as your desktop background, you can center a large picture on your desktop or tile a small picture so it repeats over the entire desktop. You can also stretch a picture to cover your desktop.

1 Right-click a blank area on your desktop. A menu appears.

2 Click **Properties**.

■ The Display Properties dialog box appears.

3 Click the **Desktop** tab.

4 Click the picture you want to display on your desktop.

5 Click this area to select how you want to display the picture on your desktop.

6 Click the way you want to display the picture.

Center – Places the picture in the middle of your desktop.

Tile – Repeats the picture until it covers your entire desktop.

Stretch – Stretches the picture to cover your entire desktop.

Did You Know? If you want to use a picture that is not stored in the My Pictures folder as a desktop background, you can click the Browse button in the Display Properties dialog box to locate the picture you want to use.

Use a Web Picture! To use a picture displayed on a Web page as a desktop background, right-click the picture. In the menu that appears, click Set as Background.

Try This! To quickly use a picture as a desktop background, display the contents of the folder that contains the picture. Right-click the picture and then click Set as Desktop Background in the menu that appears. The Set as Desktop Background option is not available in all folders.

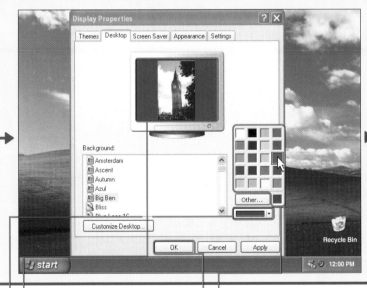

■ This area displays how the picture will appear on your desktop.

7 To select a color that will fill any space on your desktop not covered by the picture, click this area to display a list of the available colors.

8 Click the color you want to use.

9 Click **OK** to add the picture to your desktop.

■ The picture appears on your desktop.

■ To return to the original desktop background, perform steps **1** to **4**, selecting **Bliss** in step **4**. Then perform step **9**.

Have your desktop display Web content

You can customize your desktop to include content from the Web, such as your favorite Web page. Adding Web content to your desktop allows you to quickly access items on the Web that you frequently use. For example, you may want to add a Web page that displays the current news or a search tool, such as Yahoo! or Google, to search for topics of interest on the Web. You may also want to display a Web page that contains personalized information, such as your horoscope or a local weather report.

When adding a Web page to your desktop, you can choose to add your current home page or you can specify the address of another Web page. Your current home page is the first page that appears when you start your Web browser.

You must be connected to the Internet to add Web content to your desktop.

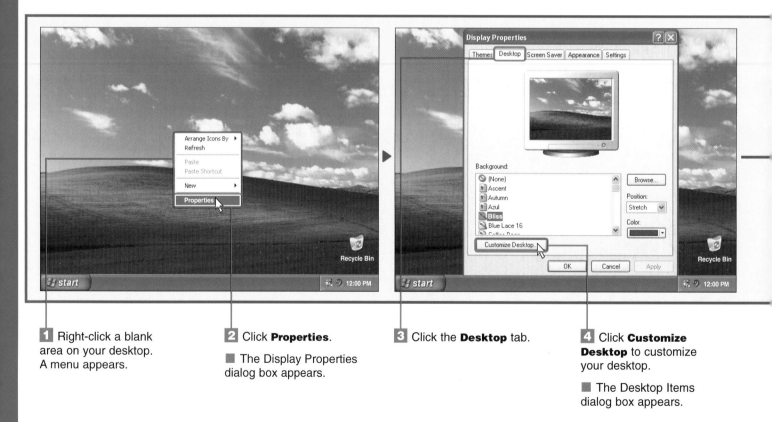

1 Right-click a blank area on your desktop. A menu appears.

2 Click **Properties**.

■ The Display Properties dialog box appears.

3 Click the **Desktop** tab.

4 Click **Customize Desktop** to customize your desktop.

■ The Desktop Items dialog box appears.

Did You Know? You can visit the Internet Explorer 4.0 Desktop Gallery Web site, which offers items, such as a stock ticker, that you can add to your desktop. Perform steps 1 to 6 below to display the New Desktop Item wizard and then click the Visit Gallery button. Click the Add to Active Desktop button for an item of interest and then follow the instructions on your screen to add the item to your desktop.

Try This! To quickly add a Web page displayed in Internet Explorer to your desktop, use the right mouse button to drag the Web page icon (🦴) from the Address bar to your desktop. Then choose "Create Active Desktop items Here" from the menu that appears. To add an item, such as an animation, from a Web page to your desktop, right-click the item and choose "Set as Desktop Item" from the menu that appears. After choosing to add a desktop item, click Yes and then OK in the dialog boxes that appear.

CONTINUED ▶

5 Click the **Web** tab.

■ This area lists the Web pages you can display on your desktop.

Note: My Current Home Page will display your home page, which is the first Web page that appears when you start your Web browser. To display this Web page on your desktop, skip to step 10 on page 78.

6 To add a Web page to the list of Web pages, click **New**.

■ The New Desktop Item wizard appears.

7 Click this area and type the address of the Web page you want to display on your desktop.

8 Click **OK** to confirm the Web page address you typed.

33

Have your desktop display Web content

When you add a Web page to your desktop, the Web page is copied to your computer and automatically appears on your desktop. Windows makes the Web page available offline, which allows the Web page to be displayed on your desktop even when you are not connected to the Internet.

When you are connected to the Internet, you can update a Web page displayed on your desktop. Many Web pages, such as Web pages that report the news, contain information that must be updated regularly in order to continue being useful.

After you add a Web page to your desktop, you may notice that Windows changes the background of the text for the icons on your desktop to make the text easier to read when appearing over the Web page.

You can click links and work with a Web page you add to your desktop the same way you would click links and work with a Web page when viewing the page in your Web browser.

CONTINUED ▶

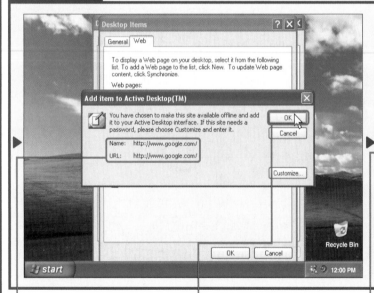

■ The Add item to Active Desktop dialog box appears.

■ This area displays the name and address of the Web page you specified.

9 Click **OK** to continue.

■ Windows copies the Web page to your computer.

■ The Web page appears in the list of Web pages you can display on your desktop.

10 Each Web page that displays a check mark (☑) will appear on your desktop. To add or remove a check mark, click the box beside the Web page.

11 Click **OK** to confirm your changes.

12 Click **OK** to close the Display Properties dialog box.

Customize It! You can easily change the size of a Web page displayed on your desktop. Position the mouse ⌖ over an edge of the Web page (⌖ changes to ↕, ↔, ⤢ or ⤡) and then drag the Web page to the size you want. To have the Web page fill the screen, position the mouse ⌖ over the top of the Web page. On the gray bar that appears, click □. To return the Web page to its previous size, position the mouse ⌖ over the top of the page and then click ▣ on the gray bar.

Delete It! To permanently delete a Web page from your computer, perform steps 1 to 5, starting on page 76. Then select the Web page you want to delete and click the Delete button. You cannot delete the My Current Home Page item.

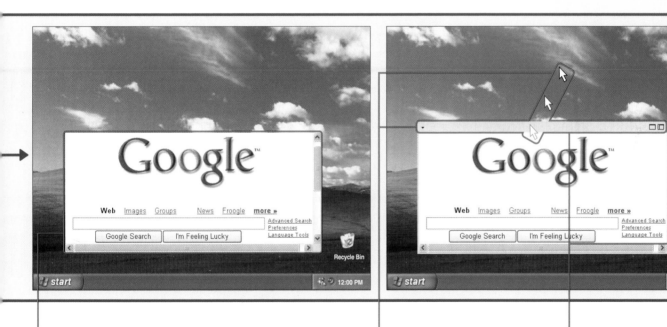

■ The Web page you selected appears on your desktop.

■ To immediately update the contents of the Web page, click a blank area on your desktop and then press the **F5** key.

MOVE A WEB PAGE ON THE DESKTOP

1 Position the mouse ⌖ over the top edge of the Web page. A gray bar appears.

2 Drag the Web page to a new location on your desktop.

REMOVE A WEB PAGE FROM THE DESKTOP

1 Position the mouse ⌖ over the top edge of the Web page. A gray bar appears.

2 Click ×.

34

Display cool shortcut icons

You can change the icons for shortcuts on your desktop as well as the shortcuts stored in other locations on your computer. Changing your shortcut icons can help personalize your computer.

A shortcut provides a quick way of opening an item you use regularly. You can easily recognize a shortcut icon by its arrow (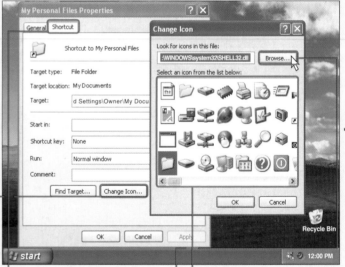) in the bottom left corner. Changing a shortcut icon will not affect the original file the shortcut refers to on your computer.

When changing shortcut icons, Windows provides you with icons you can choose from. Icons included with Windows are stored on your computer at C:\WINDOWS\system32\shell32.dll and C:\WINDOWS\system32\moricons.dll.

You can also find free icons on the Web that you can use to customize your shortcut icons. For example, you can find icons at the www.iconarchive.com and www.icons.cc Web sites. When downloading icons from the Web for your shortcut icons, make sure the icons have either the .exe, .dll or .ico extension.

1 Right-click the shortcut whose icon you want to change. A menu appears.

Note: A shortcut icon displays an arrow ( ).

2 Click **Properties** to view the properties of the shortcut.

■ The Properties dialog box appears.

3 Click the **Shortcut** tab.

4 Click **Change Icon** to change the icon for the shortcut.

■ The Change Icon dialog box appears.

5 Click the icon you want to use for the shortcut. Then skip to step **9**.

6 If you do not see the icon you want to use, click **Browse** to locate the icon you want to use on your computer.

Try This! You can change the icon for a folder on your computer that is not a shortcut. Right-click the folder you want to change and select Properties. In the Properties dialog box, click the Customize tab and click the Change Icon button. Then perform steps 5 to 10 below.

Did You Know? You can change all the icons representing a type of file, such as all the WordPad icons (📄). Open any folder on your computer, select the Tools menu and click Folder Options. In the Folder Options dialog box, click the File Types tab, click the type of file you want to change and click the Advanced button. In the Edit File Type dialog box, click the Change Icon button. Then perform steps 5 to 9 below and click OK to close the Edit File Type and Folder Options dialog boxes.

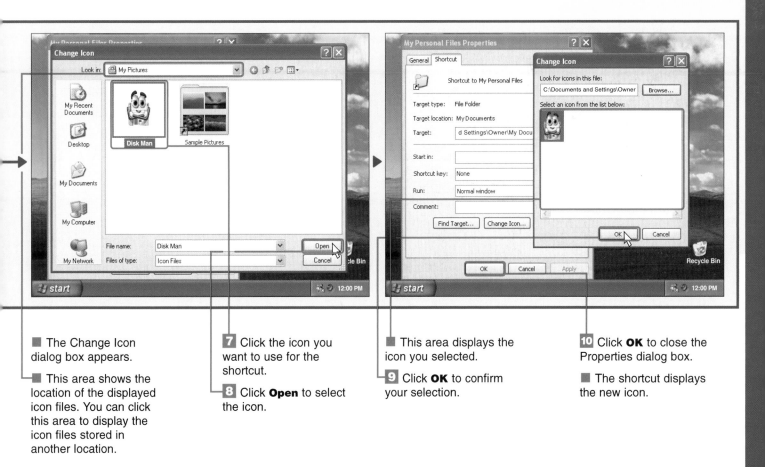

■ The Change Icon dialog box appears.

■ This area shows the location of the displayed icon files. You can click this area to display the icon files stored in another location.

7 Click the icon you want to use for the shortcut.

8 Click **Open** to select the icon.

■ This area displays the icon you selected.

9 Click **OK** to confirm your selection.

10 Click **OK** to close the Properties dialog box.

■ The shortcut displays the new icon.

#35

Set up a screen saver slide show

You can use a screen saver in Windows XP that will showcase your own pictures in a slide show. A screen saver is useful for hiding your work while you are away from your desk and also for making your screen look more interesting when your computer is not in use.

The My Pictures Slideshow screen saver uses the pictures stored in your My Pictures folder as your screen saver. When your screen saver is active, Windows will rotate through all the pictures in the folder, displaying each picture on your screen for six

seconds at a time. Using the My Pictures Slideshow screen saver is a good way to showcase photos you have copied to your My Pictures folder from a digital camera, downloaded from the Internet or scanned into your computer.

A screen saver can use a substantial amount of your computer's resources when displayed on your screen. You should turn off the screen saver if your computer will be performing unattended tasks that require a lot of processing power, such as copying files to a recordable CD.

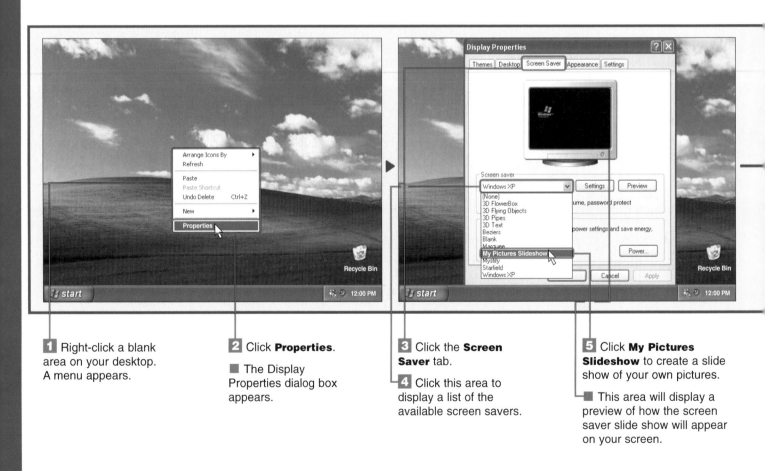

1 Right-click a blank area on your desktop. A menu appears.

2 Click **Properties**.

■ The Display Properties dialog box appears.

3 Click the **Screen Saver** tab.

4 Click this area to display a list of the available screen savers.

5 Click **My Pictures Slideshow** to create a slide show of your own pictures.

■ This area will display a preview of how the screen saver slide show will appear on your screen.

Did You Know? You can display your pictures as a slide show without creating a screen saver. In a folder that contains pictures, click the View as a slide show link to display all the pictures in the folder as a full-screen slide show. While viewing the slide show, you can move the mouse to display a toolbar that contains buttons you can use to pause, restart, move through or end the slide show.

Customize It! You can change the length of time each picture is displayed in a screen saver slide show. Perform steps 1 to 3 below and then click the Settings button. Drag the slider ( ) below "How often should pictures change?" to the right or left to increase or decrease the length of time each picture appears on the screen.

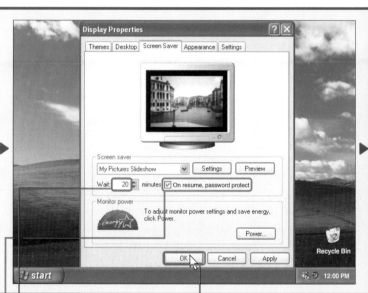

6 To specify the number of minutes your computer must be inactive before the screen saver slide show will begin, double-click this area. Then type the number of minutes.

7 This option requires you to log on to Windows each time you want to remove the screen saver. You can click this option to turn the option on (☑) or off (☐).

Note: The name of the option is different if multiple users are set up on your computer.

8 Click **OK**.

■ The screen saver slide show begins when you do not use your computer for the number of minutes you specified.

■ You can move the mouse or press a key on the keyboard to remove the screen saver from your screen.

■ To turn off the screen saver slide show, perform steps 1 to 5, selecting **(None)** in step 5. Then perform step 8.

83

36

Improve the appearance of text by using ClearType

You can use ClearType to smooth the edges of fonts, making text on your screen easier to read. Using ClearType can allow your computer screen to display a greater degree of detail, which makes the text on your screen appear clearer and sharper, almost like printed text.

The ClearType smoothing method is useful for portable computers and flat panel desktop monitors. Portable computers and flat panel desktop monitors both use LCD (Liquid Crystal Display) technology.

Most older desktop monitors use CRT (Cathode Ray Tube) technology, whereas many new desktop monitors use LCD technology. You can easily identify CRT monitors by their bulky appearance, while LCD monitors are flat and thin.

By default, Windows selects the Standard smoothing method, which is most appropriate for CRT desktop monitors. Using the ClearType option on a CRT monitor may make text appear slightly blurry.

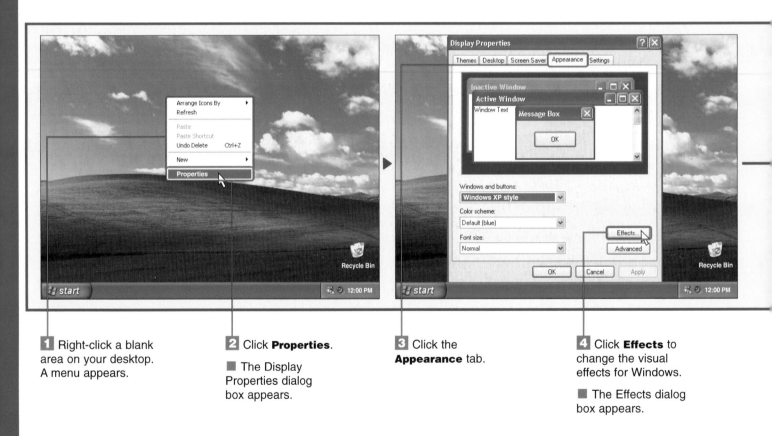

1 Right-click a blank area on your desktop. A menu appears.

2 Click **Properties**.

■ The Display Properties dialog box appears.

3 Click the **Appearance** tab.

4 Click **Effects** to change the visual effects for Windows.

■ The Effects dialog box appears.

Did You Know?   To ensure the best results when using ClearType on an LCD monitor, your display should be set at its native resolution, which is the resolution that best suits your monitor and video card. To change the resolution, perform steps 1 and 2 below and then click the Settings tab. Then drag the slider (🖢) under "Screen resolution" to select the resolution specified by the monitor's manufacturer.

Attention!   To use ClearType, your computer's monitor and video card must support a color setting of at least 256 colors (8-bit). For the best results, use the High (24-bit) or Highest (32-bit) color setting. To change the color setting, perform steps 1 and 2 below and then click the Settings tab. Then click the area below "Color quality" and select the highest color setting available.

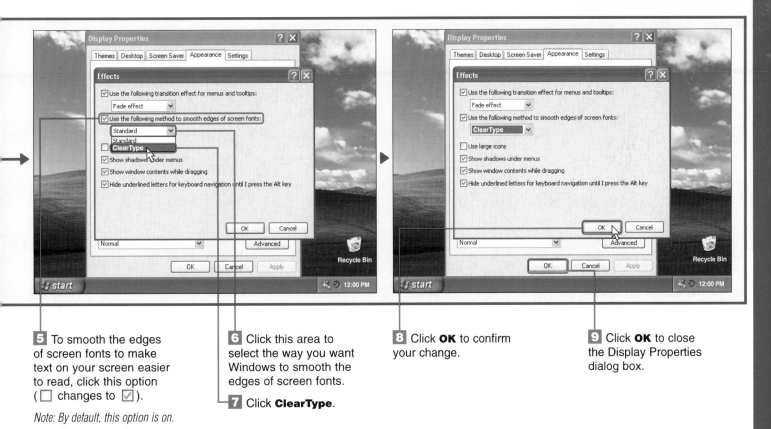

5 To smooth the edges of screen fonts to make text on your screen easier to read, click this option (☐ changes to ☑).

Note: By default, this option is on.

6 Click this area to select the way you want Windows to smooth the edges of screen fonts.

7 Click **ClearType**.

8 Click **OK** to confirm your change.

9 Click **OK** to close the Display Properties dialog box.

37

Change the picture beside your user name

When you first set up your user account, Windows automatically assigns a picture to your account. You can select a different picture for your user account to better suit your personality or interests.

If you have a computer administrator account, you can change the picture for any account set up on your computer. If you have a limited account, you can change the picture for only your own account.

Windows provides pictures that you can choose from for your user account. You can also select a picture you have stored on your computer to place beside your user name.

When you select a new picture for your user account, the new picture will appear on the Welcome screen each time you log on to your computer. The Welcome screen displays all the user accounts that are set up on your computer and allows you to select the account you want to use.

The new picture will also appear at the top of the Start menu when you are logged on to Windows.

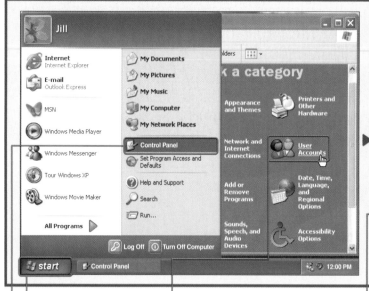

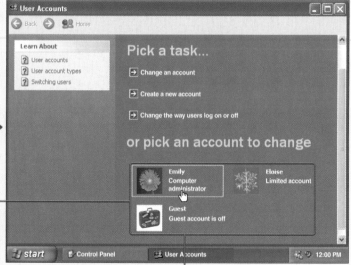

1 Click **start**.

2 Click **Control Panel** to change your computer's settings.

■ The Control Panel window appears.

3 Click **User Accounts** to work with the user accounts set up on your computer.

■ The User Accounts window appears.

■ If you have a computer administrator account, this area displays the accounts that are set up on your computer. The picture for each account appears beside each account name.

■ If you have a limited account, skip to step **5**.

4 Click the account you want to use a different picture.

Try This! You can also use a picture stored in another location on your computer to place beside your user name. Click the Browse for more pictures link in the User Accounts window. In the Open dialog box that appears, locate the picture you want to use for the user account and then double-click the picture.

Download It! You can download pictures from the Internet to use as the picture beside your user name. Right-click the picture of interest on a Web page and then click Save Picture As in the menu that appears. Type a name for the picture and then click the Save button. Your picture will be saved in the My Pictures folder.

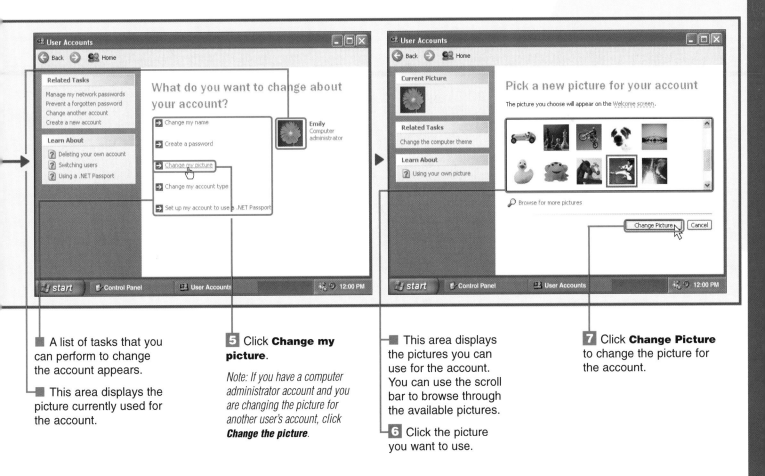

■ A list of tasks that you can perform to change the account appears.

■ This area displays the picture currently used for the account.

5 Click **Change my picture**.

Note: If you have a computer administrator account and you are changing the picture for another user's account, click ***Change the picture***.

■ This area displays the pictures you can use for the account. You can use the scroll bar to browse through the available pictures.

6 Click the picture you want to use.

7 Click **Change Picture** to change the picture for the account.

#38 Customize the mouse for left-handed users

If you are left-handed, you may want to change the way your mouse works to make the mouse easier to use.

By default, the left mouse button is the primary mouse button, while the right mouse button is the secondary mouse button. You use the primary mouse button to select and drag items and the secondary mouse button to display a list of commands for a selected item. When using the mouse with their left hand, left-handed users may find the mouse easier to use when the primary button is below their left index finger rather than below their left middle finger.

When you switch the functions of the left and right mouse buttons in the Mouse Properties dialog box, Windows immediately changes the way your mouse works.

Once you have changed the way your mouse works, keep in mind that following the instructions for using the mouse must be done opposite to the way you previously used the mouse. For example, to right-click, you must now click the left mouse button. To click or double-click, you must now click or double-click the right mouse button.

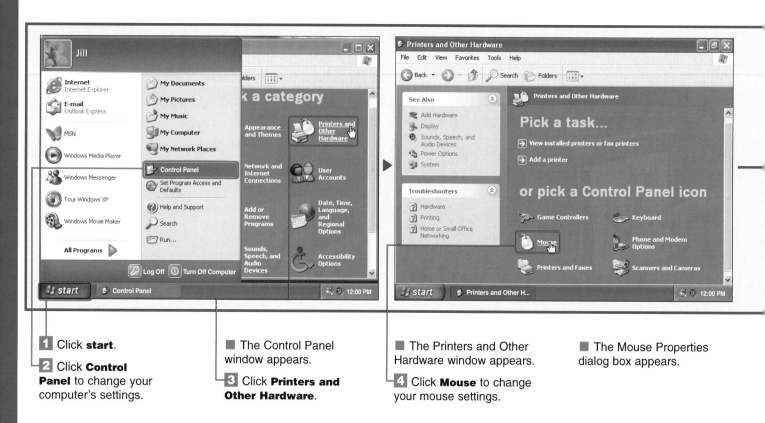

■ 1 Click **start**.

2 Click **Control Panel** to change your computer's settings.

■ The Control Panel window appears.

3 Click **Printers and Other Hardware**.

■ The Printers and Other Hardware window appears.

4 Click **Mouse** to change your mouse settings.

■ The Mouse Properties dialog box appears.

Did You Know? You can change the amount of time that can pass between two clicks of the mouse button for Windows to recognize a double-click. On the Buttons tab, drag the slider ( ) to a new position. Then double-click the yellow folder ( ) to test the new double-click speed.

Try This! The ClickLock mouse setting allows you to select text without having to continuously hold down the mouse button. On the Buttons tab, select the Turn on ClickLock option (□ changes to ☑). To select text using ClickLock, position the mouse pointer to the left of the text you want to select and then hold down the mouse button for a moment. Then click at the end of the text.

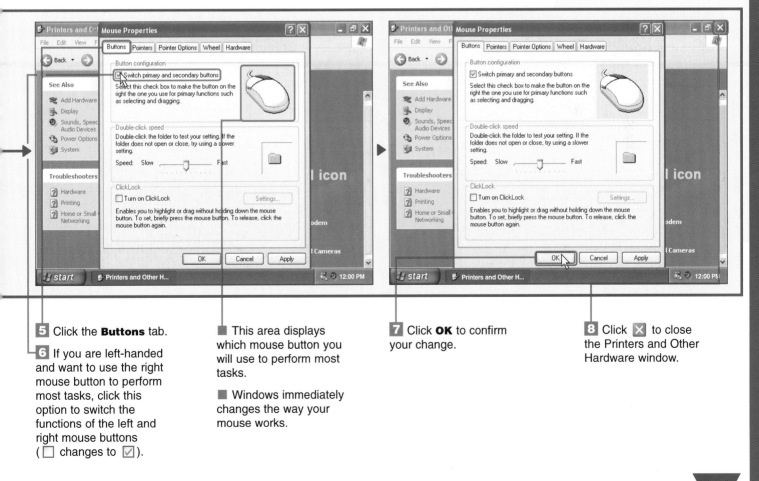

5 Click the **Buttons** tab.

6 If you are left-handed and want to use the right mouse button to perform most tasks, click this option to switch the functions of the left and right mouse buttons (□ changes to ☑).

■ This area displays which mouse button you will use to perform most tasks.

■ Windows immediately changes the way your mouse works.

7 Click **OK** to confirm your change.

8 Click ✕ to close the Printers and Other Hardware window.

Add extra fonts to your computer

Windows comes with a number of fonts, but you can add extra fonts to your computer to increase your choices when creating documents. The fonts included with Windows and any other fonts you add will be available in all Windows-based programs on your computer.

There are thousands of fonts available that you can add to your computer. You can usually buy fonts at computer stores or obtain fonts on the Internet. Many fonts on the Internet are free. When obtaining fonts, look for OpenType and TrueType fonts, since these are the most commonly used

fonts in Windows. You should also make sure the fonts you choose are designed for Windows.

There is no limit to the number of fonts you can add, but keep in mind that fonts take up storage space on your computer. You may also find that a long list of fonts becomes cluttered and difficult to use.

After you add fonts to your computer, you can delete fonts you added as you would delete any file on your computer. You should only delete fonts that you added to your computer.

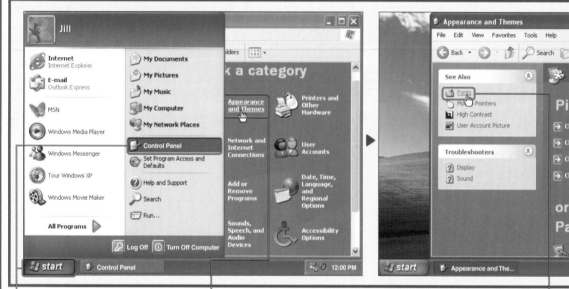

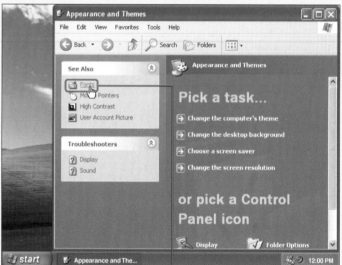

■ If the fonts you want to add are stored on a floppy disk or CD, insert the disk into the appropriate drive on your computer.

1 Click **start**.

2 Click **Control Panel** to change your computer's settings.

■ The Control Panel window appears.

3 Click **Appearance and Themes**.

■ The Appearance and Themes window appears.

4 Click **Fonts** to add new fonts to your computer.

Extract It! Fonts you downloaded to your computer from the Internet may be stored in a compressed folder (📁). You need to extract the fonts before you can add the fonts to your computer. To extract a font from a compressed folder, drag the font from the folder to a new location outside the folder.

View Samples! You can view samples of the fonts on your computer. In the Fonts window, double-click the font of interest. A window appears, displaying information about the selected font and samples of the font in various sizes. Click Done to close the window.

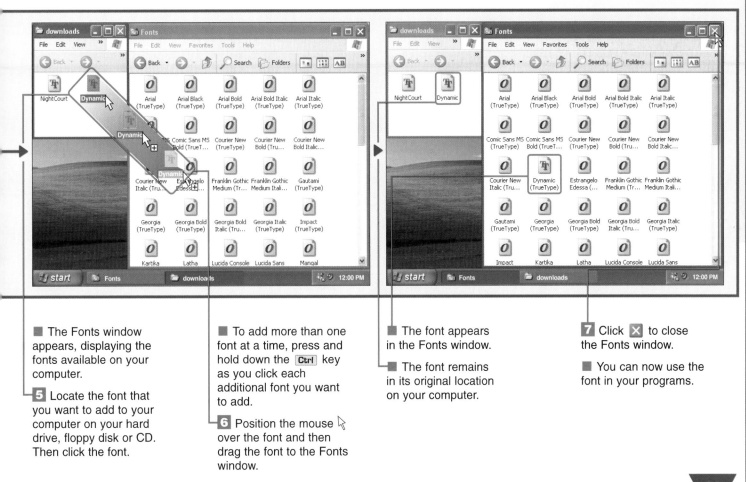

■ The Fonts window appears, displaying the fonts available on your computer.

5 Locate the font that you want to add to your computer on your hard drive, floppy disk or CD. Then click the font.

■ To add more than one font at a time, press and hold down the **Ctrl** key as you click each additional font you want to add.

6 Position the mouse over the font and then drag the font to the Fonts window.

■ The font appears in the Fonts window.

■ The font remains in its original location on your computer.

7 Click ✕ to close the Fonts window.

■ You can now use the font in your programs.

#40 Enter text in a different language

If you need to create documents in more than one language, you can set up Windows to allow you to enter text in a different language. This feature is useful for students who are required to write reports in a different language or for business people who must correspond with international contacts. You must be logged on to Windows as a computer administrator to perform this task.

When you set up your computer to enter text in a new language, your menus and toolbars will still be displayed in the original language, but your keyboard layout will be different. When you type in the new language, any special characters or accented characters used by the new language will be available on the keyboard. Some standard characters may be in a different position than they would be on your usual keyboard layout.

After you set up your computer to enter text in another language, you may notice that some of your programs also include features to help you use the new language, such as a spell checker for the new language.

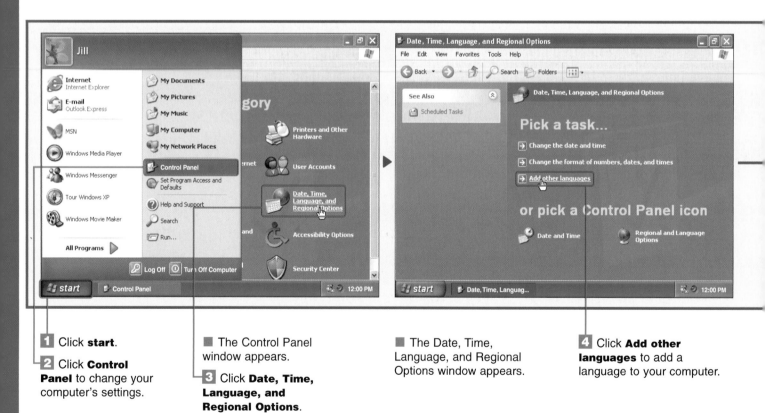

1 Click **start**.

2 Click **Control Panel** to change your computer's settings.

■ The Control Panel window appears.

3 Click **Date, Time, Language, and Regional Options**.

■ The Date, Time, Language, and Regional Options window appears.

4 Click **Add other languages** to add a language to your computer.

Attention! You should add to your computer only the languages you need. Since the information for each language is loaded into your computer's memory each time you start your computer, adding too many languages may affect your computer's performance.

Add More! If you would like to enter text in an East Asian language or a language that enters characters from right to left or uses complex script, such as Arabic or Hebrew, you must add files to your computer before you can add the language to your computer. In the Regional and Language Options dialog box, click the option for the type of language you want to add (☐ changes to ☑). Click OK in the dialog box that appears and then click OK in the Regional and Language Options dialog box. Insert your Windows XP CD into your CD drive and then click Yes when asked to restart your computer. You can now add the language to your computer.

CONTINUED ►

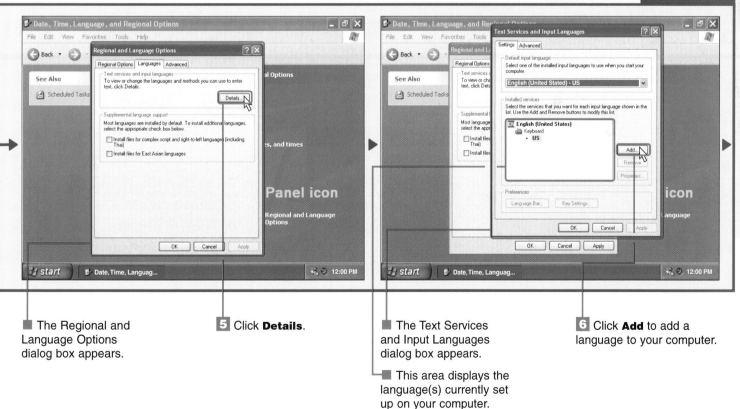

■ The Regional and Language Options dialog box appears.

5 Click **Details**.

■ The Text Services and Input Languages dialog box appears.

■ This area displays the language(s) currently set up on your computer.

6 Click **Add** to add a language to your computer.

When you choose a different language in which to enter text, Windows automatically selects a keyboard layout for the language. You can choose a different keyboard layout if the selected layout does not suit your needs.

After you set up another language on your computer, you can choose which language you want to use. A language indicator appears on the taskbar, indicating the current language, such as **EN** for English.

To switch to a different language, you can click the language indicator and then select the language you want to use from the displayed list of available languages. You can also switch between languages by pressing and holding down the Alt key as you press the Shift key.

You can view all the languages you have set up on your computer and the keyboard layout for each language in the Text Services and Input Languages dialog box.

CONTINUED ►

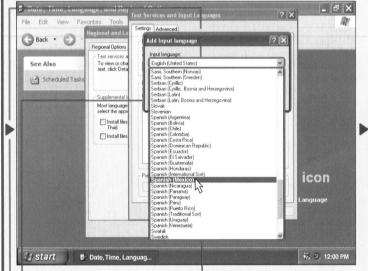

■ The Add Input language dialog box appears.

7 Click this area to display a list of languages you can choose from.

8 Click the language you want to use.

■ This area displays the keyboard layout Windows will use for the language you selected. You can click this area to choose a different keyboard layout.

Note: The keyboard layout determines how the characters used by the language are positioned on the keyboard.

9 Click **OK** to confirm your change.

Remove It! To remove a language you added, perform steps 1 to 5 starting on page 92 to display the Text Services and Input Languages dialog box. Select the language you added and then click the Remove button to remove the language.

Did You Know? Before entering text in a new language, you can use the On-Screen Keyboard to determine which character each key on the keyboard will type. To open the On-Screen Keyboard, click start, All Programs, Accessories, Accessibility, On-Screen Keyboard. Perform steps 1 to 3 below to select the program and language in which you want to enter text. The On-Screen Keyboard will display which character each key on the keyboard will type. When you finish using the On-Screen Keyboard, click ☒ to close the window.

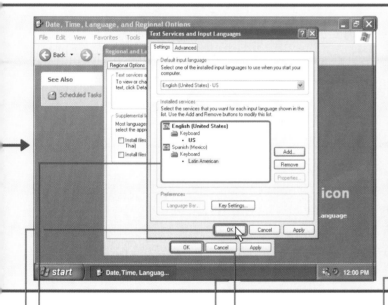

◾ The language you selected and the keyboard layout for the language appear in this area.

10 Click **OK** to close the Text Services and Input Languages dialog box.

11 Click **OK** to close the Regional and Language Options dialog box.

12 Click ☒ to close the Date, Time, Language, and Regional Options window.

ENTER TEXT IN A DIFFERENT LANGUAGE

◾ A language indicator appears on your taskbar, indicating the current language.

1 Open the program in which you want to enter text in a different language.

Note: For example, to open WordPad, click start, All Programs, Accessories, WordPad.

2 Click the language indicator to display a list of the available languages.

3 Click the language you want to use to enter text.

41

Remove the animated dog from the Search Companion

When you search for items in Windows, an animated dog automatically appears in the Search Companion to work as your search assistant. If you find the animated dog annoying or distracting, you can remove it from the Search Companion.

To remove the animated dog screen character from the Search Companion, you need to change your search preferences. The available search options will not be affected when you remove the animated screen character. Keep in mind that removing the animated

screen character from the search feature in Windows will also remove the character from the search feature in Internet Explorer.

Removing the animated character from the Search Companion will not affect the other user accounts set up on your computer. Each person with a user account set up on your computer can choose to display or hide the animated character to suit their preferences.

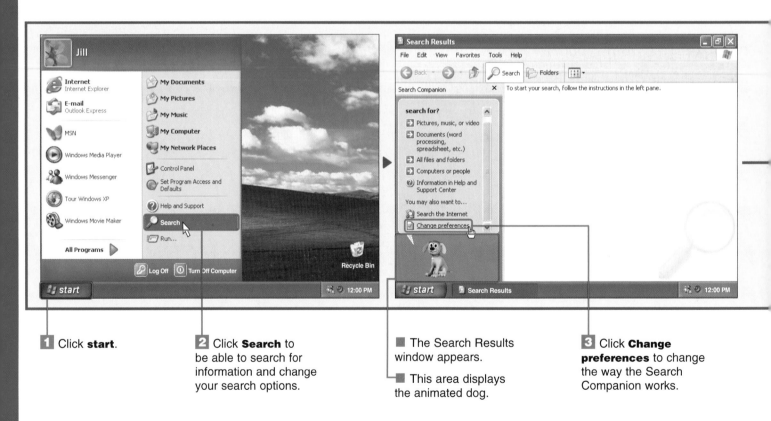

1 Click **start**.

2 Click **Search** to be able to search for information and change your search options.

■ The Search Results window appears.

■ This area displays the animated dog.

3 Click **Change preferences** to change the way the Search Companion works.

Undo It! You can bring back the animated dog at any time. To once again display the animated dog, perform steps 1 to 3 below and then click "With an animated screen character." If you changed to a different screen character before turning the character off, the last screen character you used will reappear.

Customize It! If you decide to keep an animated character in the Search Companion, but do not want to use the animated dog, you can choose from several other search characters. To display a different animated character, perform steps 1 to 3 below and then click "With a different character." Use the Back and Next buttons to move through the available characters and then click OK to select the one you want to use.

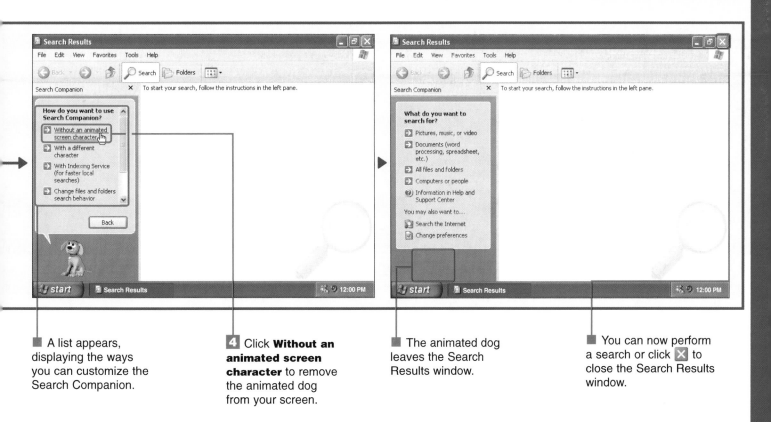

■ A list appears, displaying the ways you can customize the Search Companion.

4 Click **Without an animated screen character** to remove the animated dog from your screen.

■ The animated dog leaves the Search Results window.

■ You can now perform a search or click ⊠ to close the Search Results window.

42

Set up your computer for visitors

You can turn on the Guest account to allow a person who does not have a user account set up on your computer to use the computer. For example, a visiting friend may want to use the Guest account to check their e-mail.

Windows automatically creates the Guest account on your computer. As a security precaution, the Guest account is initially turned off. You must be logged on to Windows as a computer administrator to turn on the Guest account.

For security reasons, a guest can perform only certain tasks on your computer. For example, a guest can run programs already installed on your computer, but cannot install new programs. A guest also cannot create new user accounts or modify existing user accounts.

If your computer uses the NTFS file system, a guest will not be able to view the personal files of other users set up on your computer. If your computer uses the FAT file system, a guest will be able to view the personal files of other users. Most new computers use the NTFS file system.

1 Click **start**.

2 Click **Control Panel** to change your computer's settings.

■ The Control Panel window appears.

3 Click **User Accounts** to work with the user accounts set up on your computer.

Did You Know? There is only one Guest account available. Every person who logs on to your computer as a guest must use the same Guest account. You cannot change the name of the Guest account.

Customize It! You can change the picture for the Guest account when logged on to Windows as a computer administrator or as a guest. For information on changing the picture for an account, see task #37.

Turn It Off! To turn off the Guest account at any time, perform steps 1 to 4 below and then click the "Turn off the guest account" option. You must be logged on to Windows as a computer administrator to turn off the Guest account.

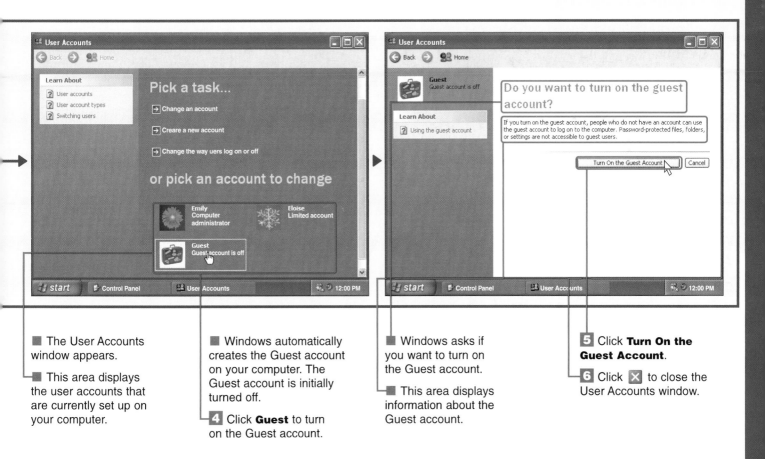

■ The User Accounts window appears.

■ This area displays the user accounts that are currently set up on your computer.

■ Windows automatically creates the Guest account on your computer. The Guest account is initially turned off.

4 Click **Guest** to turn on the Guest account.

■ Windows asks if you want to turn on the Guest account.

■ This area displays information about the Guest account.

5 Click **Turn On the Guest Account**.

6 Click ✕ to close the User Accounts window.

Boost Your Efficiency

Have you been looking for ways that you can use Windows XP to work smarter and faster? The tasks in this chapter will show you how Windows can help boost your efficiency.

You can customize Windows XP's taskbar in several ways to help you more quickly access items you frequently use. For example, you can place items on the taskbar so you can access the items with a single click of your mouse.

Do you want to customize the Start menu so you can find items you need more quickly? Read on to learn how to arrange Start menu items in alphabetical order and display the contents of your frequently used folders on the Start menu.

Do you find the balloon tips Windows XP displays on the taskbar distract you or slow down your work? Find out how to pop those balloons and get rid of them forever.

If clutter is getting in your way, review the tasks in this chapter. You will learn how to hide icons to clean up your desktop, how to perform housekeeping on your computer and how to remove unneeded programs to free up disk space so your computer can run more efficiently.

Using keyboard shortcuts to replace mouse clicks can also speed up your work. Check out this chapter to learn how to use keyboard shortcuts to lock your computer and perform many other common tasks.

101 Hot Tips

Place items on the taskbar for quick access

If you frequently use Internet Explorer, the desktop or Windows Media Player, you can add the Quick Launch toolbar to the taskbar so you can quickly access these items. The Quick Launch toolbar may also display icons for additional programs you have installed on your computer, such as Microsoft Outlook.

You can add your own items to the Quick Launch toolbar, such as files, folders and programs you want to be able to quickly access. To add an item to the toolbar,

you drag the item to the toolbar. If the item appears on the Start menu, you can drag the item from the Start menu to the Quick Launch toolbar.

You can also rearrange the items on the Quick Launch toolbar by dragging each item to a new location on the toolbar. When you drag an item, a black line indicates where the item will appear on the toolbar.

1 Right-click an empty area on the taskbar. A menu appears.

2 Click **Toolbars**.

3 Click **Quick Launch** to display the Quick Launch toolbar on the taskbar.

■ The Quick Launch toolbar appears on the taskbar.

■ The Quick Launch toolbar contains icons that allow you to quickly access Internet Explorer (▨), your desktop (▨) and Windows Media Player (▨).

Display It! If some items on the Quick Launch toolbar are not displayed, you can click ▓ at the right of the toolbar to display the hidden items.

To permanently display all the items on the Quick Launch toolbar, right-click an empty area on the taskbar. On the menu that appears, click Lock the Taskbar to remove the check mark (✔) beside the option. Then position the mouse ⌖ over the right border of the toolbar (⌖ changes to ↔) and drag the border until all the toolbar items are displayed.

Delete It! You can remove an item from the Quick Launch toolbar. To remove an item, right-click the icon for the item and then click Delete on the menu that appears. Click Yes or Delete Shortcut in the confirmation dialog box that appears.

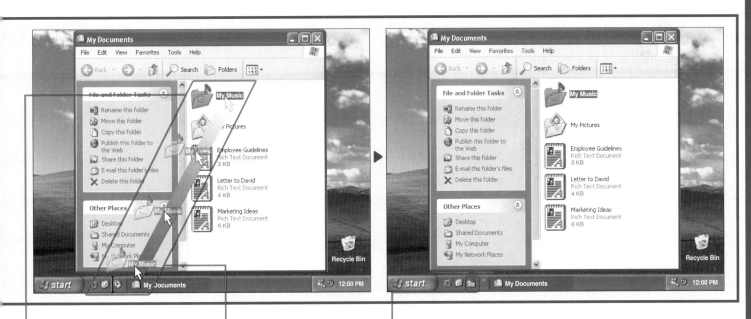

ADD ITEM TO QUICK LAUNCH TOOLBAR

1 Locate the item, such as a program, file or folder, you want to add to the Quick Launch toolbar.

2 Position the mouse ⌖ over the item.

3 Drag the item to the Quick Launch toolbar. A black line indicates where the shortcut for the item will appear.

■ Windows places a shortcut to the item on the Quick Launch toolbar.

Note: To add an item displayed on the Start menu to the Quick Launch toolbar, locate the item on the Start menu. Press and hold down the Ctrl *key as you drag the item from the Start menu to the toolbar.*

You can create a new toolbar for any folder on your computer and place the toolbar on the taskbar. Toolbars include items you can click to provide easy access to files and programs.

You may want to create a toolbar for the Control Panel or My Documents folder to quickly access the items in the folders. If many of the documents you frequently use are stored in one folder, such as a folder for a specific project, you can create a toolbar for the folder for quick access. You may also want to

create a toolbar for your My Music folder to allow you to quickly access and play your favorite songs.

When you create a new toolbar for a folder, the original folder remains in the same location on your computer.

After you add a toolbar that displays the contents of a folder to the taskbar, any files that you add to the folder will automatically appear on the toolbar.

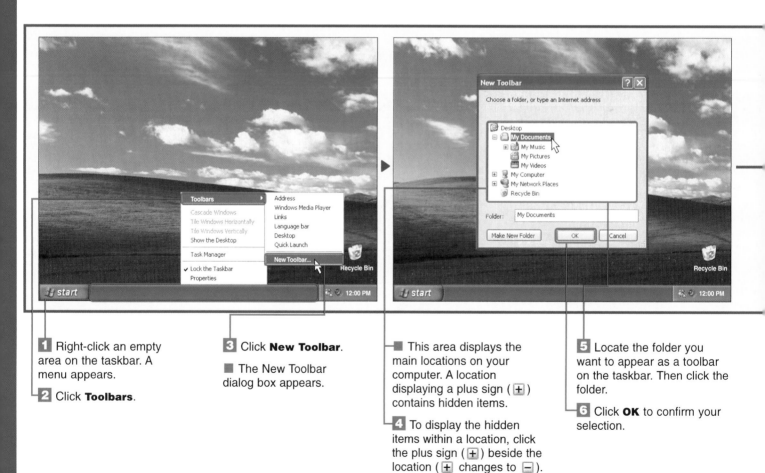

1 Right-click an empty area on the taskbar. A menu appears.

2 Click **Toolbars**.

3 Click **New Toolbar**.

■ The New Toolbar dialog box appears.

■ This area displays the main locations on your computer. A location displaying a plus sign (+) contains hidden items.

4 To display the hidden items within a location, click the plus sign (+) beside the location (+ changes to −).

5 Locate the folder you want to appear as a toolbar on the taskbar. Then click the folder.

6 Click **OK** to confirm your selection.

Move It! To move a toolbar, right-click an empty area on the taskbar and select Lock the Taskbar from the menu that appears, unlocking the taskbar. Position the mouse ⬚ over the name of the toolbar you want to move and then drag the toolbar to any edge of your screen. You can also drag a toolbar to the middle of your screen to create a floating toolbar. To move a toolbar back onto the taskbar, position the mouse ⬚ over the name of the toolbar and then drag the toolbar back to the taskbar.

Try This! To quickly create a toolbar for a folder, position the mouse ⬚ over the icon for a folder and then drag the icon to the left, right or top edge of your screen. You can drag the folder icon from a window or from your desktop.

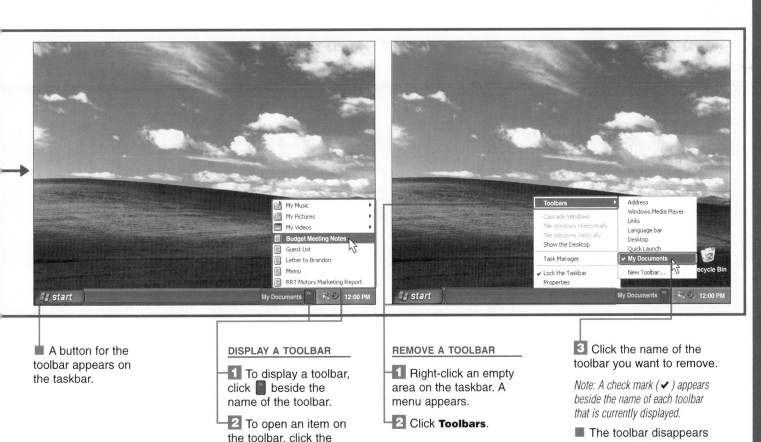

■ A button for the toolbar appears on the taskbar.

DISPLAY A TOOLBAR

1 To display a toolbar, click ⬛ beside the name of the toolbar.

2 To open an item on the toolbar, click the item.

REMOVE A TOOLBAR

1 Right-click an empty area on the taskbar. A menu appears.

2 Click **Toolbars**.

3 Click the name of the toolbar you want to remove.

Note: A check mark (✔) appears beside the name of each toolbar that is currently displayed.

■ The toolbar disappears from the taskbar.

Stop Windows from grouping taskbar buttons

If you have many windows open, Windows may group some of the buttons for open windows on the taskbar to reduce clutter and help you easily find documents. You can stop Windows from grouping buttons so you will always see a separate button for each open document. Keeping buttons separate on the taskbar allows you to see at a glance how many windows are open and quickly switch between windows with one click.

Windows generally groups the buttons for windows that are related. For example, if you

have several WordPad documents open, all the buttons for the documents may be grouped as a single button on the taskbar. The button for a group of windows displays a small triangle and a number indicating how many windows are grouped on the button.

After you ungroup buttons, the taskbar may become crowded. To quickly identify a button, you can position the mouse over the button to display its full name.

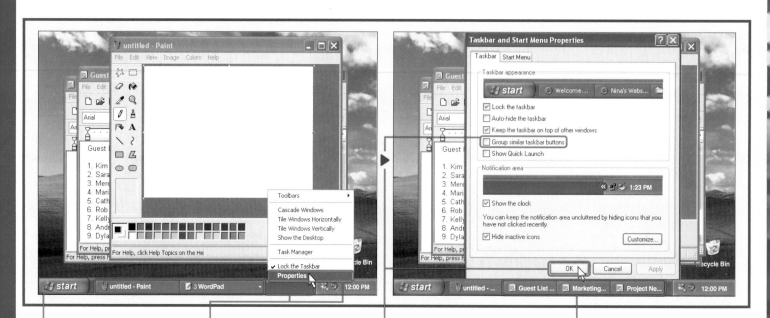

■ The taskbar displays a button for each open window. If you have many windows open, all the buttons for a program may appear as a single button on the taskbar.

1 If you do not want Windows to group related taskbar buttons, right-click an empty area on the taskbar. A menu appears.

2 Click **Properties**.

■ The Taskbar and Start Menu Properties dialog box appears.

3 Click this option if you do not want Windows to group related taskbar buttons (☑ changes to ☐).

4 Click **OK** to confirm your change.

■ Windows will no longer group related taskbar buttons.

■ To once again have Windows group related taskbar buttons, repeat steps **1** to **4** (☐ changes to ☑ in step **3**).

You can arrange items on the Start menu in alphabetical order to help you more easily locate items you want to use on the Start menu. Arranging items on the Start menu is especially useful if you have moved items around on the Start menu.

Arranging the items on the All Programs menu does not automatically arrange the items in its submenus. To alphabetically arrange items in a submenu, you must first display the submenu. For example, to alphabetically arrange the items on the Accessories

submenu, you must first click Accessories on the All Programs menu.

When you sort items on the Start menu by name, folders appear at the top of the menu in alphabetical order, followed by programs.

If the "Sort by Name" option does not appear when you right-click an area of the Start menu, you cannot sort the items displayed on that menu.

■1 Click **start**.

■2 Click **All Programs** to display a list of the programs on your computer.

■3 To sort the All Programs menu, right-click the menu. A menu appears.

Note: To sort another menu, click the menu name and then right-click the submenu.

■4 Click **Sort by Name** to alphabetically arrange the items on the menu.

■ The items on the menu are sorted by name.

■5 To close the Start menu, click outside the menu area.

Display folder contents on the Start menu

You can customize the way an item is displayed on the Start menu to suit your preferences. For example, if you frequently access items in a folder, such as the My Documents folder, you can have the contents of the folder appear in a submenu on the Start menu. This allows you to easily view the items the folder contains without having to open the folder. You can also open items in the folder more quickly by simply clicking the item of interest in the submenu.

By default, the Control Panel, My Computer, My Documents, My Music and My Pictures folders are all shown as links on the Start menu. When you click an item displayed as a link on the Start menu, a window displaying the item's contents appears. You can specify that you want to display an item as a menu, so the item's contents will appear in a submenu when you position the mouse over the item on the Start menu. You can also choose to remove any of these items from the Start menu to reduce clutter on the Start menu.

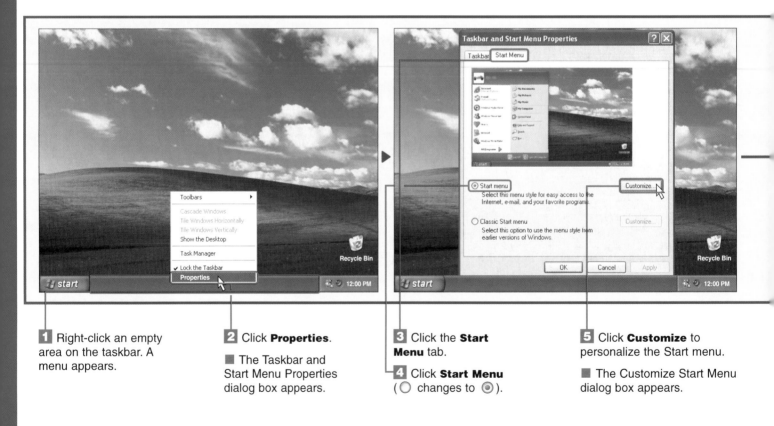

1 Right-click an empty area on the taskbar. A menu appears.

2 Click **Properties**.

■ The Taskbar and Start Menu Properties dialog box appears.

3 Click the **Start Menu** tab.

4 Click **Start Menu** (○ changes to ⊙).

5 Click **Customize** to personalize the Start menu.

■ The Customize Start Menu dialog box appears.

Further Customize! You can choose to hide or display other items on the Start menu, such as the Favorites menu, Help and Support, My Network Places, Printers and Faxes and the Run command. Perform steps 1 to 6 below. In the Start menu items area, click an item to hide (☐) or display (☑) the item on the Start menu.

Shorten It! If your All Programs menu is very long, items on the menu are displayed in several columns. To make the menu look less cluttered, you can have items on the menu appear in a single column that you can scroll through. Perform steps 1 to 6 below and then click Scroll Programs in the Start menu items area (☐ changes to ☑).

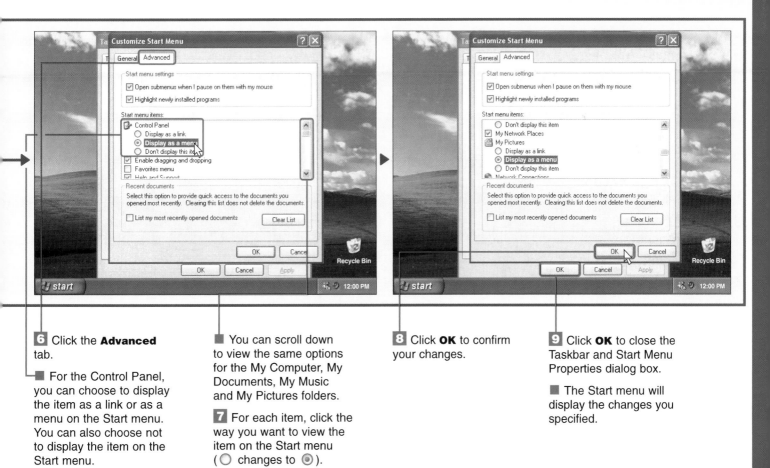

6 Click the **Advanced** tab.

■ For the Control Panel, you can choose to display the item as a link or as a menu on the Start menu. You can also choose not to display the item on the Start menu.

■ You can scroll down to view the same options for the My Computer, My Documents, My Music and My Pictures folders.

7 For each item, click the way you want to view the item on the Start menu (○ changes to ◉).

8 Click **OK** to confirm your changes.

9 Click **OK** to close the Taskbar and Start Menu Properties dialog box.

■ The Start menu will display the changes you specified.

#48 Pop the balloon tips

Windows periodically displays balloon tips on your screen. Balloon tips can appear for many different reasons, such as to display a warning that your computer might be at risk due to your security settings or to display a notification that Windows has detected a new piece of hardware connected to your computer.

If you find the balloon tips annoying or distracting, you can turn them off permanently for your user account. Turning off balloon tips for your user account will not affect the other user accounts set up on your computer.

To disable the balloon tips, you need to edit the registry using the Registry Editor. The registry contains

important information about your computer's setup and is continuously used by Windows to operate. If you make a mistake when editing the registry, you could severely damage your computer.

Before making any changes to the registry, you should create a backup copy of the files on your computer (see task #74). You should also create a restore point that will allow you to restore your computer to a time before you made changes to the registry (see task #71).

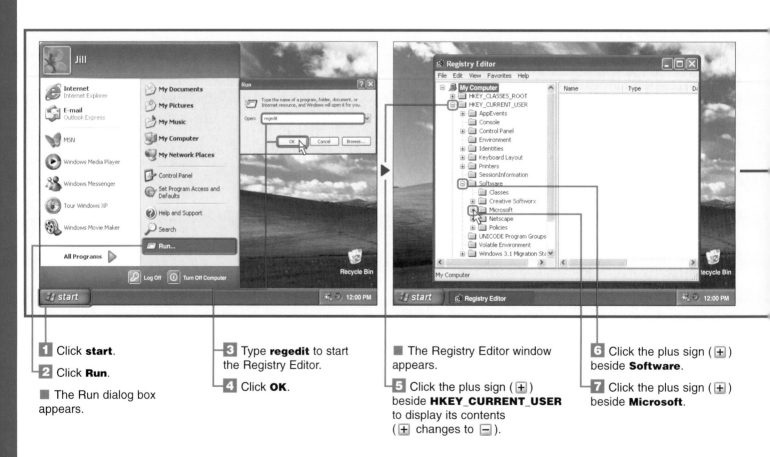

1 Click **start**.

2 Click **Run**.

■ The Run dialog box appears.

3 Type **regedit** to start the Registry Editor.

4 Click **OK**.

■ The Registry Editor window appears.

5 Click the plus sign (⊞) beside **HKEY_CURRENT_USER** to display its contents (⊞ changes to ⊟).

6 Click the plus sign (⊞) beside **Software**.

7 Click the plus sign (⊞) beside **Microsoft**.

Turn Off Tool Tips! You can also turn off the tool tips that appear when you position the mouse pointer over certain items on your screen, including files and items on the Start menu. To stop tool tips from appearing, perform steps 1 to 11 below. Then right-click the ShowInfoTip value in the right side of the window and select Modify from the menu that appears. In the dialog box that appears, type 0 in the Value data area and then click OK. The next time you start Windows, the tool tips will not appear.

Undo It! If you later want to turn the balloon tips back on, perform steps 1 to 11 below, then right-click the EnableBalloonTips value that you created and select Modify from the menu that appears. In the dialog box that appears, type 1 in the Value data area and then click OK. The next time you start Windows, the balloon tips will once again appear.

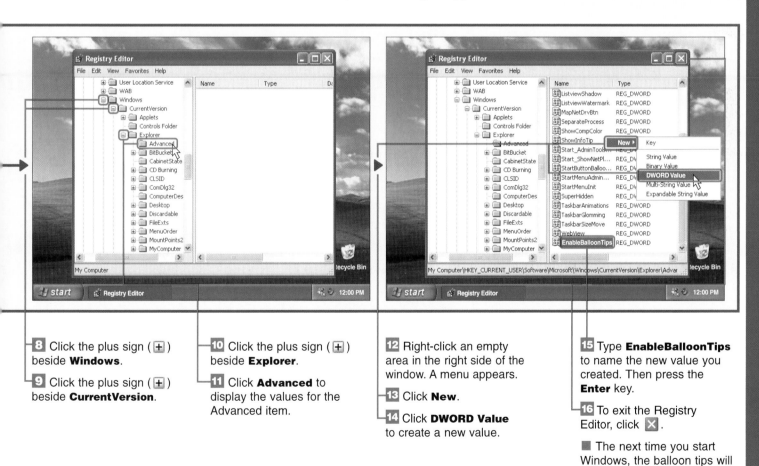

8 Click the plus sign (⊞) beside **Windows**.

9 Click the plus sign (⊞) beside **CurrentVersion**.

10 Click the plus sign (⊞) beside **Explorer**.

11 Click **Advanced** to display the values for the Advanced item.

12 Right-click an empty area in the right side of the window. A menu appears.

13 Click **New**.

14 Click **DWORD Value** to create a new value.

15 Type **EnableBalloonTips** to name the new value you created. Then press the **Enter** key.

16 To exit the Registry Editor, click ✕.

■ The next time you start Windows, the balloon tips will not appear.

You can create a shortcut on your desktop that allows you to quickly shut down Windows with a double-click instead of having to use the Start menu.

When you create a shortcut to shut down Windows, you can have Windows count down a specific number of seconds before shutting down or you can have Windows shut down immediately. If you set Windows to count down before shutting down, a warning dialog box appears when you double-click the shortcut. The warning dialog box counts down the number of seconds left before the computer will shut down.

If you set Windows to shut down immediately instead of counting down, the warning dialog box does not appear when you double-click the shortcut and Windows shuts down immediately.

The shortcut you create for shutting down Windows works just like any other shortcut. You can rename or delete the shortcut the same way you would rename or delete any file.

You must be logged on to Windows as a computer administrator to use a shortcut to shut down Windows.

1 Right-click a blank area on your desktop. A menu appears.

2 Click **New**.

3 Click **Shortcut** to create a shortcut on your desktop.

■ The Create Shortcut dialog box appears.

4 To have Windows shut down immediately when you double-click the shortcut, click this area and type **shutdown -s -t 00**.

Note: To have Windows count down for a specific number of seconds before shutting down, type the number of seconds instead of 00 in step 4.

5 Click **Next** to continue.

Change Your Mind! If you want to be able to stop Windows from shutting down once you double-click the shutdown shortcut, you can create an abort shortcut. To create an abort shortcut, perform the steps below, except type "shutdown -a" in step 4. If you set Windows to count down before shutting down, you can double-click the abort shortcut during the countdown to stop Windows from shutting down.

Try This! You can create shortcuts on your desktop that allow you to log off Windows or restart your computer. Perform the steps below, except in step 4, type "shutdown -l -t 00" to have the shortcut log you off Windows or type "shutdown -r -t 00" to have the shortcut restart your computer.

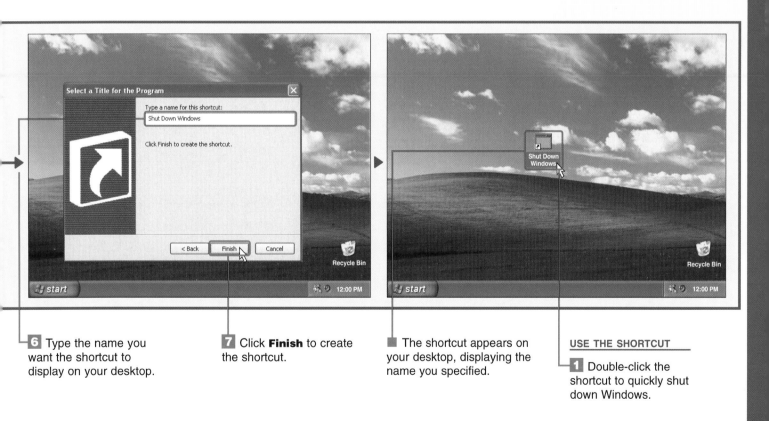

6 Type the name you want the shortcut to display on your desktop.

7 Click **Finish** to create the shortcut.

■ The shortcut appears on your desktop, displaying the name you specified.

USE THE SHORTCUT

1 Double-click the shortcut to quickly shut down Windows.

#50 Quickly lock your computer

You can quickly lock your computer to secure it from unauthorized users while you are away from your desk.

Locking your computer can be more practical than logging off or shutting down your computer. When you lock your computer, you can keep your programs running so you will not lose your place in your work. In order to log off or shut down your computer, you must close all of your open programs. Locking your computer

saves you time because you do not have to restart your programs when you start working on your computer again.

As long as every user account on your computer has a password, only people who know the password to one of the user accounts can access the computer once you lock the computer. For information on adding a password to a user account, see the top of page 29.

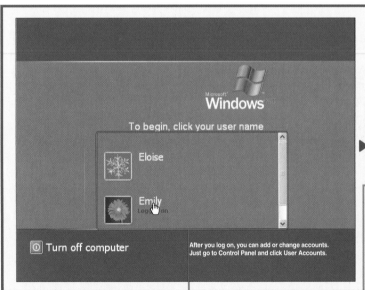

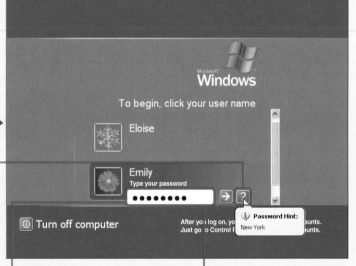

1 To lock your computer, press and hold down the ⊞ key as you press the **L** key.

■ The Welcome screen appears and the computer is locked.

■ This area displays the user accounts set up on your computer.

2 To access your programs and files, click the name of your user account.

■ A box appears that allows you to enter your password.

■ If you cannot remember your password, click ? to display the password hint you entered when you created the password.

3 Click this area and type your password. Then press the **Enter** key.

■ Windows starts, displaying your programs and files the way you left them.

#51 Instantly clean up your desktop by hiding icons

You may want to temporarily hide all the icons on your desktop to reduce clutter on your screen or to clearly display a desktop background. You can once again display the icons when you need them.

Over time, your desktop can become cluttered with icons as you work with various programs on your computer and download information from the Internet. You also may have created several desktop shortcuts for files and folders you

frequently use. Hiding numerous icons can create a clutter-free workspace when someone else, such as a colleague, needs to work with your computer.

You may also find that hiding the icons on your desktop is useful when you have customized your desktop to include content from the Web and you want to be able to clearly view the Web content. For information on adding Web content to your desktop, see task #33.

1 Right-click a blank area on your desktop. A menu appears.

2 Click **Arrange Icons By**.

3 Click **Show Desktop Icons**.

■ All the icons on your desktop temporarily disappear.

■ To once again display all the icons on your desktop, repeat steps **1** to **3**.

You can free up disk space on your computer by using Disk Cleanup to remove unnecessary files. You can select the types of files you want Disk Cleanup to remove. The available file types depend on the types of unnecessary files stored on your computer.

Downloaded program files are program files transferred automatically from the Internet and stored on your computer when you view certain Web pages.

Temporary Internet files are Web pages that Windows stores on your computer while you are browsing the Web so you can quickly view the pages again.

The Recycle Bin contains files you have deleted. Selecting the Recycle Bin option will permanently delete these files from your computer.

Temporary files are files created by programs to store temporary information.

WebClient/Publisher temporary files are copies of files you have accessed on your computer.

The Catalog files for the Content Indexer option removes files previously used to speed up and improve file searches.

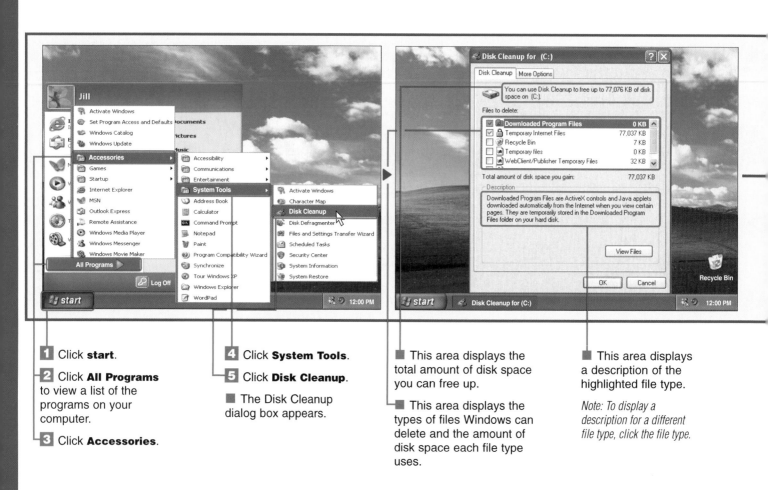

1 Click **start**.

2 Click **All Programs** to view a list of the programs on your computer.

3 Click **Accessories**.

4 Click **System Tools**.

5 Click **Disk Cleanup**.

■ The Disk Cleanup dialog box appears.

■ This area displays the total amount of disk space you can free up.

■ This area displays the types of files Windows can delete and the amount of disk space each file type uses.

■ This area displays a description of the highlighted file type.

Note: To display a description for a different file type, click the file type.

View It!   Before allowing Disk Cleanup to remove files from your computer, you can see which files will be removed. In the Disk Cleanup dialog box, select a file type and then click the View Files button. A window appears, displaying the files that will be removed. The View Files button is not available for some file types.

Did You Know?   You can free up even more disk space using Disk Cleanup. In the Disk Cleanup dialog box, click the More Options tab. This tab can help you remove Windows components and programs you do not use, as well as remove files used by the System Restore feature. The More Options tab is available only if you are using a computer administrator account.

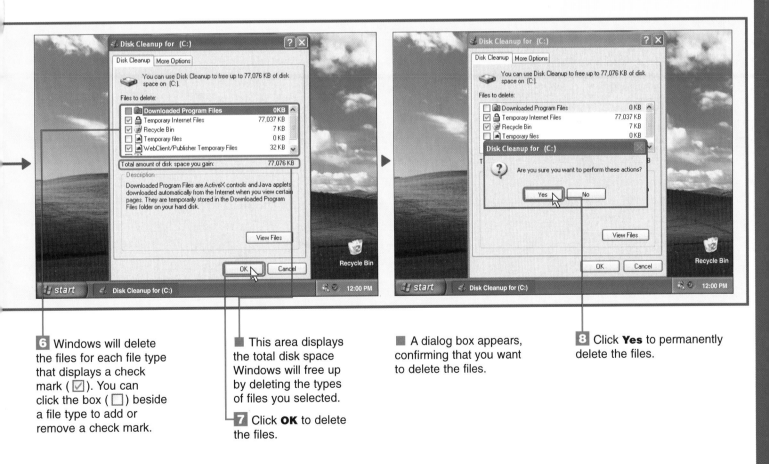

■ 6 Windows will delete the files for each file type that displays a check mark (☑). You can click the box (☐) beside a file type to add or remove a check mark.

■ This area displays the total disk space Windows will free up by deleting the types of files you selected.

■ 7 Click **OK** to delete the files.

■ A dialog box appears, confirming that you want to delete the files.

■ 8 Click **Yes** to permanently delete the files.

Remove a program to save hard disk space

If you no longer use a program installed on your computer, you can remove the program to free up space on your hard disk. If you are using a limited user account, you can only remove programs you installed yourself.

You can select the program you want to remove from a list and have Windows automatically remove the program from your computer. Keep in mind, however, that some programs do not appear in the list and cannot be removed using the method described below. Windows can only automatically remove a program that is designed for Windows.

When you remove a program from your computer, Windows deletes the program's files and may reverse the computer settings that were changed when the program was installed. However, if another program on your computer requires files that are associated with the program you are removing, Windows may leave the required files on your computer.

1 Click **start**.

2 Click **Control Panel** to change your computer's settings.

■ The Control Panel window appears.

3 Click **Add or Remove Programs**.

Program Not Listed? If the program you want to remove does not appear in the list of programs, you can check the documentation supplied with the program to determine how to remove the program.

More Space! You can help free up more hard disk space by removing Windows components you do not use, such as games. Perform steps 1 to 3 below and click Add/Remove Windows Components. In the Windows Components Wizard, click the box beside the component you want to remove (☑ changes to ☐). For some components, you can double-click the component to display its subcomponents. When displaying subcomponents, click the box beside the subcomponent you want to remove and then click OK. Click Next and then click Finish to close the wizard.

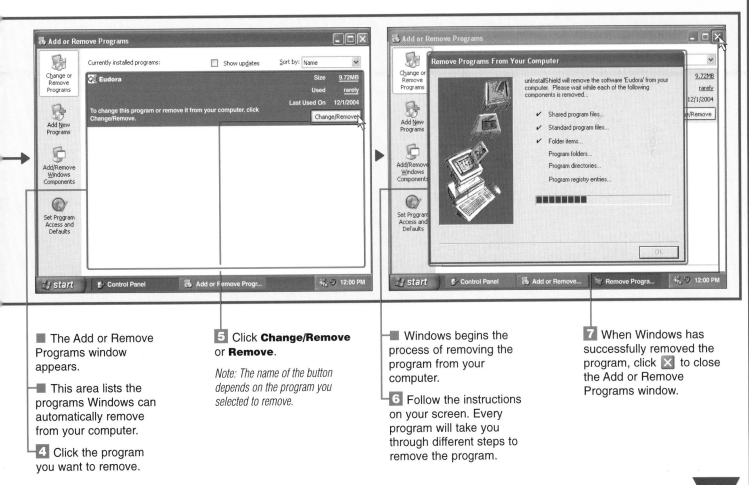

■ The Add or Remove Programs window appears.

■ This area lists the programs Windows can automatically remove from your computer.

4 Click the program you want to remove.

5 Click **Change/Remove** or **Remove**.

Note: The name of the button depends on the program you selected to remove.

■ Windows begins the process of removing the program from your computer.

6 Follow the instructions on your screen. Every program will take you through different steps to remove the program.

7 When Windows has successfully removed the program, click ☒ to close the Add or Remove Programs window.

Using keyboard shortcuts is a great way to save time when working in Windows. You can perform many tasks more quickly by pressing keys on your keyboard compared to using the mouse.

For example, you can press and hold down the ⊞ key and then press the D key to immediately minimize all items to display your desktop.

WHEN PERFORMING GENERAL TASKS

To do this	Press these keys
Select additional items in a window or on the desktop.	Shift + →, ←, ↑ or ↓
Select all items in a window or on the desktop.	Ctrl + A
Delete the selected item.	Delete
Permanently delete the selected item without placing the item in the Recycle Bin.	Shift + Delete
Rename the selected item.	F2
Display the properties of the selected item.	Alt + Enter
Update the contents of the active window.	F5
Switch between open windows.	Alt + Tab
Move through items in a window or on the desktop.	F6
View the shortcut menu for the active window.	Alt + Spacebar
View the shortcut menu for the selected item.	Shift + F10 or ▤
Close the active item.	Alt + F4

To do this	Press these keys
Close the active document in a program that allows you to have multiple documents open.	Ctrl + F4
Move to the menu bar of the active window.	F10
View a menu.	Alt + Underlined letter in menu name
Open the menu to the right of the selected menu or open a submenu.	→
Open the menu to the left of the selected menu or close a submenu.	←
Perform a command displayed on a menu.	Underlined letter in command name
Display the folder one level above the folder you are viewing.	←Backspace
Cancel the current task.	Esc
Minimize all items to display the desktop.	⊞ + D
Minimize all windows.	⊞ + M
Restore all minimized windows.	⊞ + Shift + M
Switch users.	⊞ + L

TO OPEN OR FIND COMMON ITEMS

To do this	Press these keys
Display Windows Help.	`F1`
Open the My Computer window.	`⊞` + `E`
Open the Run dialog box.	`⊞` + `R`
Open Utility Manager.	`⊞` + `U`
Open the System Properties dialog box.	`⊞` + `Break`
Search for a file.	`F3`
Search for a computer on your network.	`Ctrl` + `⊞` + `F`
Display or hide the Start menu.	`Ctrl` + `Esc` *or* `⊞`

WHEN EDITING DOCUMENTS

To do this	Press these keys
Select text by highlighting one letter or line at a time.	`Shift` + `→`, `←`, `↑` or `↓`
Select all text in a document.	`Ctrl` + `A`
Move the insertion point to the start of the next word.	`Ctrl` + `→`
Move the insertion point to the start of the previous word.	`Ctrl` + `←`
Move the insertion point to the start of the next paragraph.	`Ctrl` + `↓`
Move the insertion point to the start of the previous paragraph.	`Ctrl` + `↑`
Select text by highlighting an entire word or paragraph at a time.	`Ctrl` + `Shift` + `→`, `←`, `↑` or `↓`
Copy the selected information.	`Ctrl` + `C`
Cut the selected information.	`Ctrl` + `X`
Paste information you cut or copied.	`Ctrl` + `V`
Undo your last change.	`Ctrl` + `Z`

WHEN USING A DIALOG BOX

To do this	Press these keys
Move forward through tabs.	`Ctrl` + `Tab`
Move backward through tabs.	`Ctrl` + `Shift` + `Tab`
Move forward through options.	`Tab`
Move backward through options.	`Shift` + `Tab`
Perform a command or select an option.	`Alt` + *Underlined letter in command or option name*
Perform the command for the active option or button.	`Enter`
Add or remove the check mark if the active option has a check box (☑).	**Spacebar**
Select a button from a group of radio buttons (◉).	`→`, `←`, `↑` or `↓`
View the items in the active drop-down menu.	`F4`
Display help information for the active item.	`F1`

Boost Your Computer's Fun Factor

When you want to take a break from your work and have some fun on your computer, this chapter is the place to look!

You can learn how to copy pictures onto your computer from your digital camera so you can work with the pictures and even make them available to other people online.

If you are tired of listening to the same old sounds Windows uses to notify you of system events, you can create a new sound scheme for your computer using your own sounds.

Want to do more than just listen to your music CDs on your computer? Read on to find out how to copy songs from your CDs onto your computer and create your own playlists to personalize your music.

You can also learn how to burn your own music CDs, copy songs to an MP3 player or place 100 or more music files on a single CD so you can have hours of listening enjoyment even when you're away from your computer.

Windows XP also allows you to quickly and easily turn your computer into a radio, so you can use the Internet to listen to your favorite radio stations from around the world at any time.

You can use Windows XP's video capabilities to turn your computer into a complete home entertainment center. This chapter will show you how to play DVD movies on your computer.

101 Hot Tips

55

Copy pictures from your digital camera

After you take pictures using a digital camera, you can use the Scanner and Camera Wizard to copy the pictures from the camera to your computer.

Copying pictures to your computer from a digital camera offers many advantages. For example, after you copy pictures from a digital camera to your computer, you can print your own pictures to avoid paying a company to develop your pictures. Also, you can use the pictures in documents, publish the pictures to the Web or send the pictures in e-mail messages to friends and family members around the world.

To copy pictures from a digital camera, the camera must be installed, connected to your computer and turned on. You may also need to set the camera to a specific mode, such as the Connect mode, before you can copy pictures to your computer. By default, the Scanner and Camera Wizard will copy all the pictures on your digital camera to your computer. If you want to copy only specific pictures, you can select the pictures.

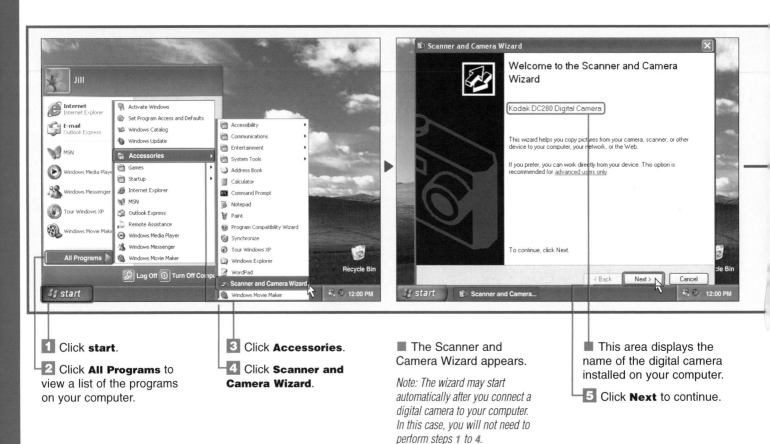

1 Click **start**.

2 Click **All Programs** to view a list of the programs on your computer.

3 Click **Accessories**.

4 Click **Scanner and Camera Wizard**.

■ The Scanner and Camera Wizard appears.

Note: The wizard may start automatically after you connect a digital camera to your computer. In this case, you will not need to perform steps 1 to 4.

■ This area displays the name of the digital camera installed on your computer.

5 Click **Next** to continue.

Try This! Most new digital cameras include a memory card, or flash card, which is a small card that stores pictures on a digital camera. You can remove the memory card from your digital camera and then insert the card into a memory card reader on your computer to copy pictures from the memory card to the computer. Many new computers come with a memory card reader.

When you insert a memory card from your digital camera into your computer's memory card reader, a dialog box appears, asking what you want Windows to do. Click the "Copy pictures to a folder on my computer" option and then click OK. The Scanner and Camera Wizard will appear, helping you copy pictures stored on the memory card to your computer.

CONTINUED ▶

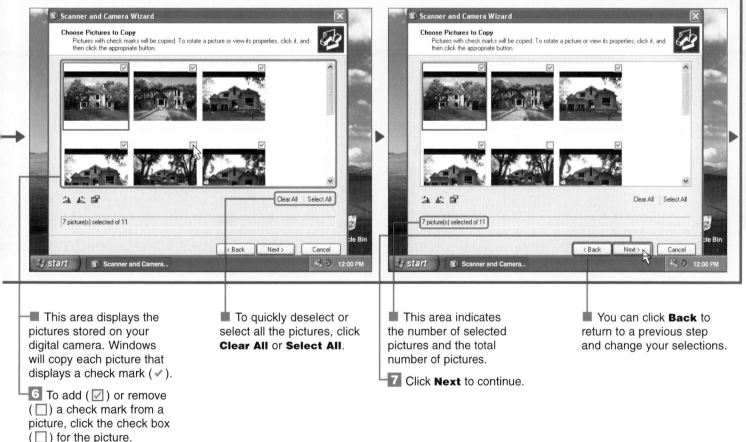

■ This area displays the pictures stored on your digital camera. Windows will copy each picture that displays a check mark (✔).

6 To add (☑) or remove (☐) a check mark from a picture, click the check box (☐) for the picture.

■ To quickly deselect or select all the pictures, click **Clear All** or **Select All**.

■ This area indicates the number of selected pictures and the total number of pictures.

7 Click **Next** to continue.

■ You can click **Back** to return to a previous step and change your selections.

#55 | Copy pictures from your digital camera

When you copy pictures from a digital camera, you can specify the name you want to use to save the pictures on your computer. Windows allows you to select the folder on your computer where you want to store the pictures. For example, you can store the pictures in a subfolder Windows creates in the My Pictures folder or directly in the My Pictures folder.

You can also specify if you want to delete the pictures from the digital camera once the pictures have been copied to your computer. Pictures you delete from the camera cannot be recovered.

Once the pictures have been copied, you can specify whether you want to publish the pictures to a Web site, order prints of the pictures from a photo printing Web site or finish working with the pictures.

When you close the wizard, Windows automatically displays the contents of the folder that contains the pictures. Each picture in the folder displays the name you specified for the pictures. Windows also sequentially numbers the pictures so that each picture is saved as a separate file with a unique name.

CONTINUED ▶

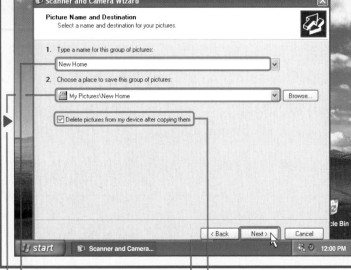

8 Type a name for the group of pictures.

9 This area displays the name of the folder where Windows will store the pictures. You can click this area to select a different folder.

10 To delete the pictures from the camera after the pictures are copied to your computer, click this option (☐ changes to ☑).

11 Click **Next** to copy the pictures to your computer.

■ This message appears when your pictures have been successfully copied to your computer.

12 Click an option to specify what you want to do with the pictures (◯ changes to ◉).

13 Click **Next** to continue.

Note: If you chose to publish the pictures or order prints in step 12, follow the instructions in the wizard.

Work With Them! The folder where you stored your pictures provides options that allow you to work with the pictures. For example, the "View as a slide show" option allows you to display your pictures as a full-screen slide show. You can also order prints of your pictures online, set a picture as your desktop background, print the pictures or publish the pictures to the Web.

Display Them! If you saved your pictures in the My Pictures folder or one of its subfolders, you can use the My Pictures Slideshow screen saver, which displays a slide show of all the pictures stored in the My Pictures folder and its subfolders. For more information on using the My Pictures Slideshow screen saver, see task #35.

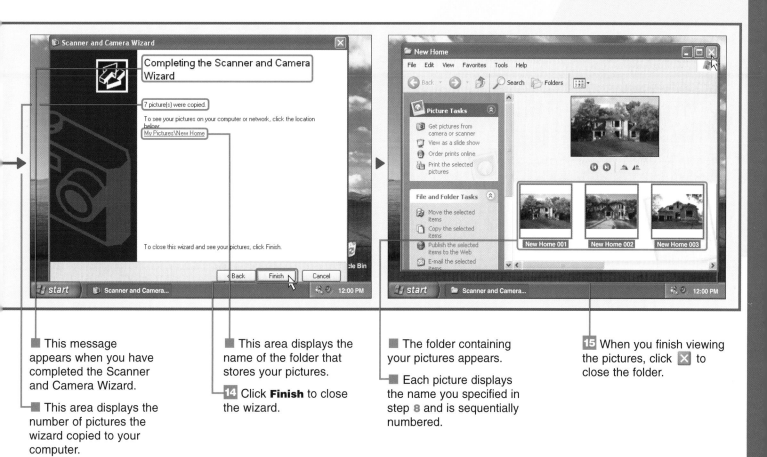

■ This message appears when you have completed the Scanner and Camera Wizard.

■ This area displays the number of pictures the wizard copied to your computer.

■ This area displays the name of the folder that stores your pictures.

14 Click **Finish** to close the wizard.

■ The folder containing your pictures appears.

■ Each picture displays the name you specified in step **8** and is sequentially numbered.

15 When you finish viewing the pictures, click ✕ to close the folder.

56

Create a personalized sound scheme for your computer

You can create a personalized sound scheme for your computer by having Windows play specific sounds when certain events occur. Assigning sounds to events can make working with Windows more entertaining and interesting.

You can assign sounds to up to 40 different events on your computer. For example, you may want to play music from a cartoon when you exit Windows, hear a sigh of relief when you restore a window or play chimes when you receive a new e-mail message.

When assigning sounds to events, you can use sound files included with Windows, purchase collections of sound files from computer stores or use sound files you have created. You can also use sound files you download from Web sites, such as www.favewavs.com and www.wavlist.com. Many of the sound files available on the Internet can be downloaded for free. Keep in mind the sounds you use must be in the Wave format. Wave files have the .wav extension, such as chimes.wav.

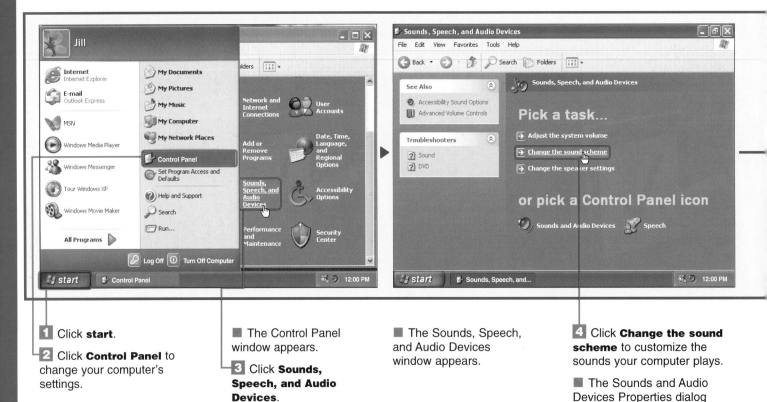

1 Click **start**.

2 Click **Control Panel** to change your computer's settings.

■ The Control Panel window appears.

3 Click **Sounds, Speech, and Audio Devices**.

■ The Sounds, Speech, and Audio Devices window appears.

4 Click **Change the sound scheme** to customize the sounds your computer plays.

■ The Sounds and Audio Devices Properties dialog box appears.

Remove It! To remove a sound you assigned to an event,
perform steps 1 to 5 below, selecting the event
you no longer want to play a sound in step 5.
Click ⌄ below Sounds and select (None) from
the list that appears.

Save It! After you have assigned sounds to events on your computer,
you can save the collection of sounds as a personalized
sound scheme. To do so, perform steps 1 to 4 below and
then click the Save As button. In the dialog box that appears,
type a name for the sound scheme and then click OK. If
you later make more sound changes that you regret, you
can return to the sound scheme you saved. To return to the
saved sound scheme, select the name of the sound scheme
from the list of available sound schemes in the Sounds and
Audio Devices Properties dialog box.

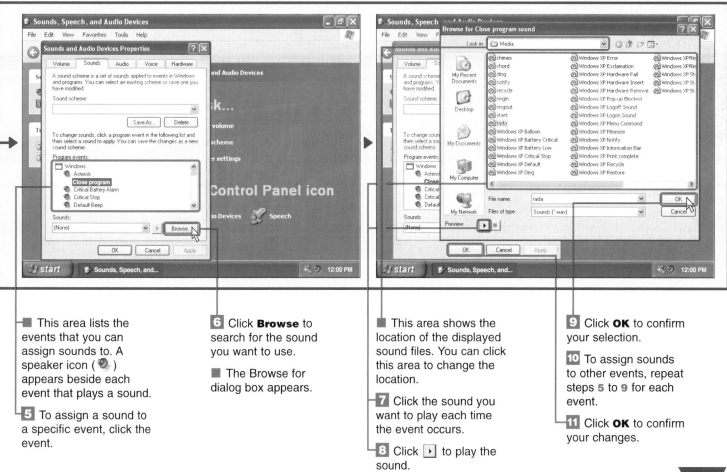

■ This area lists the
events that you can
assign sounds to. A
speaker icon (🔊)
appears beside each
event that plays a sound.

5 To assign a sound to
a specific event, click the
event.

6 Click **Browse** to
search for the sound
you want to use.

■ The Browse for
dialog box appears.

■ This area shows the
location of the displayed
sound files. You can click
this area to change the
location.

7 Click the sound you
want to play each time
the event occurs.

8 Click ▶ to play the
sound.

9 Click **OK** to confirm
your selection.

10 To assign sounds
to other events, repeat
steps **5** to **9** for each
event.

11 Click **OK** to confirm
your changes.

#57 Change the size of Windows Media Player

You can change the amount of space Windows Media Player takes up on your screen by switching between three different display modes—full, skin and mini player.

Windows Media Player initially appears in the full mode, which allows you to access all the features Windows Media Player provides. When you want to be able to access all the available menus and commands in Windows Media Player, you should work in the full mode.

The skin mode offers a distinct design. The skin mode usually takes up less room on your screen than the full mode, but offers fewer features.

The mini player mode displays only the most commonly used Windows Media Player playback controls in a toolbar on the taskbar. This mode is useful when you want to perform other tasks on your computer, but want quick access to playback controls when playing music on your computer.

You need an updated version of Windows Media Player to perform the steps as shown below. To obtain an updated version of Windows Media Player, you can visit the www.microsoft.com Web site.

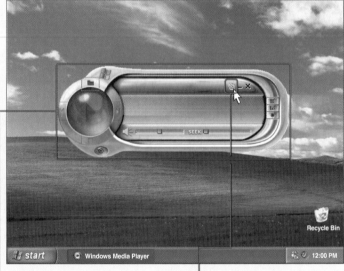

FULL MODE

■ Windows Media Player initially appears in the full mode. The full mode allows you to access all the features that Windows Media Player provides.

*Note: To start Windows Media Player, click **start** and then click **All Programs**. Then select **Windows Media Player**.*

1 To display Windows Media Player in the skin mode, click 🔽.

SKIN MODE

■ The skin mode offers a distinct design. This mode usually takes up less room on your screen but offers fewer features than the full mode.

1 To once again display Windows Media Player in the full mode, click 🔲.

Did You Know? Windows Media Player offers many different skins that you can choose from. Each skin offers its own distinct design and features. You can even obtain more skins on the Internet. To change the skin used by Windows Media Player, see task #58.

Check It Out! When you display Windows Media Player in the mini player mode, you can play, stop or browse through music or videos you are playing by clicking the play (▶), stop (■), previous (◀◀) or next (▶▶) buttons on the toolbar. You can instantly turn the sound on or off by using the mute (◀×) button or use the volume button (▾) to display or hide a volume slider (⬤) that you can drag to change the volume. To display or hide a small window that shows the currently playing video or a visualization for the currently playing sound, click ⬍.

MINI PLAYER MODE

■ The mini player mode displays the most commonly used Windows Media Player playback controls in a toolbar on the taskbar.

1 To turn on the Windows Media Player mini player mode, right-click a blank area on the taskbar. A menu appears.

2 Click **Toolbars**.

3 Click **Windows Media Player**.

Note: You only need to perform steps 1 to 3 once.

4 To display Windows Media Player in the mini player mode, click ▬ to minimize the window.

■ Windows Media Player appears as a toolbar on the taskbar. The toolbar displays the most commonly used playback controls.

■ To return Windows Media Player to the full or skin mode, click ▣. Windows Media Player will appear in the mode the player was previously in.

Note: If you want Windows Media Player to once again appear as a regular button on the taskbar when you minimize the window, repeat steps 1 to 3 to turn off the mini player mode.

#58 Change how Windows Media Player looks with skins

You can change the skin of Windows Media Player to customize how the player looks and functions.

Windows Media Player includes several skins that you can choose, including Bluesky, Headspace and Radio. Each skin offers a distinct design.

When you apply a skin, Windows Media Player automatically switches to the skin mode to display the new skin. The skin mode displays a smaller player window, which provides more room on your screen for using other programs. In skin mode, however, you do not have access to all the features

available in Windows Media Player. The number of features available in skin mode depends on the skin you select. You can switch to the full mode at any time to access all the features Windows Media Player offers.

You need an updated version of Windows Media Player to perform the steps as shown below. To obtain an updated version of Windows Media Player, you can visit the www.microsoft.com Web site.

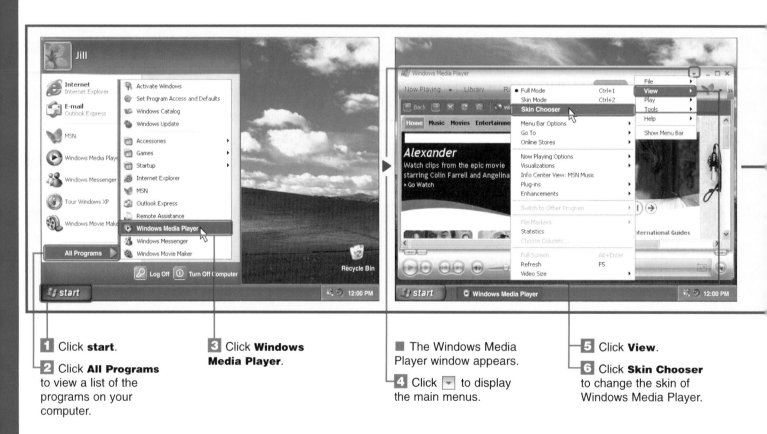

1 Click **start**.

2 Click **All Programs** to view a list of the programs on your computer.

3 Click **Windows Media Player**.

■ The Windows Media Player window appears.

4 Click ▼ to display the main menus.

5 Click **View**.

6 Click **Skin Chooser** to change the skin of Windows Media Player.

Get More Skins! You can obtain more skins for Windows Media Player on the Internet. When viewing the list of skins in Windows Media Player, click More Skins at the top of the window. Windows will open Internet Explorer and display a Web page that offers skins you can choose from. Click Download beside the skin you want to use and then click Yes and Close in the dialog boxes that appear. The skin will transfer to your computer and appear in your list of available skins.

Delete a Skin! If your list of skins becomes cluttered, you can delete skins you no longer use. When viewing the list of skins in Windows Media Player, select the skin you want to delete and then click ✕ at the top of the window. In the confirmation dialog box that appears, click Yes to delete the skin.

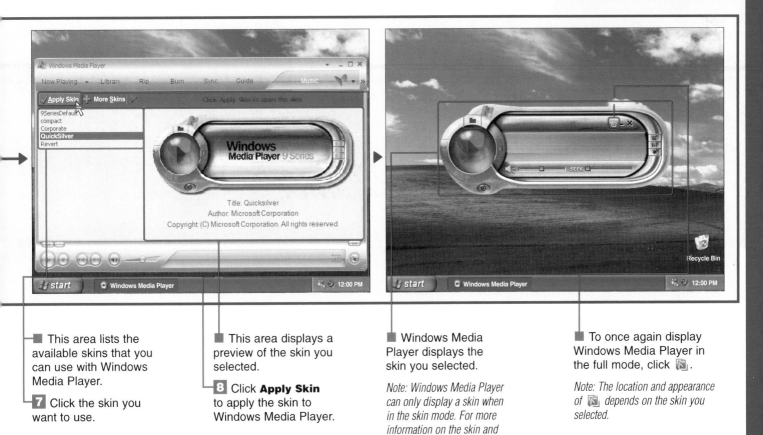

■ This area lists the available skins that you can use with Windows Media Player.

7 Click the skin you want to use.

■ This area displays a preview of the skin you selected.

8 Click **Apply Skin** to apply the skin to Windows Media Player.

■ Windows Media Player displays the skin you selected.

Note: Windows Media Player can only display a skin when in the skin mode. For more information on the skin and other display modes, see task #57.

■ To once again display Windows Media Player in the full mode, click 🖻.

Note: The location and appearance of 🖻 depends on the skin you selected.

#59 | Copy songs from a music CD to your computer

You can copy songs from a music CD onto your computer. Copying songs from a music CD, also known as "ripping music," allows you to play the songs at any time without having to insert the CD into your computer. Copying songs from a music CD also allows you to later copy the songs to a recordable CD or a portable device, such as an MP3 player.

If you are connected to the Internet when you insert the CD, Windows Media Player attempts to obtain information about the CD from the Internet. If you are not connected to the Internet or information about the CD is unavailable, Windows Media Player displays the track number of each song instead.

You can select the songs on a CD that you want to copy to your computer. Depending on your computer's CD drive and sound hardware, you may be able to listen to the CD while you are copying songs.

The first time you copy songs from a music CD, Windows allows you to accept or change the settings used to copy songs from music CDs. Windows currently uses the Windows Media Audio format when copying songs from a music CD. This format produces good quality sound with small file sizes and is suitable for most people.

You need an updated version of Windows Media Player to perform the steps as shown below. To obtain an updated version of Windows Media Player, you can visit the www.microsoft.com Web site.

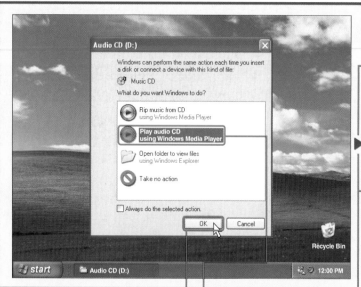

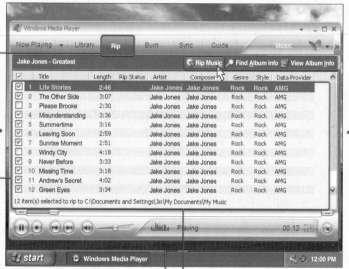

1 Insert the music CD that contains the songs you want to copy into your CD drive.

■ The Audio CD dialog box appears, asking what you want Windows to do.

2 Click this option to play the music CD.

3 Click **OK** to continue.

■ The Windows Media Player window appears and the CD begins to play.

4 Click **Rip** to copy songs from the music CD.

■ This area displays information about each song on the CD. Windows Media Player will copy each song that displays a check mark (☑) to your computer.

5 To add (☑) or remove (☐) a check mark beside a song, click the box beside the song.

6 Click **Rip Music** to start copying the selected songs to your computer.

Play It! The My Music folder contains a subfolder for each artist whose songs you have copied to your computer. To open the My Music folder, click the start button and then click My Music. To play a song, double-click a song file (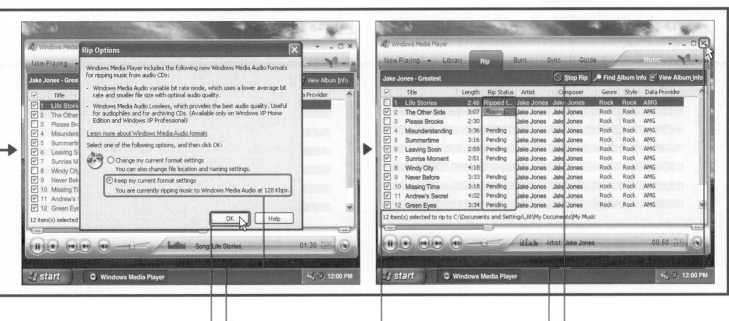) within a subfolder.

Did You Know? You can copy songs from a music CD in the MP3 format. This is useful if you later plan to copy the songs to an MP3 player that cannot play WMA files, which is the default format used by Windows Media Player. To copy songs from a music CD in the MP3 format, click ⯆ at the top of the Windows Media Player window. Click Tools and then select Options from the menus that appear. In the Options dialog box, click the Rip Music tab. Click the area below Format and then select mp3. Click OK to save your change.

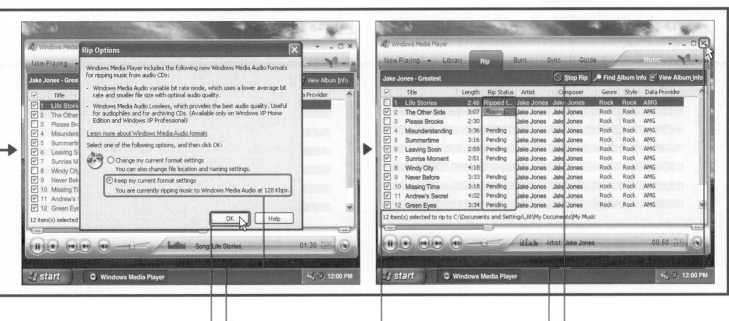

■ The first time you copy songs from a music CD, the Rip Options dialog box appears, asking if you want to change or keep the settings currently used to copy songs from a music CD.

Note: Windows currently uses the Windows Media Audio format when copying songs from a music CD. This format produces good quality sound with small file sizes and is suitable for most people.

7 Click this option to keep your current settings (○ changes to ◉).

8 Click **OK** to continue.

■ This column indicates the progress of the copy.

Note: Your computer's CD drive and sound hardware determine whether the music CD will continue playing while you copy songs from the CD.

■ To stop the copy at any time, click **Stop Rip**.

9 When you finish copying songs from the music CD, click ✕ to close the Windows Media Player window.

135

#60 Create your own music playlists

The Library in Windows Media Player displays the songs stored on your computer. You can arrange these songs into customized groups called playlists. For example, you can create a playlist named Inspirational Music that contains songs you want to listen to while working at your desk.

You can obtain songs from many sources, such as the Web or from music CDs. To add songs from a music CD to the Library, see task #59.

Windows Media Player will also allow you to add any media files you have stored on your computer to the list of files in the Library the first time you visit the Library.

You can add any number of songs to a playlist. You can also add a song to multiple playlists. The songs in a playlist will play in the order they appear in the list.

You need an updated version of Windows Media Player to perform the steps as shown below. To obtain an updated version of Windows Media Player, you can visit the www.microsoft.com Web site.

1 In the Windows Media Player window, click **Library** to view all the sound and video files on your computer.

*Note: To start Windows Media Player, click **start** and then click **All Programs**. Then select **Windows Media Player**.*

2 To create a playlist, click this button. A menu appears.

3 Click **New List**.

4 Click **Playlist**.

5 To add a song to your playlist, locate a song in the Library and then click the song.

Note: Your songs are located in the All Music category. To display the items in a category, click the plus sign (☐) beside the category.

6 Click 📝 to add the song to the playlist.

■ The song appears in the New Playlist area.

7 Repeat steps **5** and **6** for each song you want to add to the playlist.

Note: To move a song to a different location in your playlist, you can drag the song to a new location in the list of songs.

Play It! You can easily play all the songs in a playlist. Click the plus sign (⊞) beside My Playlists to view all the playlists you have created. To start playing all the songs in a playlist, double-click the name of the playlist.

Did You Know? Windows Media Player can automatically create playlists for you. The playlists are stored in the Auto Playlists category in the Library. For example, Windows Media Player creates a playlist of the songs you play most often on weekdays and another playlist of songs you play most often at night.

Delete It! You can delete a song from a playlist without removing the song from your computer or from Windows Media Player. Click the plus sign (⊞) beside My Playlists and then click the playlist that contains the song you want to delete. Click the song you want to delete and then press the Delete key.

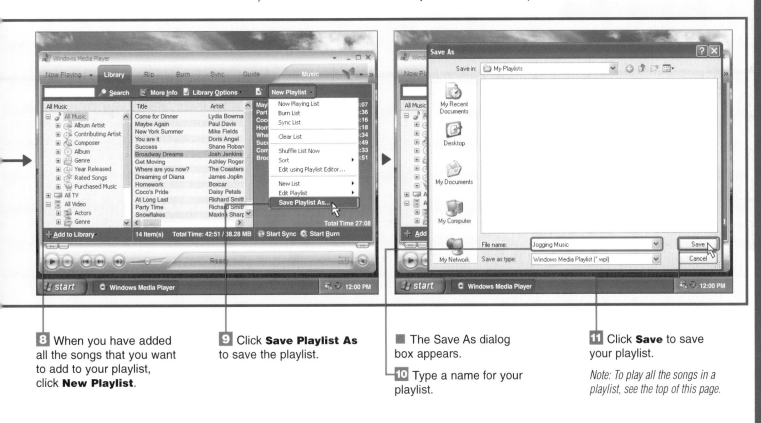

8 When you have added all the songs that you want to add to your playlist, click **New Playlist**.

9 Click **Save Playlist As** to save the playlist.

■ The Save As dialog box appears.

10 Type a name for your playlist.

11 Click **Save** to save your playlist.

Note: To play all the songs in a playlist, see the top of this page.

#61 Burn your own music CD

Windows Media Player allows you to copy songs on your computer to a recordable CD. This allows you to create your own music CDs. Copying songs to a CD is also known as "burning" a CD.

Before you burn your own music CD, you will need to create a playlist that contains the songs you want to copy onto the CD. A playlist is a personalized list of your favorite sound files. You can choose a playlist you created, such as a collection of your favorite rock songs, or choose a playlist set up for you by Windows Media Player. To create a playlist, see task #60.

A CD can store approximately 80 minutes of music. If you try to copy more songs than a CD can hold, Windows will mark the songs left over as "Will not fit" in the Windows Media Player window.

You need an updated version of Windows Media Player to perform the steps as shown below. To obtain an updated version of Windows Media Player, you can visit the www.microsoft.com Web site.

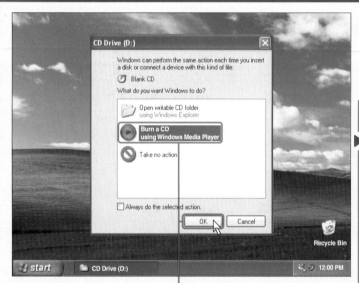

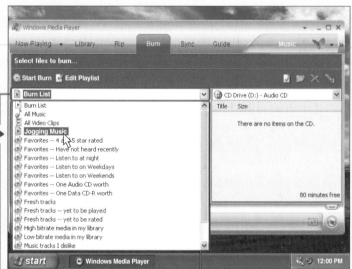

■ Before copying songs to a CD, you must create a playlist that contains all the songs you want to copy to the CD. To create a playlist, see task #60.

1 To copy songs to a CD, insert a blank, recordable CD into your recordable CD drive.

■ A dialog box appears, asking what you want Windows to do.

2 Click **Burn a CD** to copy songs to the CD using Windows Media Player.

3 Click **OK** to continue.

■ The Windows Media Player window appears.

4 Click this area to display a list of all the items in the Library, including the playlists you have created and the playlists that Windows Media Player has automatically created for you.

5 Click the playlist containing the songs you want to copy to the CD.

138

Important! You need a recordable CD drive, such as a CD-R (Compact Disc-Recordable) or CD-RW (Compact Disc-ReWritable) drive, to copy songs to a CD. A CD-R drive allows you to permanently record songs on CD-R discs. You cannot erase a CD-R disc. A CD-RW drive allows you to record songs on CD-RW or CD-R discs. You can erase a CD-RW disc in order to copy new songs to the disc. Recordable CDs you create may not play in some older CD or DVD drives or players.

Did You Know? You can copy songs to a CD only once using Windows Media Player. Since you must copy all the songs to a CD at the same time, make sure you carefully select all the songs you want to copy.

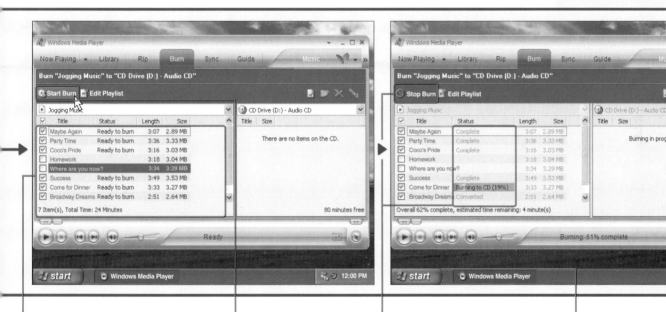

■ This area displays the songs in the playlist you selected. Windows Media Player will copy each song that displays a check mark (☑).

6 To add (☑) or remove (☐) a check mark, click the box (☐) beside the song.

7 Click **Start Burn** to start copying the songs to the CD.

■ This column indicates the progress of the copy.

■ To cancel the copy at any time, click **Stop Burn**.

■ While songs are copying to a CD, you should not perform other tasks on your computer, since Windows Media Player may stop working.

■ When the copy is complete, the CD is automatically ejected from your CD drive.

8 Click ✖ to close the Windows Media Player window.

#62 | Copy songs to your MP3 player

You can use Windows Media Player to copy songs on your computer to your MP3 player, including songs you have copied from a music CD or songs you have downloaded from the Internet. Copying songs to an MP3 player is also known as "synchronizing" or "syncing" songs.

Before copying songs to an MP3 player, you must first create a playlist that contains all the songs you want to copy to the player. To create a playlist, see task #60.

The number of songs you can copy to an MP3 player depends on the amount of storage space the MP3 player has. In general, an MP3 player requires between 500 kilobytes (KB) and 1 megabyte (MB) of storage space for each minute of music.

You need an updated version of Windows Media Player to perform the steps as shown below. To obtain an updated version of Windows Media Player, you can visit the www.microsoft.com Web site.

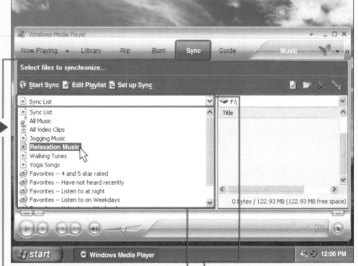

■ Before copying songs to an MP3 player, you must create a playlist that contains all the songs you want to copy. To create a playlist, see task #60.

1 To start Windows Media Player, click **start**.

2 Click **All Programs** to view a list of the programs on your computer.

3 Click **Windows Media Player**.

■ The Windows Media Player window appears.

4 Connect the MP3 player to your computer.

Note: The first time you connect an MP3 player to your computer, the Device Setup wizard may appear. For information on the Device Setup wizard, see the top of page 141.

5 Click **Sync** to be able to copy songs to the MP3 player.

6 Click this area to display a list of all the items in the Library, including the playlists you have created.

7 Click the playlist containing the songs you want to copy to your MP3 player.

Attention! The first time you connect an MP3 player to your computer, the Device Setup wizard may appear, allowing you to specify how you want to copy, or synchronize, songs to the player. To be able to follow the steps below and select the songs you want to copy to the MP3 player each time you connect the player to your computer, click Manual (○ changes to ◉) and then click Finish to continue.

Did You Know? Some new MP3 players can connect wirelessly to a computer. If your MP3 player has a removable memory card, you can insert the card into your computer's memory card reader to transfer music to the card. If your MP3 player has a flash drive, you can plug the flash drive into the computer's USB port to transfer music onto the flash drive. Once you have transferred music to the memory card or flash drive, you can re-insert the card or flash drive back into the MP3 player to enjoy the music on the player.

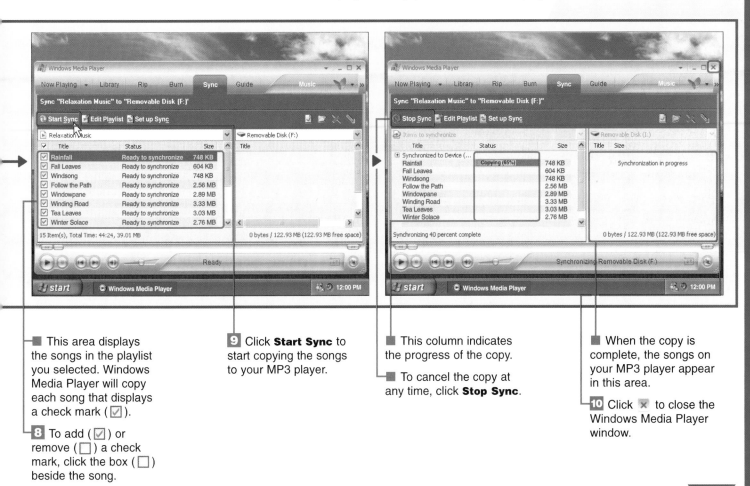

■ This area displays the songs in the playlist you selected. Windows Media Player will copy each song that displays a check mark (☑).

8 To add (☑) or remove (☐) a check mark, click the box (☐) beside the song.

9 Click **Start Sync** to start copying the songs to your MP3 player.

■ This column indicates the progress of the copy.

■ To cancel the copy at any time, click **Stop Sync**.

■ When the copy is complete, the songs on your MP3 player appear in this area.

10 Click ✖ to close the Windows Media Player window.

You can copy music files in the MP3 or WMA format from your computer to a CD. MP3 and WMA are the two most common digital music formats. Copying music files from your computer directly to a CD allows you to store several hours of music on a single CD. If you were to copy music files to a CD using Windows Media Player as shown in task #61, you would only be able to store just over one hour of music on a single CD.

The number of music files you can store on a CD depends on the size of the files. The size of a music file is usually dependent on the recording quality and the length of a song. You may be able to store over 100 MP3 files or over 200 WMA files on a typical CD that stores 700 MB of data.

You need a recordable CD drive to copy music files to a CD. For more information on recordable CD drives, see the tip area for task #61. When you are ready to play the CD, the CD player you use to play the CD must be able to play MP3 or WMA files.

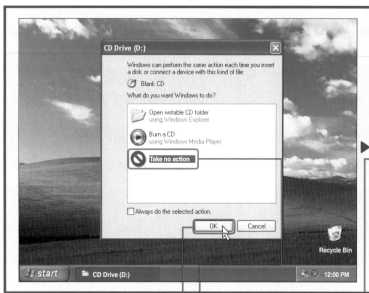

SELECT MUSIC FILES TO COPY

1 Insert a recordable CD into your recordable CD drive.

■ A dialog box may appear, asking what you want Windows to do.

2 Click **Take no action**.

3 Click **OK** to continue.

4 Select the music files you want to copy to the CD. To select multiple music files, press and hold down the **Ctrl** key as you click each file you want to copy.

5 Click **Copy the selected items**.

*Note: If you selected only one file, click **Copy this file** in step 5.*

Try This! You can copy a folder that contains music files to a CD the same way you copy music files to a CD. When you copy a folder to a CD, Windows will copy all the files in the folder. To copy a folder to a CD, perform steps 1 to 7 starting on page 142, except select the "Copy this folder" option in step 5. Then perform steps 1 to 10 starting on page 143.

Watch Out! If you download music files from the Web, make sure you are not breaking the law by copying the files. Beware of downloading music files that contain copyrighted material. Also, watch out for people who illegally distribute music files through popular Web-based, file-sharing programs.

CONTINUED ►

■ The Copy Items dialog box appears.

6 Click the recordable CD drive that contains the CD you want to copy the files to.

7 Click **Copy** to place a copy of the music files in a temporary storage area on your computer where the files will be held until you copy them to the CD.

■ You can repeat steps **4** to **7** for each set of files you want to copy to the CD.

COPY SELECTED MUSIC FILES TO A CD

1 Click **start**.

2 Click **My Computer** to view the contents of your computer.

■ The My Computer window appears.

3 Double-click the recordable drive that contains the CD you want to copy the music files to.

#63 | Place 100 or more songs on a single CD

Before copying the music files you selected to a CD, Windows stores the files in a temporary storage area on your computer. This allows you to review the music files you selected before copying the files to a CD.

When you copy music files to a CD using the method in the screens below, you can copy the songs at separate times. However, each time you copy music files to a CD, approximately 20 MB of extra information is stored on the CD.

To make the best use of the storage space on the CD, you may want to copy all the music files to the CD at the same time.

Make sure no interruptions occur while the music files are being copied to the CD, since this may cause the CD to become unreadable. As a precaution, avoid running programs and screen savers while copying files to a CD.

CONTINUED ▶

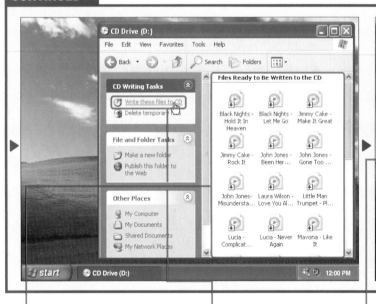

■ A window appears, displaying the files being held in a temporary storage area on your computer and any files currently stored on the CD.

4 Click **Write these files to CD** to copy the music files to the CD.

■ The CD Writing Wizard appears.

5 Type a name for the CD.

Note: The name you specify for the CD will appear in the My Computer window when the CD is in a CD drive.

6 Click **Next** to continue.

Delete It! You can remove files you no longer want to copy to a CD from the temporary storage area. When the temporary storage area is displayed, press and hold down the Ctrl key as you click each music file you no longer want to copy and then press the Delete key. To remove all the files, click the "Delete temporary files" option.

Erase It! You can erase a CD-RW disc to permanently delete all the files on the disc. You cannot erase a CD-R disc. To erase a CD-RW disc, click start and then select My Computer. In the My Computer window, right-click your recordable drive and then click Erase this CD-RW in the menu that appears. Follow the instructions in the CD Writing Wizard to erase the disc.

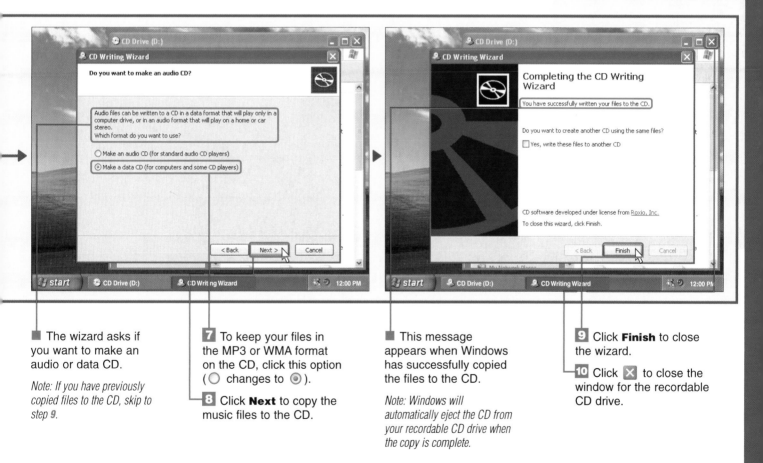

■ The wizard asks if you want to make an audio or data CD.

Note: If you have previously copied files to the CD, skip to step 9.

7 To keep your files in the MP3 or WMA format on the CD, click this option (○ changes to ◉).

8 Click **Next** to copy the music files to the CD.

■ This message appears when Windows has successfully copied the files to the CD.

Note: Windows will automatically eject the CD from your recordable CD drive when the copy is complete.

9 Click **Finish** to close the wizard.

10 Click ✕ to close the window for the recordable CD drive.

#64 | Turn your computer into a radio

When you are connected to the Internet, you can use Windows Media Player to listen to radio stations from around the world that broadcast on the Internet.

Windows Media Player allows you to find radio stations by browsing through music categories. The music categories Windows Media Player offers include top 40, country, new age, jazz, rock, hip hop and talk radio.

When you play a radio station, some radio stations offer enhanced content, such as the radio station's Web page. You can choose whether or not to display this enhanced content in Windows Media Player.

Keep in mind that the information the Radio Tuner tab contains is hosted by the WindowsMedia.com Web site and is frequently updated. This means the Radio Tuner shown below may look different than the Radio Tuner displayed on your screen.

1 In the Windows Media Player window, click the **Guide** tab to access the latest music, movies and information on the Internet.

*Note: To start Windows Media Player, click **start** and then click **All Programs**. Then select **Windows Media Player**.*

2 Click 🏠 to display the home page of the Guide.

3 Click **Radio Tuner** to access radio stations that broadcast on the Internet.

■ This area displays a list of featured radio stations. To play a radio station in the list, click the radio station and then skip to step **6**.

■ This area displays categories of radio stations.

4 Click a category to display radio stations in the category.

Search! You can search for a radio station of interest on the Internet. To display the Radio Tuner, perform steps 1 to 3 below. Drag the mouse over the text "Search Keyword" below the radio station categories to select the text. Then type information about a radio station of interest and press the Enter key. A list of radio stations matching the information you entered appears.

Save Your Favorites! You can create a list of your favorite radio stations. When you find a radio station you want to add to your list of favorites, click "Add to My Stations" instead of Play in step 6 below. To display your list of favorites, perform steps 1 to 3 below to display the Radio Tuner. Then click My Stations below the Featured Stations area to display a list of your favorite radio stations.

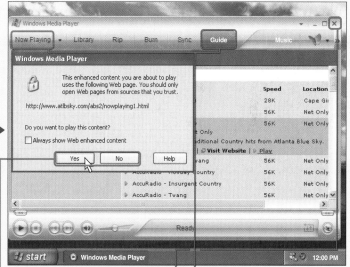

■ A list of radio stations appears.

5 Click the name of the radio station you want to play.

■ To return to the list of radio station categories at any time, click **Return to My Stations**.

■ Information about the radio station you selected appears.

6 Click **Play** to play the radio station.

*Note: If the Play option is not available, click **Visit Website to Play** to display the radio station's Web page and play the radio station.*

■ After a moment, the radio station begins to play.

■ A dialog box appears if the radio station can display enhanced content, such as the radio station's Web page.

7 Click **Yes** or **No** to specify if you want to view the enhanced content.

■ If you selected **Yes** in step **7**, the enhanced content will appear on the **Now Playing** tab. To return to the list of radio stations at any time, click the **Guide** tab.

8 When you finish listening to radio stations, click ☒ to close the Windows Media Player window.

#65 | Play DVD movies

If you have a computer with a DVD drive, you can watch DVD movies on your computer using Windows Media Player. Playing DVD movies on your computer is especially useful when traveling with a notebook computer.

You can interact with a DVD movie playing on your computer the same way you would when using a standard DVD player. Windows Media Player has many of the same controls as a standard DVD player. For example, you can use the controls in Windows Media Player to play, pause and stop a movie.

When you play a DVD movie, Windows Media Player displays a list of the titles stored on the DVD. Each title on a DVD represents a section of content. Each title can contain one or more chapters. A chapter is usually a scene in a movie.

You need an updated version of Windows Media Player to perform the steps as shown below. To obtain an updated version of Windows Media Player, you can visit the www.microsoft.com Web site.

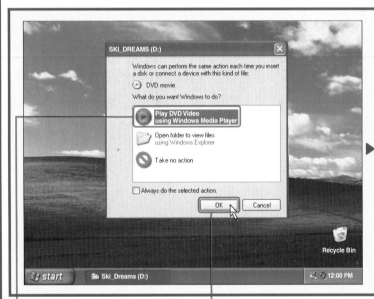

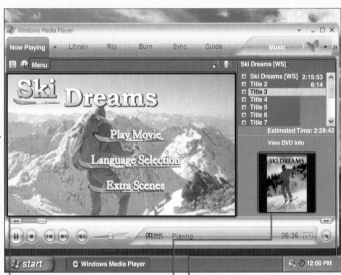

1 Insert a DVD movie into your computer's DVD drive.

■ A dialog box appears, asking what you want Windows to do.

2 Click **Play DVD Video** to play the DVD movie using Windows Media Player.

3 Click **OK** to continue.

■ The Windows Media Player window appears and the movie begins to play.

■ The DVD movie plays in this area. After a few moments, the DVD's main menu usually appears, displaying a list of options you can select, such as playing the movie or playing a specific scene. To select an option, click the option.

■ To display the DVD's main menu at any time, click **Menu**.

■ If you are connected to the Internet and information about the movie is available, this area displays the cover for the DVD.

Attention! Before you can play DVD movies, your computer must have a DVD drive and a DVD decoder installed. A DVD decoder is software that allows your computer to play DVD movies. Most new computers with a DVD drive come with a DVD decoder installed. If your computer has a DVD drive but does not have a DVD decoder installed, you can purchase a DVD decoder that is compatible with Windows XP from companies such as InterVideo (www.intervideo.com) and CyberLink (www.gocyberlink.com).

Enlarge It! You can use the entire screen to view a DVD movie that is currently playing. Click ▣ directly above the movie area. To display the controls when viewing the movie using the entire screen, move the mouse. To once again display the movie in the Windows Media Player window, press the Esc key.

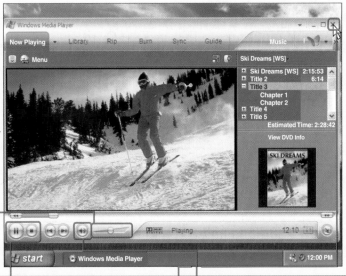

■ This area displays a list of the titles and chapters on the DVD. A title is a section of content on a DVD. Each title can contain one or more chapters, which often play specific scenes in a movie.

Note: The first title usually contains all the scenes for the entire movie.

4 To display the chapters in a title, click the plus sign (⊞) beside the title (⊞ changes to ⊟).

■ The chapters in the title appear.

5 To play a specific title or chapter, double-click the title or chapter. The title or chapter is highlighted.

6 To pause or stop the play of the movie, click the Pause (‖) or Stop (▪) button (‖ changes to ▶).

Note: You can click ▶ to resume the play of the movie.

7 To adjust the volume, drag the volume slider (◯) left or right to decrease or increase the volume.

8 To turn off the sound, click ◀)) (◀)) changes to ◀).

Note: You can click ◀ to once again turn on the sound.

9 When you finish watching the movie, click ✖ to close the Windows Media Player window.

Simple Solutions for Computer Problems

Are you looking for tips and tricks you can use to troubleshoot and fix problems you encounter with your computer? If so, then this chapter is for you!

When a program freezes, do you know what to do? This chapter includes tasks that teach you how to close a misbehaving program or capture a picture of your screen to share with a friend or colleague who can help you.

After reviewing the tasks in this chapter, you'll know how to react when Windows does not act as it should—by using safe mode to identify and fix the problem or using the System Restore feature to return your computer to a time before the problem occurred.

If you are having a problem with your computer, you can use the Help and Support Center included with Windows to get help with the problem. You can also visit the Microsoft Help and Support Web site to search the Knowledge Base for helpful information. Both of these tasks are described in this chapter.

Are you prepared for the possibility of losing important documents and information due to a computer crash? If not, read this chapter to find out how you can use Windows XP to back up your files so you can rest easier, knowing your information is safe.

101 Hot Tips

#66 | Close a misbehaving program

If a program you have open is no longer responding, you can close the program without having to shut down Windows.

When a program fails to respond to mouse or keyboard actions, Windows identifies the program as not responding. Windows may detect that a program is not responding and display a warning message before you are aware of the problem. You may also discover on your own that a program is not behaving as it should.

Windows allows you to view the status of all the programs running on your computer. You can then close a program that is no longer working properly without having to shut down Windows or any other program.

When you close a program that is not responding, you will lose any information you did not save in the program. Closing a misbehaving program should not affect the operation of Windows or any other program you have open.

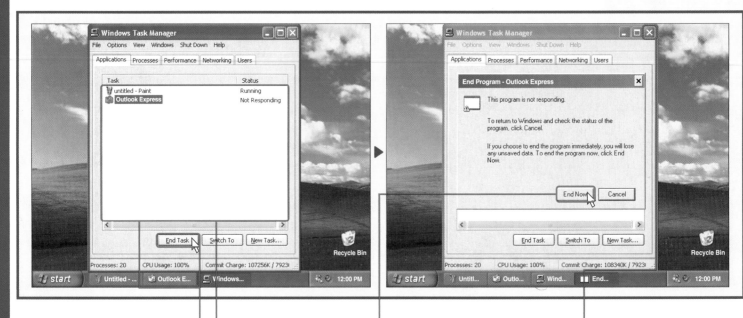

■ **1** To close a misbehaving program, press and hold down the **Ctrl** and **Alt** keys as you press the **Delete** key.

■ The Windows Task Manager window appears.

■ This area lists the programs that are currently running. The phrase "Not Responding" appears beside the name of a misbehaving program.

2 Click the program that is misbehaving.

3 Click **End Task**.

■ The End Program dialog box appears, stating that the program is not responding.

4 Click **End Now** to close the program.

5 Click ☒ to close the Windows Task Manager window.

*Note: A dialog box may appear, asking if you want to send information about the misbehaving program to Microsoft. Click **Send Error Report** or **Don't Send**.*

#67 | Use print screen to capture your screen

You can use the Print Screen feature to create a copy of all or part of your screen. Copying all or part of your screen is useful if you are trying to explain a computer problem or procedure and you want to use a visual example to illustrate what you are trying to explain. You may also find this feature useful when you want to show someone an error message that appears on your screen.

You can take a picture of the entire screen or just the active window or dialog box. After you copy all or part of the screen, you can place the image in a program such as Paint or WordPad and then print the image or e-mail the image to another person.

You may not be able to use the Print Screen feature to capture a moving image on your screen. For example, you cannot capture videos playing in Windows Media Player.

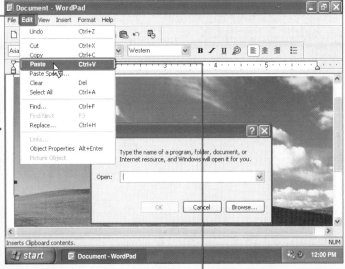

1 To copy the entire screen, press the **Print Screen** key.

■ To copy just the active window or dialog box, press and hold down the **Alt** key as you press the **Print Screen** key.

■ Windows copies the image of your screen.

2 Open the document you want to display a copy of the image. In this example, a WordPad document was opened.

3 Click **Edit**.

4 Click **Paste**.

■ The image appears in the document.

Get help information online from Microsoft

The Microsoft Help and Support Web site, located at support.microsoft.com, offers a wide range of information. Whenever you run into a problem while using Windows, you will likely find at least one article on how to fix the problem by searching this Web site.

The Knowledge Base, which is found on the Microsoft Help and Support Web site, is a database containing over 250,000 help articles. The Knowledge Base is constantly updated to offer users the most recent information.

You can search the Knowledge Base to look for articles related to a computer problem or a question that you have. The Knowledge Base is also useful if you want to search for text displayed in an error message so you can find out how to fix the problem. When conducting your search, try to use multiple words and make sure all the words you use are spelled correctly.

Since the information the Microsoft Help and Support Web site displays is frequently updated, the Web site shown below may look different than the Web site displayed on your screen.

■ Before you can use Microsoft's online help and support, you must be connected to the Internet.

1 In the Microsoft Internet Explorer window, click this area and type **support.microsoft.com**. Then press the **Enter** key.

*Note: To display the Microsoft Internet Explorer window, click **start**, select **All Programs** and then click **Internet Explorer**.*

■ The Microsoft Help and Support Web page appears, displaying many features and links to help you find help information.

2 To search the Knowledge Base for a help topic, click this area and then type a word or phrase that describes the topic of interest.

3 Click **Go** to start the search.

Did You Know? You can perform an advanced search to specify more details about the information you want to find. Click the Advanced Search option on the left side of your screen. In the Web page that appears, you can select a number of options for your search, such as specifying whether you want to search for all or any of the keywords you entered. When you finish entering the information for your search, click → to start the search.

Browse for Information! You can easily browse through help information about Windows XP. Under the Top Solution Centers heading at the left side of the Microsoft Help and Support Web page, click the Windows XP option to display a list of articles. You can find articles that cover the latest Windows XP news, how-to topics, troubleshooting and more.

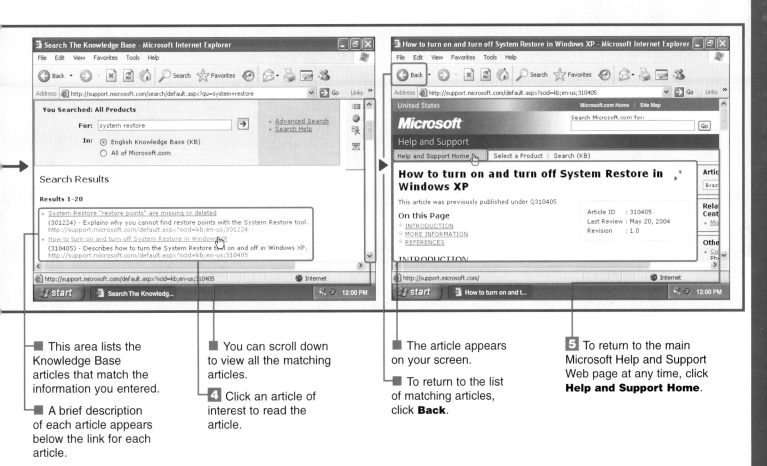

■ This area lists the Knowledge Base articles that match the information you entered.

■ A brief description of each article appears below the link for each article.

■ You can scroll down to view all the matching articles.

4 Click an article of interest to read the article.

■ The article appears on your screen.

■ To return to the list of matching articles, click **Back**.

5 To return to the main Microsoft Help and Support Web page at any time, click **Help and Support Home**.

#69 | Stop Windows from reporting errors

If you encounter a problem in Windows, such as when a program malfunctions, a message will usually appear that asks if you want Windows to send an error report to Microsoft. If you never want to send error reports, you can prevent Windows from displaying this message.

An error report provides Microsoft with information about the problem that occurred on your computer, which can help them make improvements to Windows. However, you may not want to send a report if you are concerned about security or if it is inconvenient for you. For example, if you do not have a constant connection to the Internet, you may not want to connect each time you need to send an error report. Instead of having to

choose not to send the error report each time you are asked, it is more efficient to prevent Windows from asking you at all.

After you stop Windows from sending error reports to Microsoft, you can choose whether you want Windows to notify you when a critical error occurs on your computer.

You must be using a computer administrator account to change the error reporting settings.

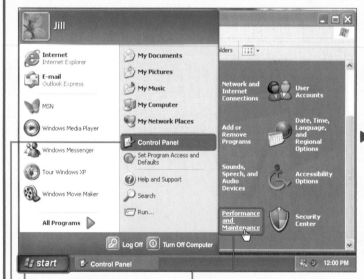

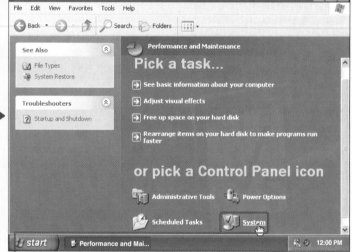

1 Click **start**.

2 Click **Control Panel**.

■ The Control Panel window appears.

3 Click **Performance and Maintenance**.

■ The Performance and Maintenance window appears.

4 Click **System** to view the settings for your computer system.

■ The System Properties dialog box appears.

Did You Know? Instead of completely disabling error reporting, you can choose to generate error reports only for Windows operating system errors or only for errors that occur in the programs installed on your computer. In the Error Reporting dialog box, click Enable error reporting (○ changes to ◉). Click Windows operating system or Programs to turn the options on (☑) or off (☐). If you choose the Programs option, Windows will create error reports for programs that came with Windows, such as WordPad and Windows Media Player, as well as for programs you installed, such as Microsoft Excel.

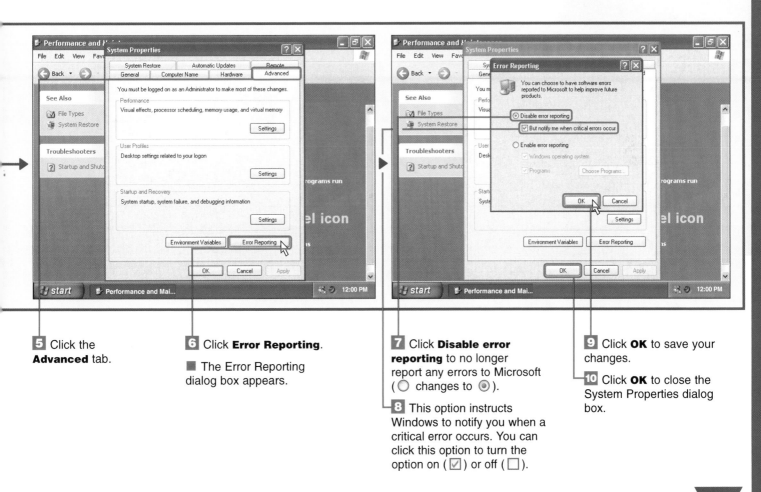

5 Click the **Advanced** tab.

6 Click **Error Reporting**.

■ The Error Reporting dialog box appears.

7 Click **Disable error reporting** to no longer report any errors to Microsoft (○ changes to ◉).

8 This option instructs Windows to notify you when a critical error occurs. You can click this option to turn the option on (☑) or off (☐).

9 Click **OK** to save your changes.

10 Click **OK** to close the System Properties dialog box.

70

Run an older program in Windows XP

If a program that was designed for a previous version of Windows does not run properly in Windows XP, you can change certain settings that will allow you to run the older program.

You can choose from several versions of Windows to run an older program. You should select the version of Windows that is recommended for the program. If you are unsure which version is recommended, you can specify the most recent version of Windows that supported the program.

Once you have specified settings for an older program, Windows will use the settings each time

you run the program. Your settings will automatically return to normal when you close the program.

You should not change the settings for older antivirus or backup programs. If you are having difficulty using one of these types of programs with Windows XP, you should contact the manufacturer to obtain a more recent version of the program. If a more recent version of the program is not available, consider obtaining a similar program designed for Windows XP.

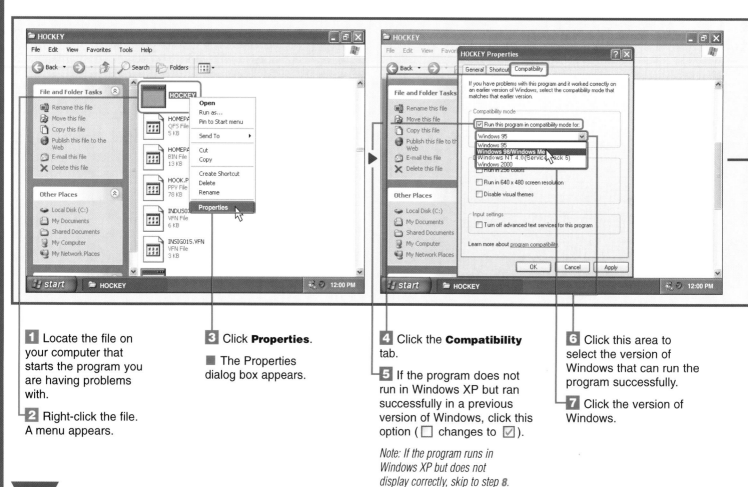

1 Locate the file on your computer that starts the program you are having problems with.

2 Right-click the file. A menu appears.

3 Click **Properties**.

■ The Properties dialog box appears.

4 Click the **Compatibility** tab.

5 If the program does not run in Windows XP but ran successfully in a previous version of Windows, click this option (☐ changes to ☑).

Note: If the program runs in Windows XP but does not display correctly, skip to step 8.

6 Click this area to select the version of Windows that can run the program successfully.

7 Click the version of Windows.

Try This! Windows also provides a Program Compatibility Wizard that can help you set up an older program to run in Windows XP. The wizard is beneficial if you need help finding the program on your computer. The wizard also allows you to test the settings you selected to determine if the problems with the program were fixed. Click start, click All Programs, select Accessories and then choose Program Compatibility Wizard. Then follow the instructions on your screen.

Still Not Working? Some older programs will not work properly with Windows XP, regardless of the settings you select. You can contact the program's manufacturer to determine if there is an updated version of the program available that is compatible with Windows XP.

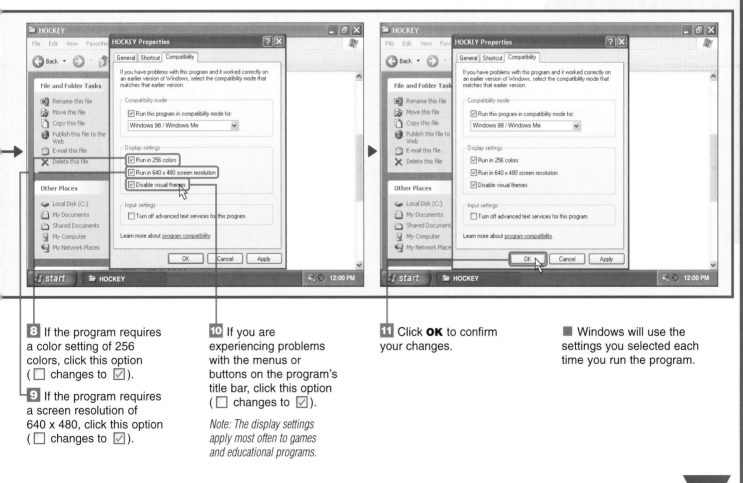

8 If the program requires a color setting of 256 colors, click this option (☐ changes to ☑).

9 If the program requires a screen resolution of 640 x 480, click this option (☐ changes to ☑).

10 If you are experiencing problems with the menus or buttons on the program's title bar, click this option (☐ changes to ☑).

Note: The display settings apply most often to games and educational programs.

11 Click **OK** to confirm your changes.

■ Windows will use the settings you selected each time you run the program.

#71 | Turn back the clock on computer troubles

If you are experiencing problems with your computer, you can use the System Restore feature to return your computer to a time before the problems occurred. For example, if you accidentally delete program files or if your computer does not work properly after you install a program, you can restore your computer to a time before you made the changes.

When you restore your computer, you return your computer to an earlier, more stable time, called a restore point. Windows creates different types of restore points. An Initial System Checkpoint is created when you first start Windows.

Windows then regularly creates new System Checkpoint restore points. Windows also creates restore points when you install certain programs. From the available restore points, you can choose the restore point when you last remember your computer working properly.

You must be using a computer administrator account to restore a computer.

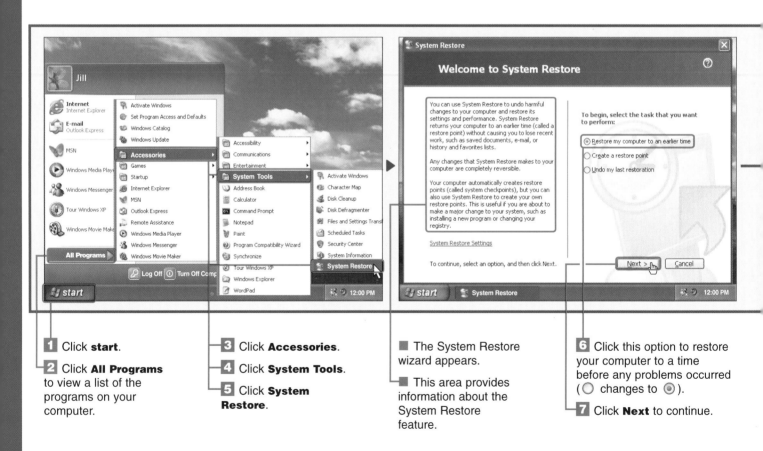

1 Click **start**.

2 Click **All Programs** to view a list of the programs on your computer.

3 Click **Accessories**.

4 Click **System Tools**.

5 Click **System Restore**.

■ The System Restore wizard appears.

■ This area provides information about the System Restore feature.

6 Click this option to restore your computer to a time before any problems occurred (○ changes to ◉).

7 Click **Next** to continue.

Customize It! You can create your own restore point if you plan to make a major change to your computer, such as installing a program. Perform steps 1 to 5 below to start the System Restore wizard. Select Create a restore point (○ changes to ◉) and then click Next. Type a description for the restore point and then click Create. Click Close to complete the wizard.

Did You Know? Windows can store between one and three weeks of restore points. The number of available restore points primarily depends on how frequently you use your computer. You may find that the days you do not use your computer do not have any restore points, while days when you perform many tasks on your computer may have several restore points.

CONTINUED ▶

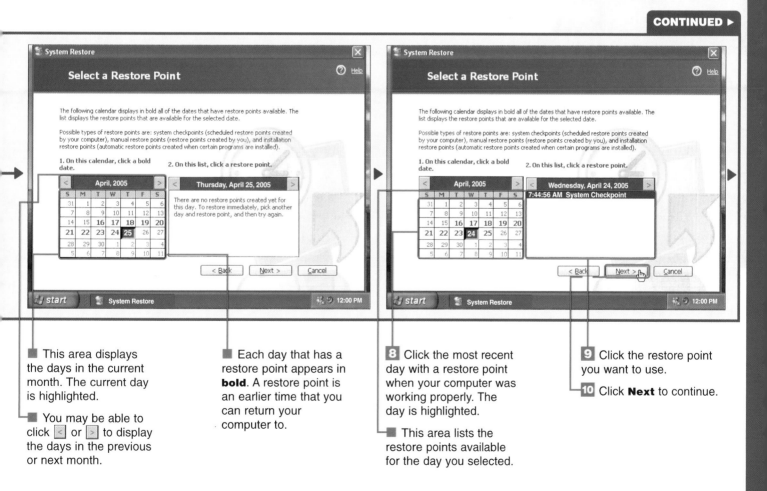

■ This area displays the days in the current month. The current day is highlighted.

■ You may be able to click < or > to display the days in the previous or next month.

■ Each day that has a restore point appears in **bold**. A restore point is an earlier time that you can return your computer to.

8 Click the most recent day with a restore point when your computer was working properly. The day is highlighted.

■ This area lists the restore points available for the day you selected.

9 Click the restore point you want to use.

10 Click **Next** to continue.

71

Turn back the clock on computer troubles

Restoring your computer will not cause you to lose any of your personal files, such as word processing documents or spreadsheet files. If you want to ensure a specific file is not affected by the restoration, you can store the file in the My Documents folder. Any files stored in the My Documents folder will not be affected. System Restore will also not affect your e-mail messages or the items in your Favorites list and History list in Internet Explorer.

Before restoring your computer to an earlier time, you should close all open files and programs. Your computer will automatically restart when the

restoration is complete. If the restoration could not be completed, System Restore will automatically undo any changes made during the restoration.

When you restore your computer to an earlier time, you will not lose the last password you specified for your user account. If the Welcome screen appears after the restoration is complete, you can type your password to log on to your user account.

CONTINUED ►

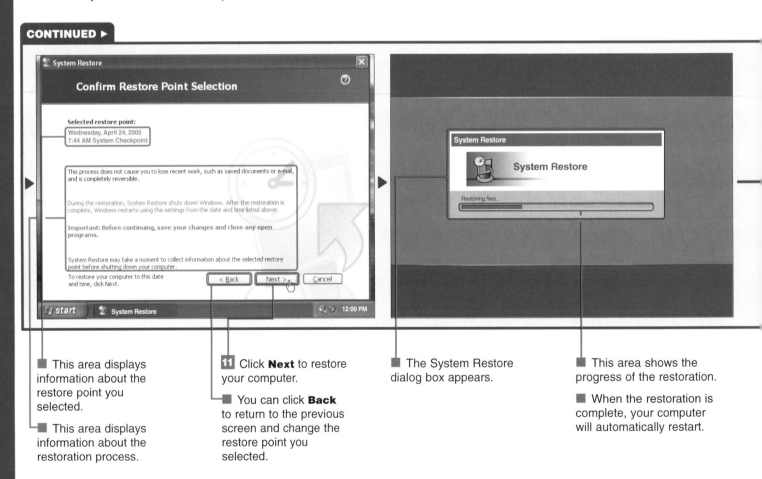

■ This area displays information about the restore point you selected.

■ This area displays information about the restoration process.

11 Click **Next** to restore your computer.

■ You can click **Back** to return to the previous screen and change the restore point you selected.

■ The System Restore dialog box appears.

■ This area shows the progress of the restoration.

■ When the restoration is complete, your computer will automatically restart.

Attention! You may need to re-install some programs after the restoration. When you restore your computer to an earlier time, any programs you installed after that date may be uninstalled. Files you created using the program will not be deleted, but you may need to re-install the program to work with the files again.

Undo It! Any changes the System Restore feature makes to your computer are completely reversible. To reverse your last restoration, perform steps 1 to 5 on page 160 to display the System Restore wizard. Select Undo my last restoration and then click Next to undo the changes Windows made during the last restoration. Then perform steps 11 to 14 below.

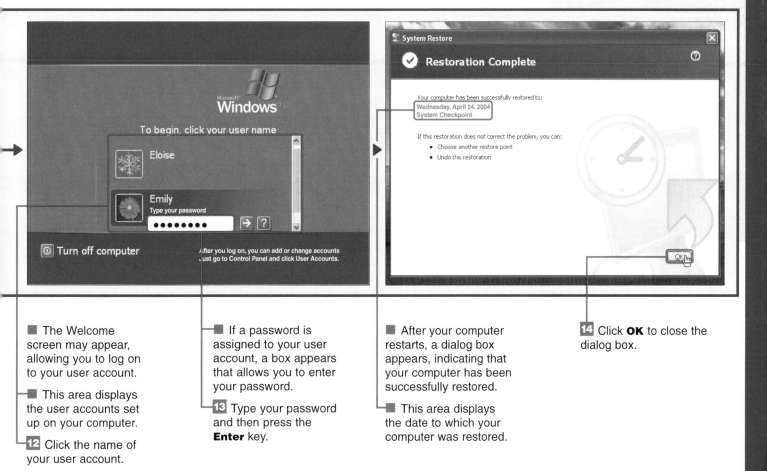

■ The Welcome screen may appear, allowing you to log on to your user account.

■ This area displays the user accounts set up on your computer.

12 Click the name of your user account.

■ If a password is assigned to your user account, a box appears that allows you to enter your password.

13 Type your password and then press the **Enter** key.

■ After your computer restarts, a dialog box appears, indicating that your computer has been successfully restored.

■ This area displays the date to which your computer was restored.

14 Click **OK** to close the dialog box.

#72 | Take action when Windows will not start properly

If Windows will not start properly, you may be able to start Windows in safe mode to try to correct the problem. Windows may not start properly for many reasons. For example, if you accidentally deleted important files, installed a program or changed certain Windows settings, Windows may not start properly.

When your computer is running in safe mode, Windows displays the words "Safe Mode" in each corner of your screen. Safe mode uses the minimum capabilities required to run Windows. For this reason, some hardware devices, such as printers, sound cards, modems and some types of mice, may not be available when you start Windows in safe mode.

To start Windows in safe mode, you must log on using a computer administrator account. Windows automatically creates an Administrator account that you can use if your account is unavailable.

When you finish fixing the problem that is preventing Windows from starting normally, you can exit safe mode and restart your computer. After restarting, your computer should function normally.

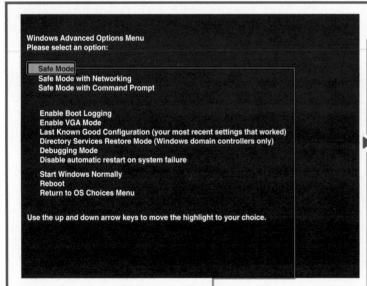

1 After you turn on your computer and monitor, immediately press and hold down the **F8** key.

■ The Windows Advanced Options Menu appears, displaying a list of options for starting Windows.

2 To start Windows in safe mode, press the ⬇ or ⬆ key until you highlight Safe Mode. Then press the **Enter** key.

■ Windows asks you to select the operating system you want to start.

3 To start Windows XP, press the ⬇ or ⬆ key until you highlight Microsoft Windows XP Home Edition. Then press the **Enter** key.

Ways to Fix It! When running your computer in safe mode, try reversing the action that may have caused the problem that is preventing Windows from starting normally. For example, if the problem occurred after you installed a program, try uninstalling the program. You can also use the System Restore feature to return your computer to a time before the problem occurred. For information about System Restore, see task #71.

Try This! If you are not sure how to fix the problem, you can start your computer using the Last Known Good Configuration option. This option allows you to restore the settings Windows used the last time your computer started successfully. To use this option, perform steps 1 to 3 below, except select Last Known Good Configuration in step 2.

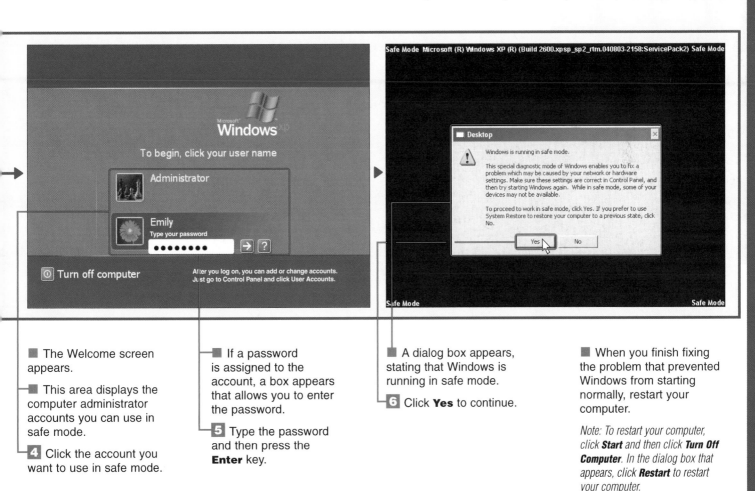

■ The Welcome screen appears.

■ This area displays the computer administrator accounts you can use in safe mode.

4 Click the account you want to use in safe mode.

■ If a password is assigned to the account, a box appears that allows you to enter the password.

5 Type the password and then press the **Enter** key.

■ A dialog box appears, stating that Windows is running in safe mode.

6 Click **Yes** to continue.

■ When you finish fixing the problem that prevented Windows from starting normally, restart your computer.

*Note: To restart your computer, click **Start** and then click **Turn Off Computer**. In the dialog box that appears, click **Restart** to restart your computer.*

165

Fix computer problems using the Help and Support Center

If you are having a problem with your computer, you can use the Help and Support Center included with Windows to get help with the problem. You can find help information on both hardware and software problems you may be experiencing. Checking the Help and Support Center provides a good starting point when you have a problem with your computer, since the problem may be easy to fix on your own.

Windows categorizes topics in the Help and Support Center window so you can quickly find the topic that best describes your problem. For example, the

Printing problems category is useful if you are having a problem installing a printer on your computer or the quality of your printed photos is poor.

The help topics in the Help and Support Center may provide a troubleshooter, which asks you a series of questions to help you fix a problem.

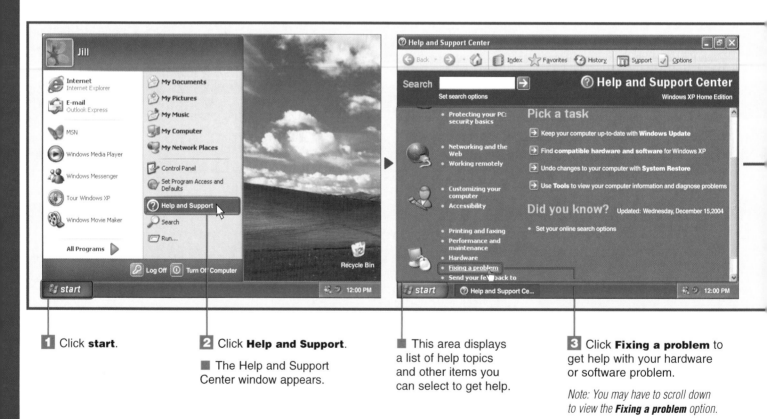

1 Click **start**.

2 Click **Help and Support**.

■ The Help and Support Center window appears.

■ This area displays a list of help topics and other items you can select to get help.

3 Click **Fixing a problem** to get help with your hardware or software problem.

*Note: You may have to scroll down to view the **Fixing a problem** option.*

Check It Out! You can view a list of troubleshooters that are available in Windows Help. At the top of the Help and Support Center window, click in the Search area, type "list of troubleshooters" and then press the Enter key. Click the List of troubleshooters option to view a list of troubleshooters that you can choose from.

Try This! You can use the Device Manager to determine if there is a problem with a hardware device. Click start, right-click My Computer and then select Properties from the menu that appears. Choose the Hardware tab and click the Device Manager button. In the Device Manager window, an exclamation mark (❗) appears over the icon for a device with a problem. Double-click the device to view the properties of the device, which indicate a suggested solution for the problem.

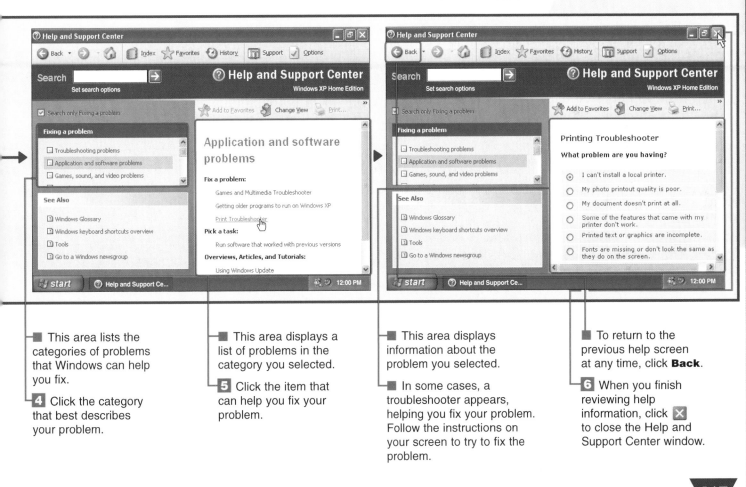

■ This area lists the categories of problems that Windows can help you fix.

4 Click the category that best describes your problem.

■ This area displays a list of problems in the category you selected.

5 Click the item that can help you fix your problem.

■ This area displays information about the problem you selected.

■ In some cases, a troubleshooter appears, helping you fix your problem. Follow the instructions on your screen to try to fix the problem.

■ To return to the previous help screen at any time, click **Back**.

6 When you finish reviewing help information, click ☒ to close the Help and Support Center window.

#74 | Rest easier by backing up your files

Backing up important information from your computer to a storage device, such as an external hard drive, a tape drive or a location on a network, allows you to rest easier knowing your information is safe. Windows XP comes with a Backup utility that allows you to easily back up your information.

If your computer's hard drive fails, you may lose valuable information stored on your computer. If you have backed up the information, however, you can use the backup copy to restore the information to your computer.

The Backup utility provides a wizard that you can use to create a backup job. A backup job allows you to indicate what information you want to back up and where you want to store the information. When creating a backup job, you can choose to back up your settings and the files in your My Documents folder, the settings and My Documents folder of every user on your computer, all the information on your computer or specific files and folders.

You must be logged on to Windows as a computer administrator to back up files and folders.

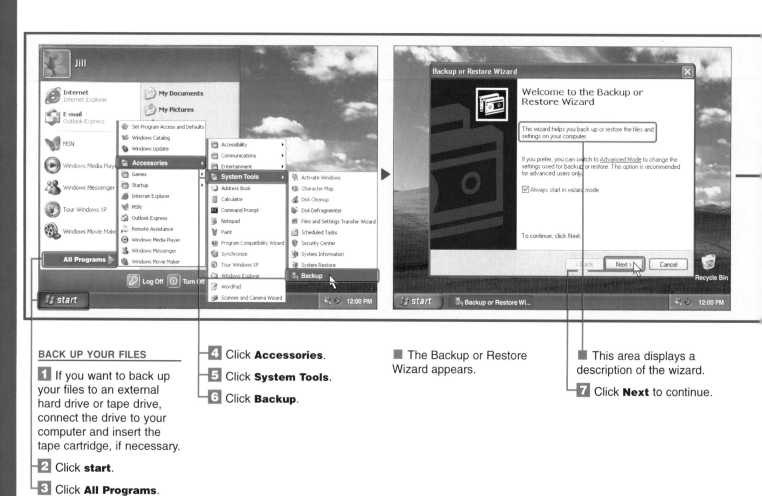

BACK UP YOUR FILES

1 If you want to back up your files to an external hard drive or tape drive, connect the drive to your computer and insert the tape cartridge, if necessary.

2 Click **start**.

3 Click **All Programs**.

4 Click **Accessories**.

5 Click **System Tools**.

6 Click **Backup**.

■ The Backup or Restore Wizard appears.

■ This area displays a description of the wizard.

7 Click **Next** to continue.

Install It! You may need to install the Backup utility. Insert the Windows XP CD-ROM disc into a drive. In the dialog box that appears, click Perform additional tasks and then click Browse this CD. In the window that appears, double-click the VALUEADD folder and then double-click the MSFT folder. Double-click the NTBACKUP folder and then double-click NTBACKUP to install the Backup utility.

Select Files! If you select the "Let me choose what to back up" option in step 10 below, a window appears after you click Next, allowing you to select the drives, folders and files you want to back up. Click ⊞ beside a drive or folder on the left to display its contents and then click the drive or folder containing the items you want to back up. On the right, click the box beside each item you want to back up (☐ changes to ☑) and then click Next to continue.

CONTINUED ▶

8 Click this option to back up the files and settings on your computer (○ changes to ◉).

9 Click **Next** to continue.

10 Click an option to specify what information you want to back up (○ changes to ◉).

11 Click **Next** to continue.

Note: If you selected the "Let me choose what to back up" option, see the top of this page for information on selecting drives, folders and files to back up.

When backing up files to an external hard drive or to a location on your network, Windows will automatically select the File backup type, which will store your backup information as a file. If you are backing up information to a tape drive, you need to select the tape drive as your backup type.

If you are backing up a large amount of information using a tape drive, the Backup utility is capable of backing up your information onto more than one tape cartridge.

When you complete the wizard, all the folders and files you specified will be backed up to the storage device you selected. If you back up information to a tape cartridge, you should label the cartridge with the name of the backup and the date. For safekeeping, you should store the external hard drive or tape cartridge containing the backup in a safe place.

CONTINUED ►

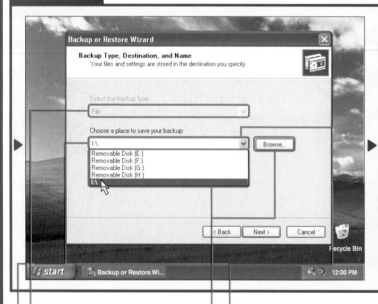

■ This area displays how Windows will store the backup. If you are using a tape drive, click ✓ to display a list that you can choose from and then select the tape drive connected to your computer.

■ This area displays the location where you will store your backup.

12 Click this area to display a list of storage locations.

13 Click the storage location you want to use.

■ You can also click **Browse** to specify a different location to store your backup.

14 Drag the mouse I over the text in this area and then type a name for the backup.

15 Click **Next** to continue.

■ You can click **Back** at any time to return to a previous step and change your selections.

Did You Know? The Backup utility does not allow you to back up your files directly onto a CD. However, you can first store a backup on your computer's hard drive and then copy the backup from your hard drive to a recordable CD. When you need to restore lost or damaged files, you can simply use the backup stored on the CD. Storing a backup on a recordable CD is useful when you want to back up a small number of files.

Protect the Registry! You can protect the data in your computer's registry, which contains the essential settings for running your computer by backing up the System State data. Perform steps 1 to 6 on page 168 and then click the "Advanced Mode" option. In the window that appears, click the Backup tab and select the box beside System State (☐ changes to ☑). Near the bottom of the window, confirm the location where the data will be backed up and then click the Start Backup button. In the dialog box that appears, click Start Backup.

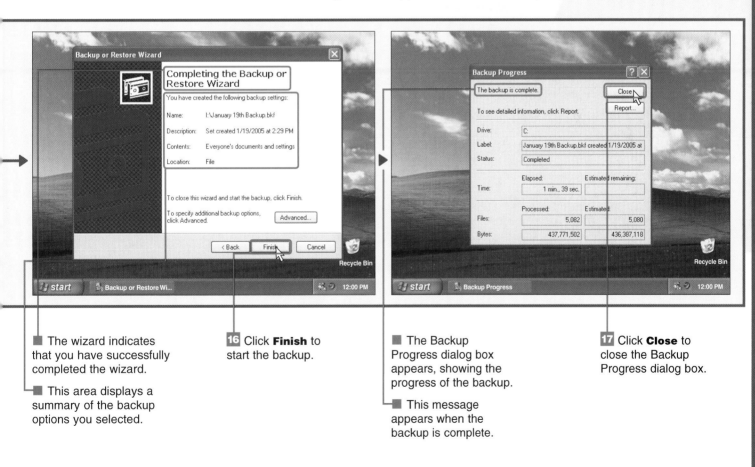

■ The wizard indicates that you have successfully completed the wizard.

■ This area displays a summary of the backup options you selected.

16 Click **Finish** to start the backup.

■ The Backup Progress dialog box appears, showing the progress of the backup.

■ This message appears when the backup is complete.

17 Click **Close** to close the Backup Progress dialog box.

If files on your computer are lost or damaged, you can use a backup you created to restore the files to your computer. For information on backing up files, see task #74.

If you backed up information to an external hard drive or to a tape drive, you will need to connect the drive and insert the tape cartridge, if necessary, that contains the information you want to restore. When restoring information from a backup that is stored on more than one tape cartridge, you must start restoring the files with the first tape cartridge. Files must be restored in the order that they were originally backed up.

The Backup or Restore Wizard displays a list of backup jobs you have performed. From this list, you can select the backup job you want to use to restore the lost or damaged information.

You must be logged on to Windows as a computer administrator to restore your backed up files. You can use your computer while the Backup utility is restoring your files, but your computer may operate more slowly than normal.

When the restore is complete, you will be able to access the restored information on your computer.

 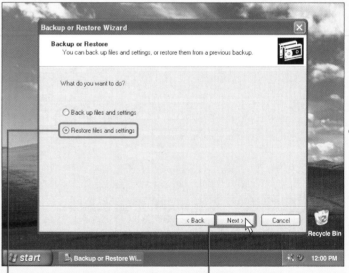

RESTORE YOUR FILES

1 If you want to restore files you backed up to an external hard drive or tape drive, connect the drive to your computer and insert the tape cartridge that contains the backup, if necessary.

2 Perform steps **2** to **6** on page 168 to start the Backup or Restore Wizard.

3 Click **Next** to continue.

4 Click this option to restore the files and settings on your computer (○ changes to ◉).

5 Click **Next** to continue.

Try This! You can specify the name and location of the backup file you want to use to restore your files. After performing step 5 below, click the Browse button. Then click the Browse button in the dialog box that appears. Locate the backup file you want and click Open. Click OK and then continue with step 9 below.

Did You Know? After performing step 9 below, you can click the Advanced button to choose options such as restoring the backup files to a different location or specifying what you want the Backup utility to do if a file you are restoring already exists on your computer.

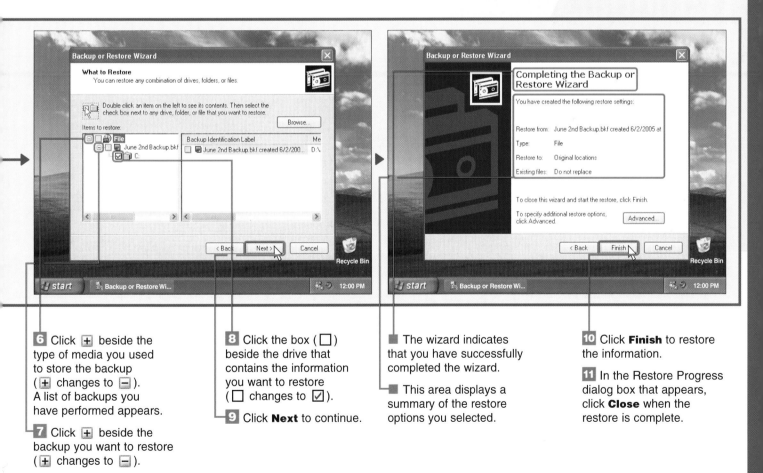

6 Click ⊞ beside the type of media you used to store the backup (⊞ changes to ⊟). A list of backups you have performed appears.

7 Click ⊞ beside the backup you want to restore (⊞ changes to ⊟).

8 Click the box (☐) beside the drive that contains the information you want to restore (☐ changes to ☑).

9 Click **Next** to continue.

■ The wizard indicates that you have successfully completed the wizard.

■ This area displays a summary of the restore options you selected.

10 Click **Finish** to restore the information.

11 In the Restore Progress dialog box that appears, click **Close** when the restore is complete.

Smart Web Browsing

Are you looking for ways to optimize the time you spend on the Web? Do you want to learn tips and tricks for working with Internet Explorer? The tasks discussed in this chapter will help you browse the Web smarter.

When browsing the Web, you can search for text of interest on a Web page or save a picture you see on a page on your computer. You can also quickly e-mail a Web page of interest to a friend or colleague to share the information.

Have you visited Web pages you do not want other people to know about? This chapter can show you how to erase the History list to delete any record of these pages.

If you have many Web pages saved in your Favorites list, over time the list may become unmanageable. This chapter will show you how to create folders to organize your favorite Web pages so you can quickly find favorite pages you want to display. You will also learn how to limit the space Internet Explorer uses to store temporary Internet files on your computer. Fewer stored temporary Internet files means Web pages will appear on your screen even faster.

If you often search the Internet for information of interest, you can set up Internet Explorer to use your favorite search engine. You will also learn how to use the Google search engine more effectively when searching for information on the Web.

101 Hot Tips

When browsing the Web, Internet Explorer sometimes blocks content on Web pages you view. You may choose to view blocked content on some Web pages.

Internet Explorer blocks most pop-up windows from appearing. Pop-up windows are small windows that often display advertisements and usually appear as soon as you visit a Web site. When blocking pop-up windows, Internet Explorer may block some useful pop-up windows. For example, if you click an image to see a larger version of the image, Internet Explorer may block the pop-up window that displays the larger image.

Internet Explorer also blocks content by preventing Web sites from downloading potentially harmful files and running software on your computer without your knowledge. When blocking content, Internet Explorer may prevent some Web pages from displaying properly.

You should be very cautious before allowing Web sites to download files and run software on your computer since Internet Explorer is designed to help protect your computer from damage. If viewing blocked content is not essential, you should avoid viewing the blocked content.

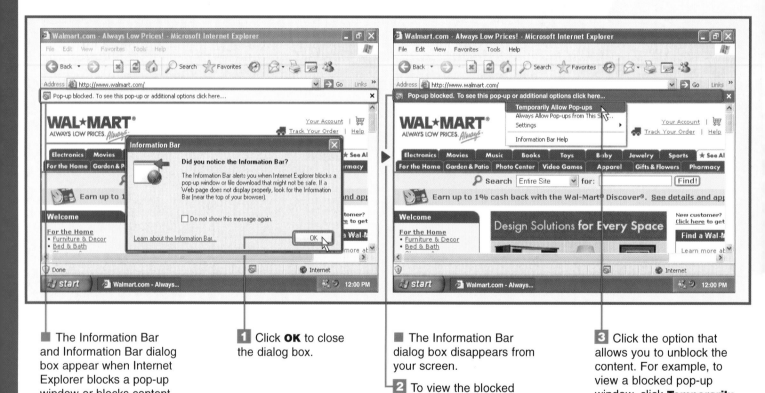

■ The Information Bar and Information Bar dialog box appear when Internet Explorer blocks a pop-up window or blocks content on a Web page that could harm your computer.

1 Click **OK** to close the dialog box.

■ The Information Bar dialog box disappears from your screen.

2 To view the blocked pop-up window or content on the displayed Web page, click the Information Bar. A menu appears.

3 Click the option that allows you to unblock the content. For example, to view a blocked pop-up window, click **Temporarily Allow Pop-ups**.

#77 E-mail a Web page to a friend

When viewing a Web page, you can quickly e-mail the Web page to another person without having to open your e-mail program. E-mailing a Web page is useful when you are browsing the Web and find something that might interest a friend or colleague.

When you e-mail a Web page, the recipient will be able to view the entire Web page within the e-mail message. You can also e-mail a link to a Web page.

In this case, the recipient will be able to click the link to open the Web page in their own Web browser.

When e-mailing a Web page, Outlook Express automatically fills in the subject of the message for you. You can use the subject Outlook Express provides or change the subject to something more personal or appropriate.

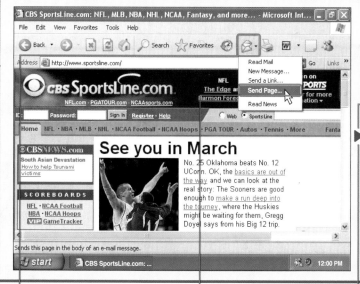

1 When you are viewing a Web page you want to e-mail to another person, click 🖃.

2 Click **Send Page** to send a copy of the Web page in an e-mail message.

*Note: If you want to send a Web page as a link in an e-mail message, click **Send a Link**.*

■ A window appears, displaying the Web page you are sending.

■ Outlook Express fills in the subject for you.

3 Type the e-mail address of the person you want to receive the message.

4 Click **Send** to send the message.

#78 | Sort Web pages you recently visited

The History list keeps track of the Web pages you have recently visited so you can quickly return to a Web page. You can sort the items displayed in the History list in different ways to help you find a Web page you want to revisit.

The History list initially sorts Web pages by the date when you visited the pages, but you might find another sorting method more useful. For example, if you know the name of a Web site but cannot remember when you visited the site,

you can sort by site to list the Web sites alphabetically by name. Alternatively, you can sort the History list so that the Web pages you visited most frequently appear at the top of the list.

To quickly find a Web page you visited today, you can have Internet Explorer arrange today's Web pages in the order in which you visited the pages, starting with the most recently visited.

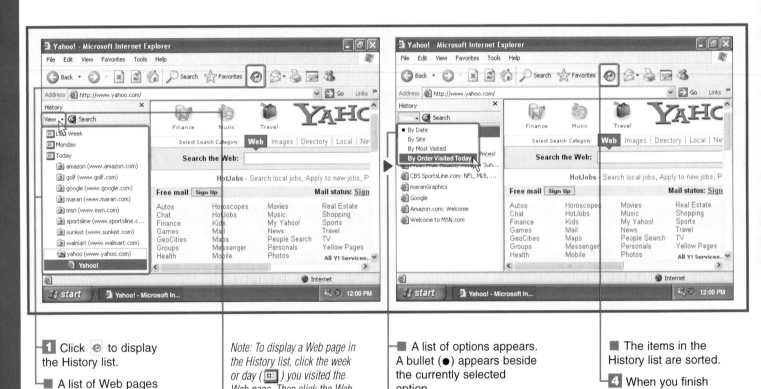

■1 Click 🕘 to display the History list.

■ A list of Web pages you have recently visited appears. The list is organized by week and day.

Note: To display a Web page in the History list, click the week or day (🗒) you visited the Web page. Then click the Web site (🖳) that offers the Web page followed by the Web page (🗐) you want to view.

■2 To change the way the History list is sorted, click **View**.

■ A list of options appears. A bullet (●) appears beside the currently selected option.

■3 Click the way you want to sort the items in the History list.

■ The items in the History list are sorted.

■4 When you finish viewing the History list, click 🕘 to hide the list.

Keep your Web browsing private

You can keep your Web browsing private by deleting the list of Web pages you visited in Internet Explorer.

As you browse the Web, Internet Explorer keeps track of the addresses of Web pages you visit and compiles them in a History list. If you visit Web pages you do not want other people to know about, you can erase the History list to delete the record of these pages. For example, if you are planning a surprise family vacation, you may not want to leave clues that you visited travel sites. To view or hide the History list, click ⊘ at the top of the Internet Explorer window.

A list of Web pages you have recently viewed will appear on the left side of your screen. The list of Web pages is organized by week and day so you can quickly find a Web page you viewed on a specific day. Internet Explorer is set up to keep track of the last 20 days of Web pages you have viewed.

Clearing the History list keeps your Web browsing private and also allows you to free up space on your computer.

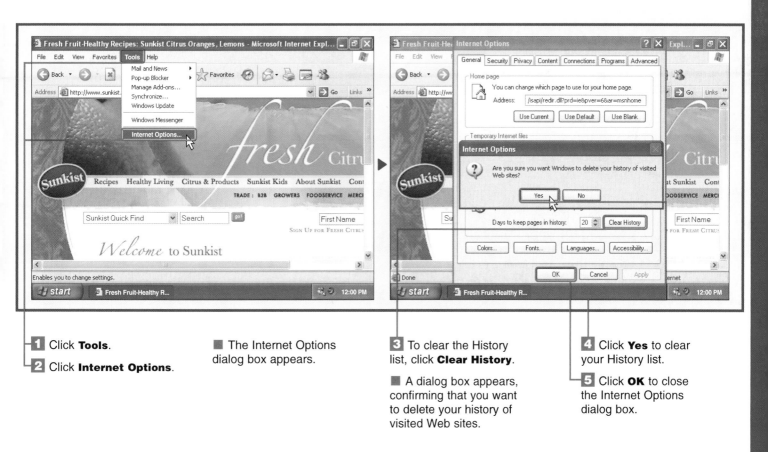

1 Click **Tools**.

2 Click **Internet Options**.

■ The Internet Options dialog box appears.

3 To clear the History list, click **Clear History**.

■ A dialog box appears, confirming that you want to delete your history of visited Web sites.

4 Click **Yes** to clear your History list.

5 Click **OK** to close the Internet Options dialog box.

When you are viewing a Web page that contains a lot of text, you can use the Find feature to quickly locate a word or phrase of interest on the Web page. For example, when you are viewing a news article, you may want to search for specific information in the article, such as "healthcare."

When you search for text on a Web page, Internet Explorer will find the text even if the text is part of a larger word. For example, if you search for "photo," Internet Explorer will also find "photograph."

The word or phrase you search for on a Web page may appear in several locations on the page. Internet Explorer will find and highlight the first instance of the word or phrase. You can continue the search to find the next instance of the word or phrase.

During your search, the Find dialog box may cover information you want to read on a Web page. To move the Find dialog box on your screen, simply position the mouse pointer over the title bar of the dialog box and then drag the dialog box to a new location.

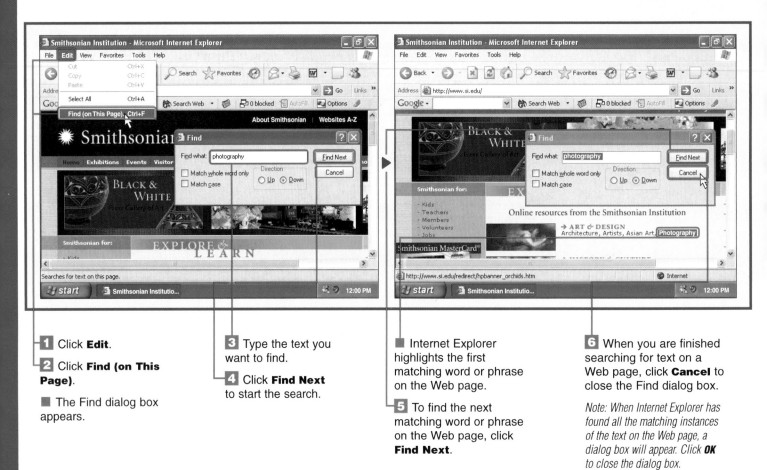

1 Click **Edit**.

2 Click **Find (on This Page)**.

■ The Find dialog box appears.

3 Type the text you want to find.

4 Click **Find Next** to start the search.

■ Internet Explorer highlights the first matching word or phrase on the Web page.

5 To find the next matching word or phrase on the Web page, click **Find Next**.

6 When you are finished searching for text on a Web page, click **Cancel** to close the Find dialog box.

Note: When Internet Explorer has found all the matching instances of the text on the Web page, a dialog box will appear. Click OK to close the dialog box.

When you see a picture you like on a Web page, you can save the picture on your computer. When browsing through Web pages, you may see a picture of your favorite celebrity, animal, painting or building that you want to save.

After you save a picture you see on a Web page, you can view and work with the picture as you would view and work with any picture stored on your computer. You can send the picture in an e-mail message to share the picture with family and friends. You can also use the picture as your desktop background, so you can see the picture as you work.

Display as Desktop Background!

To display a saved picture as your desktop background, right-click the picture on your computer and then click "Set as Desktop Background" from the menu that appears. This option is only available for pictures in folders designed to store pictures, such as the My Pictures folder. To change the way the picture appears on your desktop, such as stretching the picture to fill the desktop, perform steps 1 to 9 of task #32, leaving out step 4.

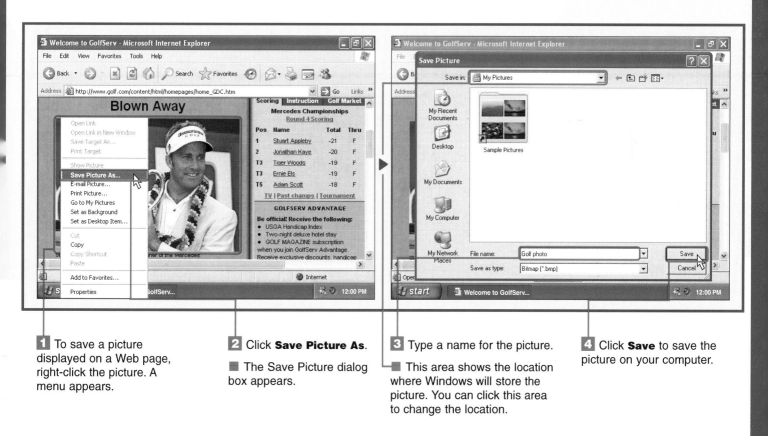

1 To save a picture displayed on a Web page, right-click the picture. A menu appears.

2 Click **Save Picture As**.

■ The Save Picture dialog box appears.

3 Type a name for the picture.

■ This area shows the location where Windows will store the picture. You can click this area to change the location.

4 Click **Save** to save the picture on your computer.

82

Organize your favorite Web pages

You can organize the Web pages in your Favorites list to help make the list easier to use. Your Favorites list contains a list of Web pages you frequently visit so you can quickly display a favorite Web page at any time.

Over time, your Favorites list may become large and unmanageable. To keep your Favorites list organized, you can create folders to arrange Web pages by topic. For example, you may want to create folders with names such as Sports, News and Shopping.

Once you have created folders, you can rearrange the Web pages in your Favorites list to move Web pages to folders you have created. You may also want to place some of the Web pages you frequently use at the top of the list for quick access.

You can sort the folders and favorite Web pages on your Favorites list in alphabetical order. All your folders will be placed at the top of the list, followed by all the Web pages.

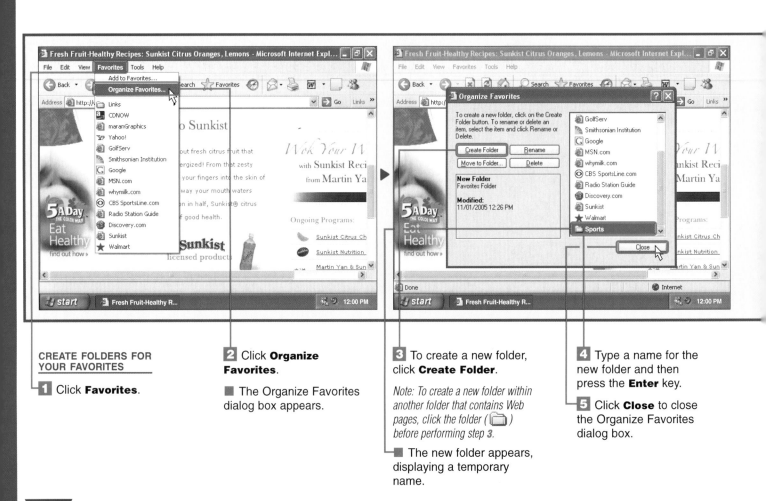

CREATE FOLDERS FOR YOUR FAVORITES

1 Click **Favorites**.

2 Click **Organize Favorites**.

■ The Organize Favorites dialog box appears.

3 To create a new folder, click **Create Folder**.

Note: To create a new folder within another folder that contains Web pages, click the folder (📁) before performing step 3.

■ The new folder appears, displaying a temporary name.

4 Type a name for the new folder and then press the **Enter** key.

5 Click **Close** to close the Organize Favorites dialog box.

Add It! You can easily add a Web page to your Favorites list. Display the Web page you want to add to your Favorites list. Click the Favorites menu and then select Add to Favorites. In the Add Favorite dialog box, click OK to add the Web page to your Favorites list.

Delete It! You can delete a Web page or folder you no longer use from your Favorites list. Click the Favorites menu to display your Favorites list. Right-click the Web page or folder you want to delete and then click Delete on the menu that appears. Click Yes in the confirmation dialog box to delete the item. Deleting a folder also deletes all the Web pages in the folder.

MOVE YOUR FAVORITES

1 Click **Favorites** to display a list of your favorite Web pages.

2 Position the mouse over the favorite Web page you want to move.

3 Drag the Web page to a new location in your list of favorites.

Note: To move a Web page to a folder, drag the Web page over the folder and then to a location in the submenu that appears.

■ A solid line indicates where the Web page will appear in the list.

SORT YOUR FAVORITES

1 Click **Favorites** to display a list of your favorite Web pages.

2 Right-click anywhere in the list of favorites. A menu appears.

3 Click **Sort by Name** to sort your list of favorites alphabetically.

Surf faster by limiting space for temporary Internet files

Internet Explorer stores temporary Internet files in the Temporary Internet Files folder on your computer. You may want to reduce the size of the folder to speed up your Web browsing and save disk space. Reducing the size of the folder is especially useful if you have a high-speed connection.

Temporary Internet files are Web pages and images Internet Explorer stores on your hard disk while you are browsing the Web. Before transferring a Web page to your computer, Internet Explorer checks whether the page is stored in the Temporary Internet Files folder. If the Web page is stored in the folder,

Internet Explorer quickly displays the stored page rather than transferring the page from the Internet. If your folder is too large, it may take longer to search for the Web page in the folder than to download the page from the Internet.

You may want to try different values for the amount of disk space set aside for the Temporary Internet Files folder. You can try a lower value, such as 1 MB, and then try a higher value, such as 50 MB, to see how the values affect your Web browsing speed.

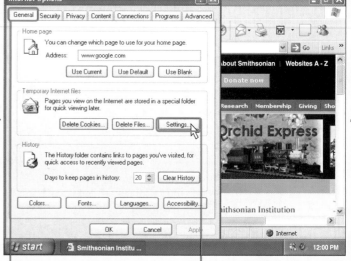

1 Click **Tools**.

2 Click **Internet Options**.

■ The Internet Options dialog box appears.

3 Click the **General** tab.

4 Click **Settings** to change the settings for the temporary Internet files stored on your computer.

■ The Settings dialog box appears.

Delete Files! You can delete all the temporary Internet files stored in your Temporary Internet Files folder. Deleting these files is useful if your computer's available disk space is low and you do not plan to browse through Web pages you have previously viewed. In the Internet Options dialog box, click the General tab and then click the Delete Files button to delete the files stored in the Temporary Internet Files folder. In the dialog box that appears, click OK to delete the files in the folder.

Surf Even Faster! If you use a modem to connect to the Internet, you can buy software such as Propel Accelerator (www.propel.com) that can dramatically increase the speed of your Web browsing experience. You can also look for an Internet Service Provider that offers this software as part of their service.

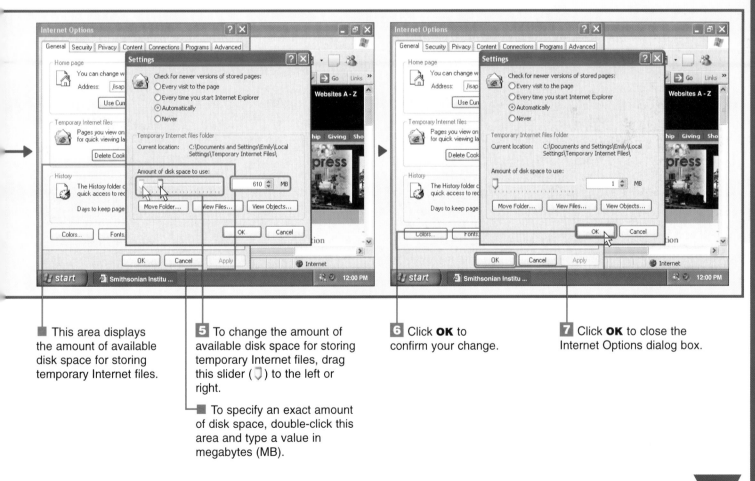

■ This area displays the amount of available disk space for storing temporary Internet files.

5 To change the amount of available disk space for storing temporary Internet files, drag this slider ( ) to the left or right.

■ To specify an exact amount of disk space, double-click this area and type a value in megabytes (MB).

6 Click **OK** to confirm your change.

7 Click **OK** to close the Internet Options dialog box.

84

Set up Internet Explorer to use your favorite search engine

When you use the Search Companion in Internet Explorer to search for Web pages, the Search Companion automatically uses the MSN search engine to search for pages. If you would prefer to use another search engine, you can specify the search engine you want to use.

Changing the search engine used by the Search Companion is useful if you always use a specific search engine, such as Google. You can quickly perform your search in the Search Companion using the search engine you specify, while benefiting from the added features the Search Companion offers, such as search refinement suggestions.

Some popular search engines you can choose as the new search engine include Google, Ask Jeeves, Yahoo! and AOL Search.

Regardless of the search engine you use, you will not find every page on the Web that discusses your topic of interest. Search engines cannot possibly catalog every page on the Web because Web pages change frequently and new pages are created every day.

1 Click **Search** to display the Search Companion.

■ The Search Companion appears.

2 Click **Change preferences** to change the way the Search Companion works.

■ A list of options appears, allowing you to change the way the Search Companion works.

3 Click **Change Internet search behavior**.

Did You Know? You can also search the Internet by entering a word or phrase in the Address bar of the Microsoft Internet Explorer window. In the Address bar, type a question mark (?) followed by a space and the word or phrase you want to search for. Then press the Enter key. Even if you changed the search engine used by the Search Companion, searches you perform using the Address bar will still be performed by the MSN search engine.

Try This! If your search using the Search Companion does not provide the results you want, you can use other search engines to find more information. In the Search Companion, click the "Automatically send your search to other search engines" option.

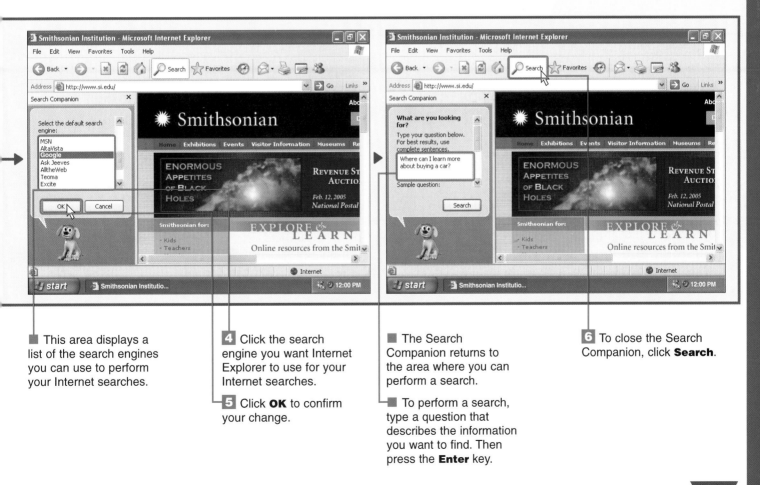

■ This area displays a list of the search engines you can use to perform your Internet searches.

4 Click the search engine you want Internet Explorer to use for your Internet searches.

5 Click **OK** to confirm your change.

■ The Search Companion returns to the area where you can perform a search.

■ To perform a search, type a question that describes the information you want to find. Then press the **Enter** key.

6 To close the Search Companion, click **Search**.

187

85

Search the Web effectively with Google

When searching for information on the Web, you can obtain comprehensive results by using Google to perform your search. Google is the most popular search Web site. You can visit Google at www.google.com.

The Google Main Page

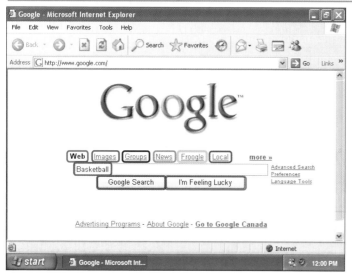

Performing a Search

To perform a search, click the search area and then type the word(s) that best describes the information you want to find. Then press the Enter key or click the Google Search button. Google will find only Web pages that contain all the words you type. You can use more words to narrow your search.

✓ Make sure the words you type are as specific as possible. For example, type "Picasso" rather than "painter."

✓ To search for a phrase, type quotation marks (" ") around the phrase. For example, type "The Wizard of Oz."

✓ You do not need to capitalize words. For example, typing "abraham lincoln" will return the same results as "Abraham Lincoln."

I'm Feeling Lucky

Click this button to bypass the search results and go directly to the first Web page that matches the information you enter.

Web

Searches for Web pages that match the information you enter.

Images

Searches for images that match the information you enter.

Groups

Allows you to browse through discussion groups and search for messages sent to discussion groups. Discussion groups allow people with similar interests to communicate.

News

Displays the top news headlines and allows you to search for a news item of interest.

Froogle

Allows you to search for products you can purchase.

Local

Allows you to search the Web for stores and businesses in your area.

Google Features

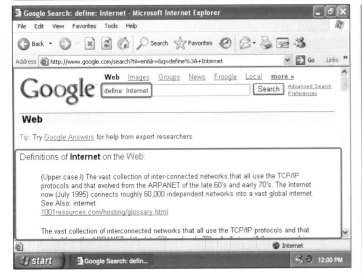

Display a Definition

To display a definition for a word or phrase, type "define:" followed by the word or phrase you want defined. For example, type "define: Internet."

Directory

You can browse through categories offered by Google to find information of interest. You can visit Google's directory at directory.google.com.

Track a Parcel

To track a parcel, type the UPS, FedEx or USPS tracking number for the parcel. For example, to track a FedEx package, type "555555555555."

Phonebook

To find the address and phone number for a business in the United States, type the business name along with the city and state or type the business name and ZIP code. For example, type "Ford Detroit Michigan." To find the address and phone number of a person in the United States, type the person's first name, last name and city.

Get Stock Quotes

To get stock or mutual fund information, type one or more NYSE, NASDAQ, AMEX or mutual fund ticker symbols or the name of a corporation traded on one of the stock indices. For example, to get stock information about Microsoft, type "MSFT."

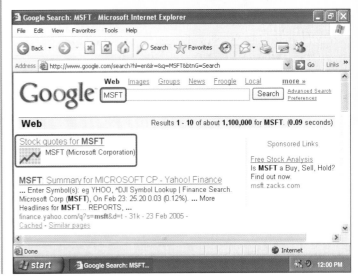

Google Features

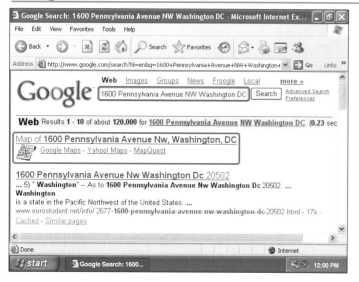

Street Map Search

To find a street map of an address in the United States, you can type the street address, including the city and state or the ZIP code.

Get Airline Flight Information

To check the status of a United States flight, type the name of the airline followed by the flight number. For example, to check the status of United Airlines flight number 162, type "United 162."

Web Site Search

You can search for information within a specific Web site. Type the word(s) you want to find and then type "site:" followed by the address of the Web site. For example, type "admissions site:www.harvard.edu."

Who Links to You?

To display a list of Web pages that contain a link to your Web page, type "link:" followed by your Web page address. For example, type "link:www.maran.com."

Perform a Calculation

Google can solve math problems, including basic arithmetic and unit conversions. For example, you can type "5+3*4," "26 miles in kilometers" or "half a cup in teaspoons."

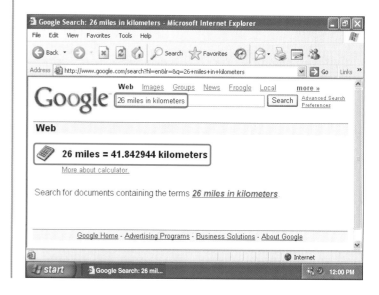

Search Results

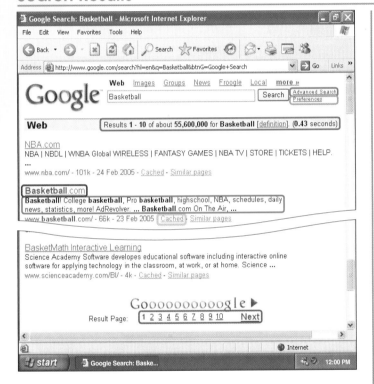

Advanced Search

Displays additional options you can use to help narrow your search.

Preferences

Allows you to specify how you want Google to work, such as specifying the number of results displayed on each results page.

Statistics Bar

Displays the number of results and a description of your search.

Web Page Title

Displays the title of a Web page Google found.

Web Page Description

An excerpt of text from a Web page Google found appears below a Web page title. Your search words appear in bold to show the context in which the words were used on a Web page.

Cached

Displays the Web page as the page appeared when it was indexed by Google. Viewing a cached Web page is useful if a Web page is no longer available.

Translate this page

If the search results contain a Web page published in a language other than English, you can view an English translation of the page.

Results Pages

Google displays ten Web pages on each results page. To display additional results pages, click a specific number or click Next to display the next results page.

Tips and Tricks for E-mail, Instant Messages and Faxes

Have you been looking for hot new tips and tricks for using your computer to exchange information with other people? This chapter is full of ways to enhance your e-mailing, instant messaging and faxing capabilities.

You can set up Outlook Express to access your Hotmail account so you can send and receive Hotmail messages without opening your Web browser!

Have you ever wondered if the e-mail messages you send actually arrive at their destinations safely? You can have Outlook Express notify you when your e-mail message has been opened by the recipient, so you'll never have to wonder if your message is lost again.

You can also set up Outlook Express to automatically send an e-mail reply to each person who sends you a message while you are on vacation or away from the office for a few days.

When using Windows Messenger to exchange instant messages, you can easily block specific people from contacting you. Windows Messenger even lets you see and talk to another person over the Internet instead of simply exchanging text messages.

Did you know that you can use your computer to send and receive faxes without a fax machine? Read on to find out how to use this great Windows XP feature!

101 Hot Tips

View blocked content in an e-mail message

You can choose to view pictures and other content that Outlook Express has blocked in an e-mail message.

Outlook Express blocks pictures and other content from appearing in your messages to help you avoid viewing potentially offensive material. Blocking content also helps reduce the amount of junk mail you receive. Junk mail can include advertisements, chain letters, fake virus warnings or petitions and is often sent to a large number of

people at once. Pictures in junk mail can transmit a message back to the sender, notifying the sender that your e-mail address works, which often results in you receiving more junk mail.

You should only view blocked content in an e-mail message when you receive a message from a person you know and trust.

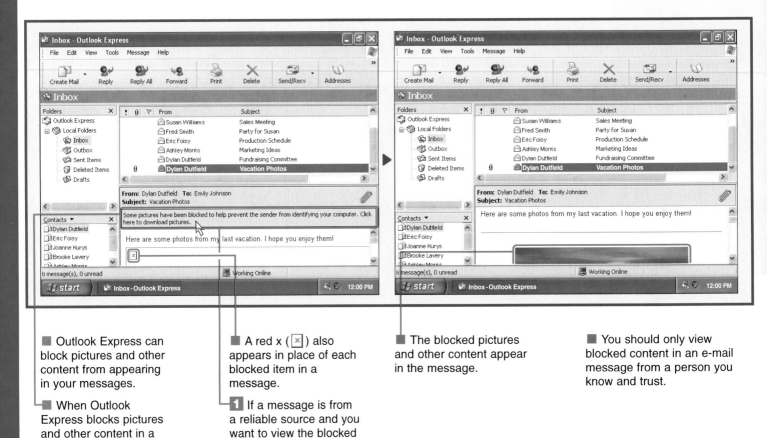

■ Outlook Express can block pictures and other content from appearing in your messages.

┗■ When Outlook Express blocks pictures and other content in a message, a banner appears in this area.

■ A red x (⊠) also appears in place of each blocked item in a message.

1 If a message is from a reliable source and you want to view the blocked content, click the banner.

■ The blocked pictures and other content appear in the message.

■ You should only view blocked content in an e-mail message from a person you know and trust.

When you send an e-mail message, you can ask Outlook Express to request a read receipt for the message. A read receipt is a confirmation e-mail message that notifies you that the person to whom you sent the message has received and read the message. Requesting a read receipt allows you to confirm that a message you sent was delivered and lets you know what time the message was opened on the recipient's computer.

Keep in mind that the recipient can choose whether or not to send a read receipt for the message. When the recipient opens a message you requested a read receipt for, a dialog box appears, asking whether the person would like to send a receipt. If the person chooses to send a receipt, you will receive an e-mail message verifying that your message was displayed on the recipient's computer. The dialog box requesting a receipt may not appear on some recipients' computers.

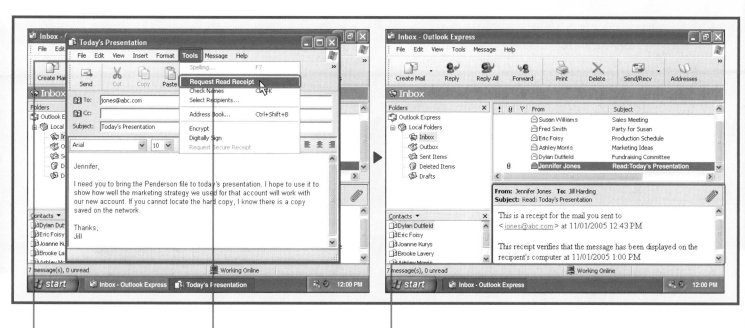

1 When composing a message, click **Tools**.

2 Click **Request Read Receipt**.

■ A check mark (✔) will appear beside the Request Read Receipt option on the Tools menu.

■ When the person reads the contents of the message, you may receive a confirmation message indicating the date and time the person read the message.

■ If you sent the message to more than one person, you will receive a separate confirmation message from each person who chose to send a confirmation.

Access your Hotmail account in Outlook Express

You can set up Outlook Express to check the e-mail messages in your Hotmail account. Hotmail is a free Web-based e-mail service, which allows you to send and receive e-mail from any computer that has access to the Web.

If you already have an e-mail account set up through your Internet Service Provider (ISP), you can have Outlook Express check that account and your Hotmail account at the same time. If you do not have another e-mail account set up, you can set up Outlook Express to only check your Hotmail account.

Working with your Hotmail account through Outlook Express can save you time because you only have to go to one location to access both of your e-mail accounts. Another advantage to working with your Hotmail account in Outlook Express is the ability to read and compose Hotmail messages when you are not connected to the Internet.

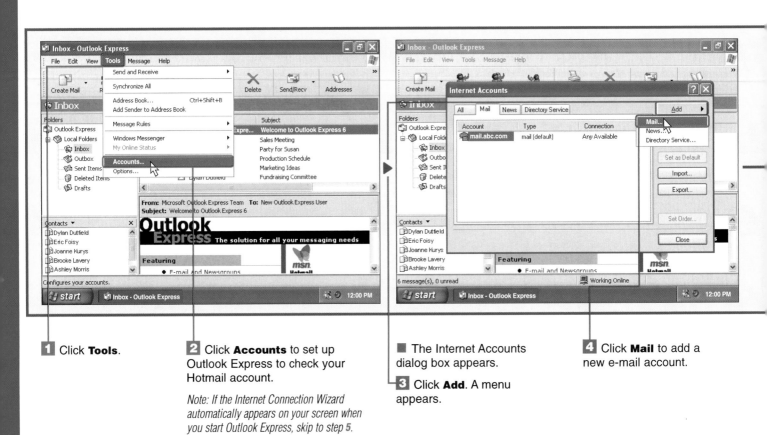

1 Click **Tools**.

2 Click **Accounts** to set up Outlook Express to check your Hotmail account.

Note: If the Internet Connection Wizard automatically appears on your screen when you start Outlook Express, skip to step 5.

■ The Internet Accounts dialog box appears.

3 Click **Add**. A menu appears.

4 Click **Mail** to add a new e-mail account.

Check It Out! You can set up Outlook Express to check other e-mail accounts. For example, you can perform the steps below to set up an account that ends with @msn.com. You can also set up e-mail accounts that are not Web-based. For example, you can set up your home computer to access your e-mail account at work. Check with your ISP or network administrator for the account's name and password, as well as the account's incoming and outgoing mail servers.

Change It! To later change the information for an e-mail account, select the Tools menu and then click Accounts. On the Mail tab, select the e-mail account you want to change and then click the Properties button. In the Properties dialog box, you can change the information for the e-mail account.

CONTINUED ▶

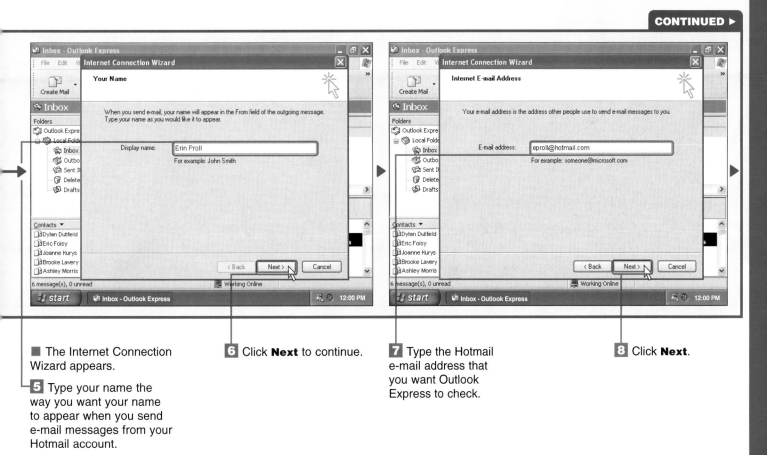

■ The Internet Connection Wizard appears.

5 Type your name the way you want your name to appear when you send e-mail messages from your Hotmail account.

6 Click **Next** to continue.

7 Type the Hotmail e-mail address that you want Outlook Express to check.

8 Click **Next**.

To set up Outlook Express to check your Hotmail account, you need to specify the account name and password you use to access your Hotmail account. The account name for a Hotmail account is the same as your Hotmail e-mail address. You can have Outlook Express remember your password so you do not have to type the password each time you connect to your Hotmail account.

Once you set up Outlook Express to check your Hotmail account, the mail folders for your Hotmail account will appear in the Outlook Express window.

Any changes you make to these folders and the e-mail messages in the folders in Outlook Express will also change on your Hotmail Web page.

Whenever your computer is connected to the Internet, Outlook Express will automatically check for new messages on your Hotmail account and any other e-mail accounts you have set up. By default, Outlook Express checks for new messages every 30 minutes.

CONTINUED ▶

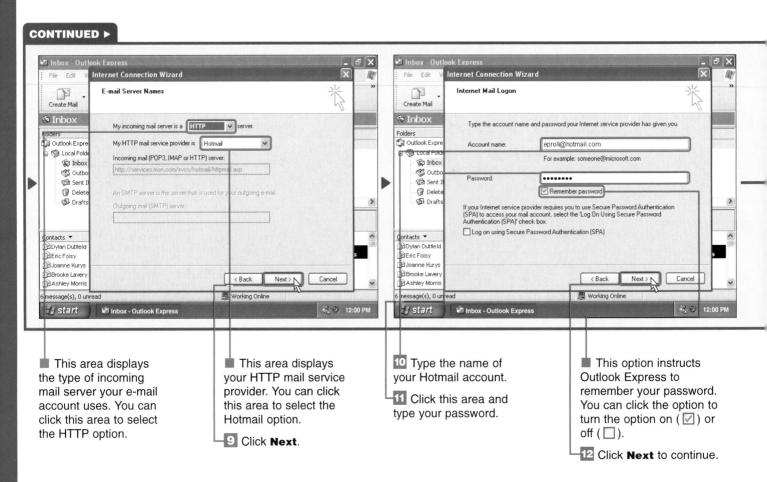

■ This area displays the type of incoming mail server your e-mail account uses. You can click this area to select the HTTP option.

■ This area displays your HTTP mail service provider. You can click this area to select the Hotmail option.

9 Click **Next**.

10 Type the name of your Hotmail account.

11 Click this area and type your password.

■ This option instructs Outlook Express to remember your password. You can click the option to turn the option on (☑) or off (☐).

12 Click **Next** to continue.

Delete It! To delete an e-mail account you no longer need, select the Tools menu and then click Accounts. On the Mail tab, click the name of the e-mail account you want to delete. Then click the Remove button. In the confirmation dialog box that appears, click Yes to confirm the deletion. Deleting your Hotmail account from Outlook Express does not affect your Hotmail account on the Web.

Did You Know? You can check for new messages on only your Hotmail account at any time. Click ▾ beside the Send/Recv button. In the menu that appears, click Hotmail to have Outlook Express check for new messages on only your Hotmail account.

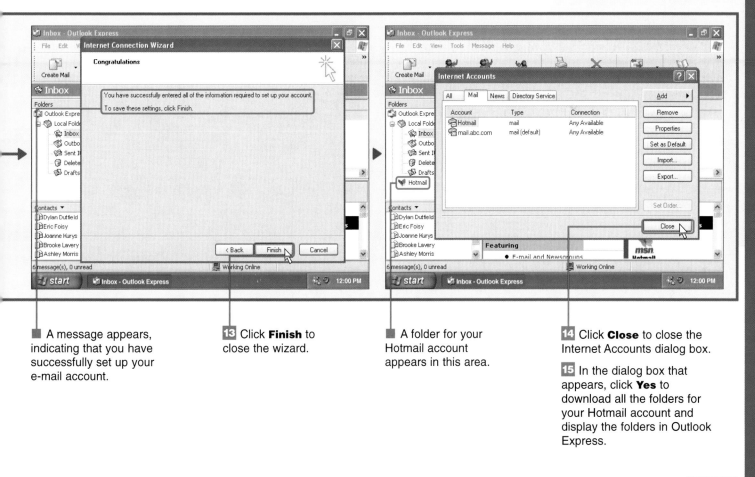

■ A message appears, indicating that you have successfully set up your e-mail account.

13 Click **Finish** to close the wizard.

■ A folder for your Hotmail account appears in this area.

14 Click **Close** to close the Internet Accounts dialog box.

15 In the dialog box that appears, click **Yes** to download all the folders for your Hotmail account and display the folders in Outlook Express.

Create an eye-catching e-mail

In the same way you would use decorative paper for written letters, you can have an e-mail message you send display attractive stationery. Using stationery can help make your e-mail messages appear more personalized and interesting to read.

Outlook Express includes several ready-made stationery designs, but you can obtain additional stationery designs at www.microsoft.com/windows/oe/features/stationery. You can also use any HTML file stored on your computer as stationery.

Each stationery design includes coordinated elements, such as a background color, background image, font style and font color. This allows you to quickly jazz up your e-mail messages without having to choose fonts, colors and a background.

When sending a message with a stationery design, in some cases an e-mail provider may remove the stationery from the message or the e-mail program used by the recipient may not display the stationery design.

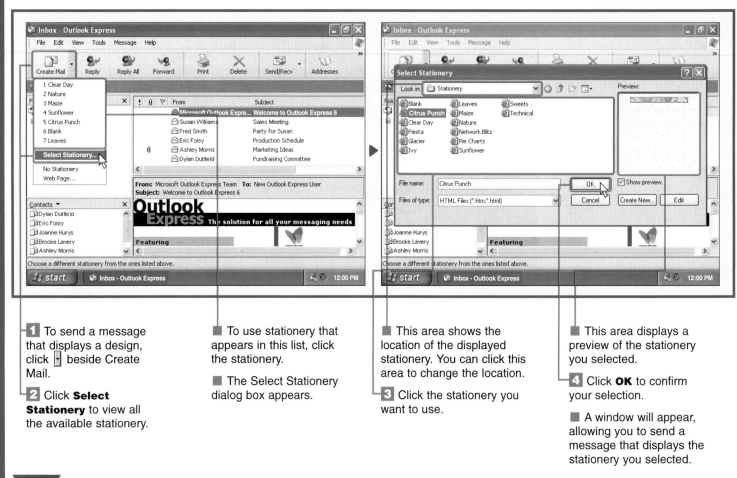

■1 To send a message that displays a design, click ⏷ beside Create Mail.

■2 Click **Select Stationery** to view all the available stationery.

■ To use stationery that appears in this list, click the stationery.

■ The Select Stationery dialog box appears.

■ This area shows the location of the displayed stationery. You can click this area to change the location.

■3 Click the stationery you want to use.

■ This area displays a preview of the stationery you selected.

■4 Click **OK** to confirm your selection.

■ A window will appear, allowing you to send a message that displays the stationery you selected.

Stop adding people to your address book automatically

When you reply to an e-mail message, Outlook Express automatically adds the person who sent you the message to your address book. If you do not want Outlook Express to automatically add people to your address book, you can turn this feature off.

When Outlook Express automatically adds people to your address book, your address book may become cluttered. For example, if a person sends you a message from a home e-mail address and then another message from a work e-mail address, Outlook Express will add each address to your address book as a separate entry when you respond to the messages. Eventually your address book may become cluttered with multiple entries for many of your contacts. Preventing Outlook Express from automatically adding people to your address book will reduce the number of entries in your address book, since only the entries you intentionally add will appear.

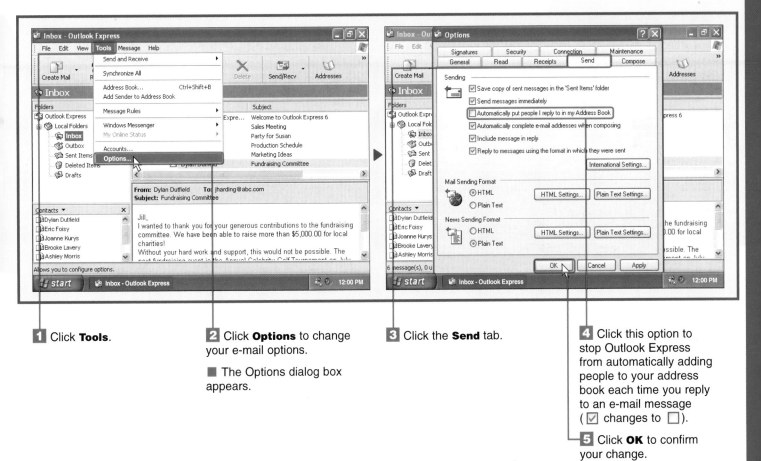

1 Click **Tools**.

2 Click **Options** to change your e-mail options.

■ The Options dialog box appears.

3 Click the **Send** tab.

4 Click this option to stop Outlook Express from automatically adding people to your address book each time you reply to an e-mail message (☑ changes to ☐).

5 Click **OK** to confirm your change.

#91 | Create multiple e-mail signatures

Creating multiple signatures allows you to choose the most appropriate signature for each message you send. For example, you may want to have one signature for business e-mails and a different signature for personal e-mails.

Using signatures saves you from having to type the same information at the end of every message, such as your name, e-mail address, occupation or Web page address. Many people also use signatures to display a favorite humorous or inspirational quotation. As a courtesy to people who will be reading your messages, you should limit your signature to four or five lines.

Each time you send a message in Outlook Express, you will be able to choose the signature you want to add to the message. By default, the signatures you create are named "Signature #1," "Signature #2" and so on. You can give each signature a descriptive name, such as Business and Personal, to make it easier to insert the correct signature into your messages.

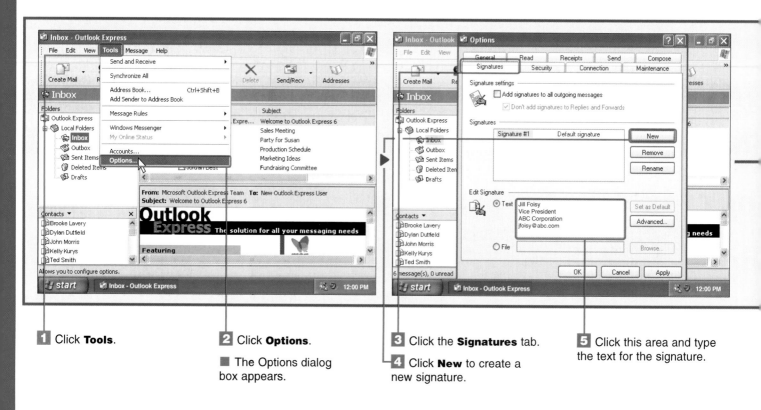

1 Click **Tools**.

2 Click **Options**.

■ The Options dialog box appears.

3 Click the **Signatures** tab.

4 Click **New** to create a new signature.

5 Click this area and type the text for the signature.

Add It Automatically! You can have Outlook Express automatically add one of your signatures to every message you send. Perform steps 1 to 3 below. If the signature you want to add to all your messages is not labeled "Default signature," click the name of the signature and then click the Set as Default button. At the top of the dialog box, click the "Add signatures to all outgoing messages" option (☐ changes to ☑). To also add the signature to messages you reply to and forward, click the "Don't add signatures to Replies and Forwards" option (☑ changes to ☐). Click OK to confirm your changes.

If you do not want the signature to appear in a message you are sending, you can drag the mouse I over the signature and then press the Delete key to remove the signature from the message.

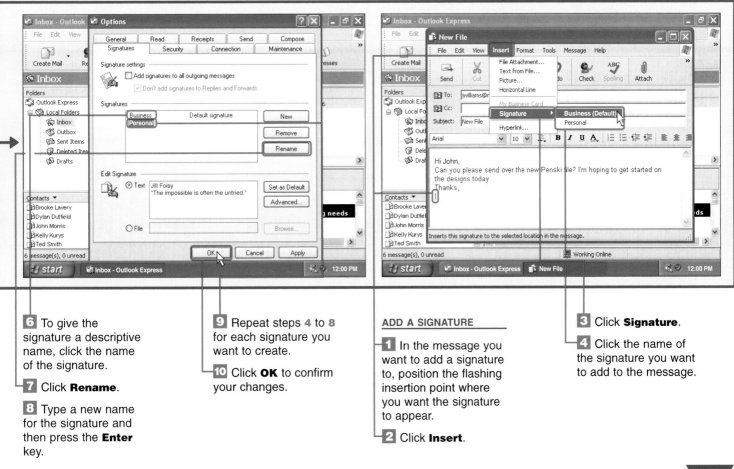

6 To give the signature a descriptive name, click the name of the signature.

7 Click **Rename**.

8 Type a new name for the signature and then press the **Enter** key.

9 Repeat steps **4** to **8** for each signature you want to create.

10 Click **OK** to confirm your changes.

ADD A SIGNATURE

1 In the message you want to add a signature to, position the flashing insertion point where you want the signature to appear.

2 Click **Insert**.

3 Click **Signature**.

4 Click the name of the signature you want to add to the message.

#92 Create a shortcut to a person you e-mail regularly

If you frequently e-mail the same person, you can create a shortcut on your desktop that will quickly address an e-mail message to that person. When you double-click the shortcut on your desktop, your default e-mail program will open, displaying a new message with the person's e-mail address filled in for you. To complete the message, you only need to type a subject and text for the message.

When entering the e-mail address of the person you e-mail regularly, if the person is in your address book, you can type the person's name instead of typing their e-mail address to create the shortcut.

You can work with a shortcut you create as you would work with a regular file on your computer. For example, you can rename or delete a shortcut as you would rename or delete any file.

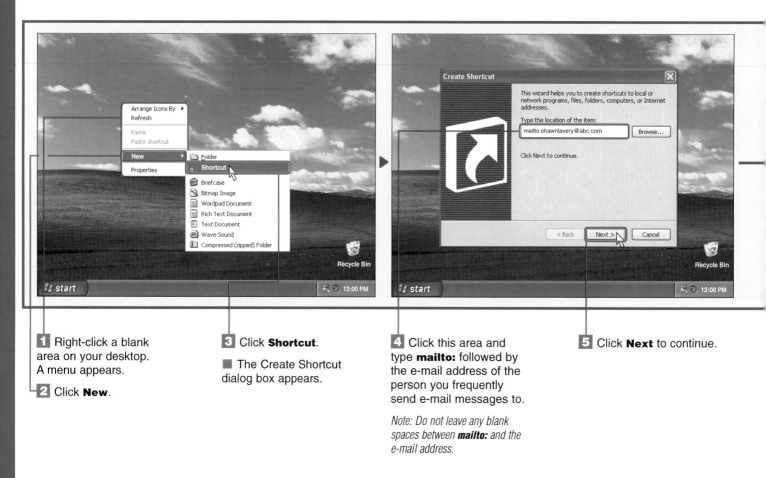

1 Right-click a blank area on your desktop. A menu appears.

2 Click **New**.

3 Click **Shortcut**.

■ The Create Shortcut dialog box appears.

4 Click this area and type **mailto:** followed by the e-mail address of the person you frequently send e-mail messages to.

*Note: Do not leave any blank spaces between **mailto:** and the e-mail address.*

5 Click **Next** to continue.

Did You Know? You can create a shortcut that will address an e-mail message to more than one person. Perform steps 1 to 7 below, entering the e-mail address of each person you want to receive the message in step 4. Make sure you separate each e-mail address with a semi-colon (;) or comma (,) and do not leave any blank spaces before or after the e-mail addresses.

Customize It! You can change the icon for the shortcut you created to give the icon a customized look. Windows provides icons for you to choose from, but you can also download fun or interesting icons from the Web. To change the icon for a shortcut, see task #34.

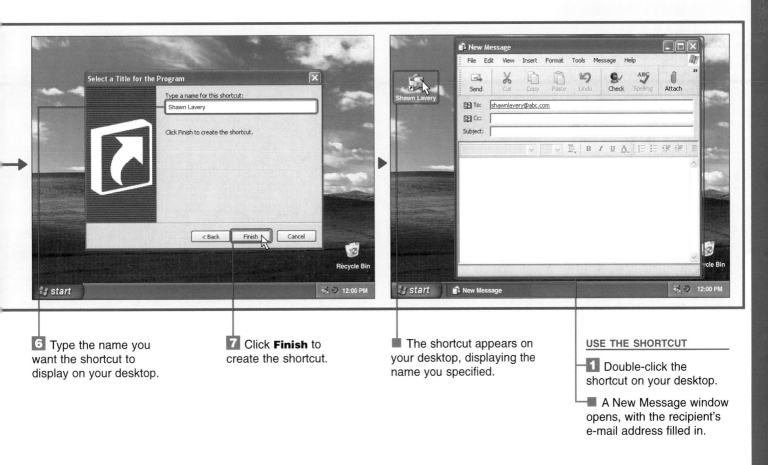

6 Type the name you want the shortcut to display on your desktop.

7 Click **Finish** to create the shortcut.

■ The shortcut appears on your desktop, displaying the name you specified.

USE THE SHORTCUT

1 Double-click the shortcut on your desktop.

■ A New Message window opens, with the recipient's e-mail address filled in.

205

When you e-mail a picture, you can have Windows reduce the size of the picture. Pictures with smaller sizes will transfer faster over the Internet and fit better on a recipient's computer screen.

Reducing the size of pictures is useful when you are e-mailing a large picture or many pictures, since many companies that provide e-mail accounts do not allow you to send or receive messages larger than a

certain file size. Reducing the size of a picture you are e-mailing does not change the original picture on your computer.

When you e-mail a picture, Windows displays text in your message and attaches the picture you selected to the message. You can replace the text Windows displays with the text you want the message to display.

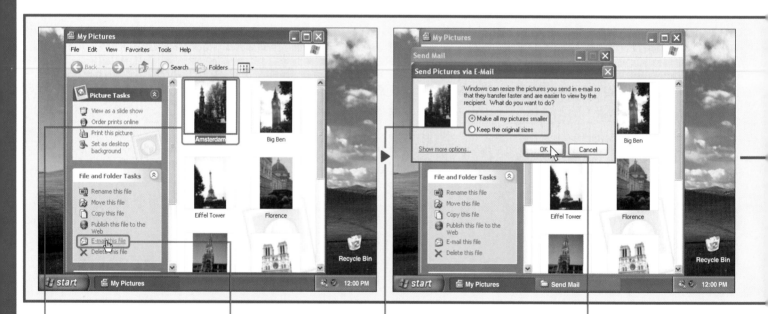

1 Click the picture you want to send in an e-mail message.

■ To send more than one picture in an e-mail message, press and hold down the **Ctrl** key as you click each picture you want to send.

2 Click **E-mail this file**.

*Note: If you selected multiple pictures, click **E-mail the selected items** in step 2.*

■ The Send Pictures via E-Mail dialog box appears, indicating that Windows can resize the picture you selected.

3 Click an option to make the picture smaller or keep the original size of the picture (○ changes to ◉).

4 Click **OK** to continue.

Did You Know? You can specify the size of a picture you selected to send in an e-mail message. In the Send Pictures via E-Mail dialog box, click the Show more options link and then click the option for the size you want to use (○ changes to ◉). You can choose a small, medium or large picture size.

Desktop Trick! If the picture you want to e-mail is located on your desktop, you can quickly e-mail the picture directly from your desktop. Right-click the picture and select Send To in the menu that appears. Then click Mail Recipient. You can then perform steps 3 to 8 below to send the message.

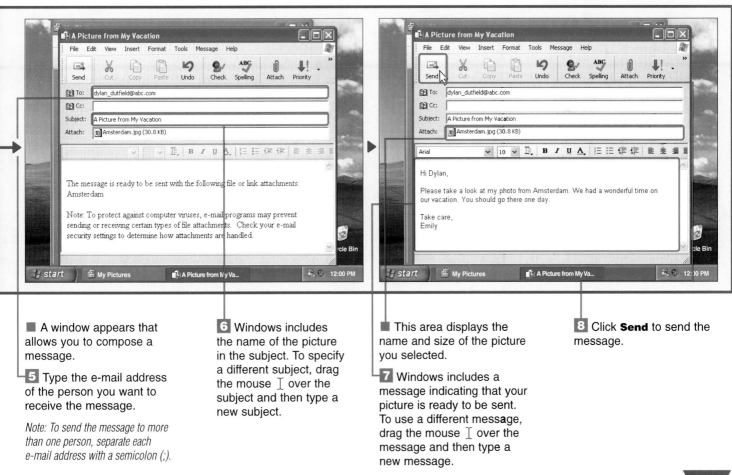

■ A window appears that allows you to compose a message.

5 Type the e-mail address of the person you want to receive the message.

Note: To send the message to more than one person, separate each e-mail address with a semicolon (;).

6 Windows includes the name of the picture in the subject. To specify a different subject, drag the mouse I over the subject and then type a new subject.

■ This area displays the name and size of the picture you selected.

7 Windows includes a message indicating that your picture is ready to be sent. To use a different message, drag the mouse I over the message and then type a new message.

8 Click **Send** to send the message.

Send an automatic e-mail reply when on vacation

You can create an e-mail message and have Outlook Express automatically deliver the message to everyone who sends you an e-mail message. This is useful if you want to send an automatic response to let people know that you are away on vacation and when you will be back.

You may also have another reason for sending the same reply to all of your e-mail messages. For example, you may have changed jobs and want to send automatic replies to let people know your new e-mail address. Keep in mind that the automatic reply will only be sent as long as your original e-mail address is active.

When creating your automatic reply, do not type any e-mail addresses in the To: or Cc: areas. Outlook Express will automatically fill in the appropriate e-mail address in the To: area each time a reply is sent.

You also do not need to type a subject in the Subject: area. When replying to a message, Outlook Express will use the subject "Re:" followed by the subject used by the sender, such as "Re: Sales Meeting."

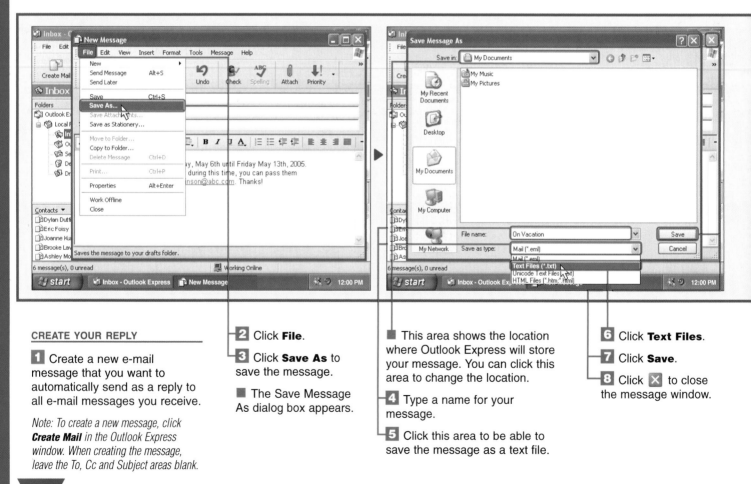

CREATE YOUR REPLY

1 Create a new e-mail message that you want to automatically send as a reply to all e-mail messages you receive.

Note: To create a new message, click ***Create Mail*** *in the Outlook Express window. When creating the message, leave the To, Cc and Subject areas blank.*

2 Click **File**.

3 Click **Save As** to save the message.

■ The Save Message As dialog box appears.

■ This area shows the location where Outlook Express will store your message. You can click this area to change the location.

4 Type a name for your message.

5 Click this area to be able to save the message as a text file.

6 Click **Text Files**.

7 Click **Save**.

8 Click ☒ to close the message window.

Attention! You will need to perform one extra step if you have previously created a rule to sort incoming messages. When you perform steps 1 to 3 on page 209, the Message Rules dialog box will appear rather than the New Mail Rule dialog box. To display the New Mail Rule dialog box to set up an automatic reply, click the New button in the Message Rules dialog box.

Did You Know? You can change how frequently Outlook Express will check for messages and send your automatic replies. In the Outlook Express window, choose the Tools menu and click Options. On the General tab, double-click the box beside "Check for new messages every" and type a new number of minutes. Then click OK to confirm your change.

CONTINUED ▶

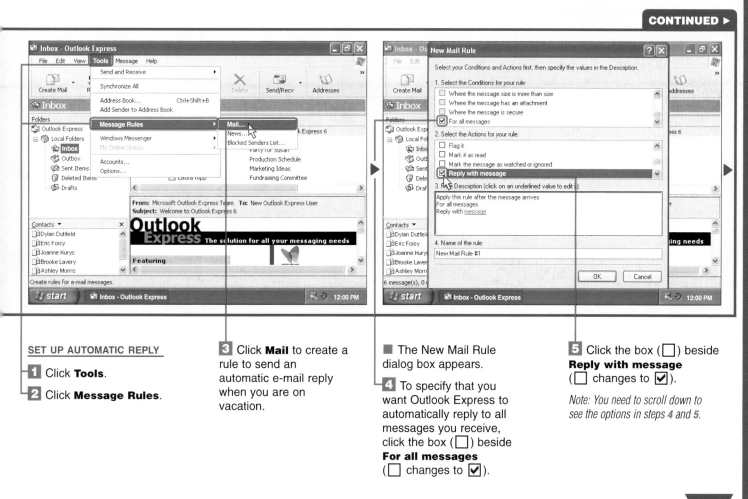

SET UP AUTOMATIC REPLY

1 Click **Tools**.

2 Click **Message Rules**.

3 Click **Mail** to create a rule to send an automatic e-mail reply when you are on vacation.

■ The New Mail Rule dialog box appears.

4 To specify that you want Outlook Express to automatically reply to all messages you receive, click the box (☐) beside **For all messages** (☐ changes to ☑).

5 Click the box (☐) beside **Reply with message** (☐ changes to ☑).

Note: You need to scroll down to see the options in steps 4 and 5.

Send an automatic e-mail reply when on vacation

You must keep Outlook Express open and your computer turned on and connected to the Internet for Outlook Express to be able to send your automatic replies. Outlook Express must also be set up to periodically check for new messages. By default, Outlook Express will automatically check for new messages every 30 minutes.

Each time you receive a message, Outlook Express will automatically send your automatic reply to your Outbox folder. When Outlook Express checks for new messages, your reply will be sent.

If you have set up Outlook Express to check your Hotmail account, Outlook Express cannot send automatic replies to messages the account receives. For information on setting up Outlook Express to check your Hotmail account, see task #88.

CONTINUED ▶

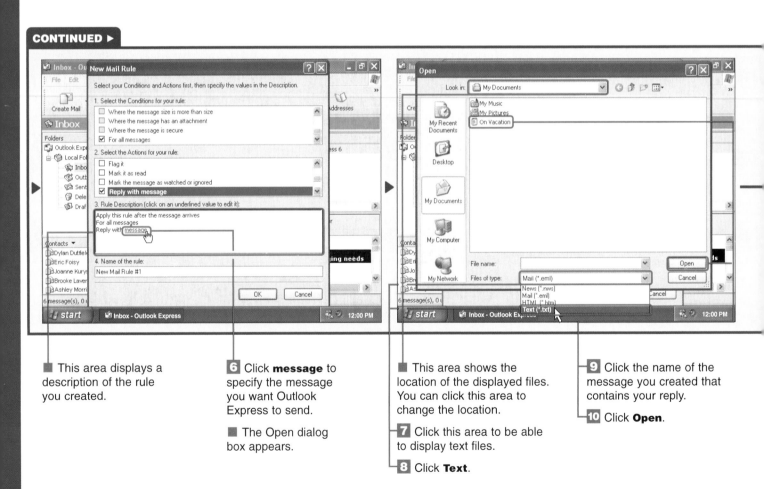

■ This area displays a description of the rule you created.

6 Click **message** to specify the message you want Outlook Express to send.

■ The Open dialog box appears.

■ This area shows the location of the displayed files. You can click this area to change the location.

7 Click this area to be able to display text files.

8 Click **Text**.

9 Click the name of the message you created that contains your reply.

10 Click **Open**.

Test It!   To test the automatic reply you set up, you need to ask another person to send you an e-mail message and then tell you if they received your automatic reply. Outlook Express will not allow you to test an automatic reply by sending yourself an e-mail message.

Stop It!   When you no longer want Outlook Express to send automatic replies, perform steps 1 to 3 on page 209 to display the Message Rules dialog box. Click the name of the rule you want to remove and then click the Remove button. In the confirmation dialog box that appears, click Yes to remove the rule. Then click OK to confirm your change.

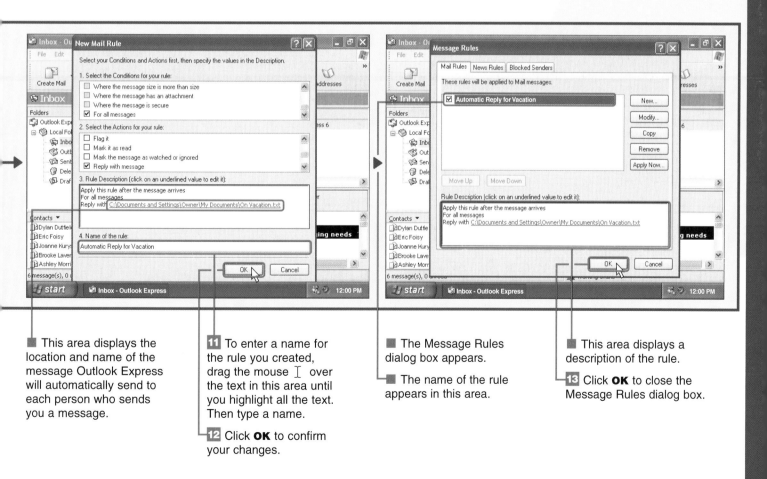

■ This area displays the location and name of the message Outlook Express will automatically send to each person who sends you a message.

11 To enter a name for the rule you created, drag the mouse I over the text in this area until you highlight all the text. Then type a name.

12 Click **OK** to confirm your changes.

■ The Message Rules dialog box appears.

■ The name of the rule appears in this area.

■ This area displays a description of the rule.

13 Click **OK** to close the Message Rules dialog box.

The address book in Outlook Express stores the contact information for people you frequently send messages to. You can print your address book to keep a printed copy of your contact information readily available. You may find printing your address book useful when you are going on vacation or a business trip.

Since your address book stores a wide variety of information, a printed copy of your address book can be a valuable resource. For example, in addition to e-mail addresses, your address book may include home and business addresses and phone numbers.

When printing your address book, you can choose to print the contact information for every contact or only a specific contact. You can also specify if you want to print all the contact information, only business-related information or just the phone numbers in your address book.

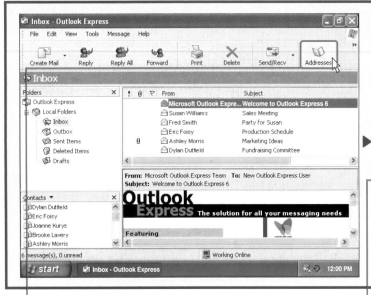

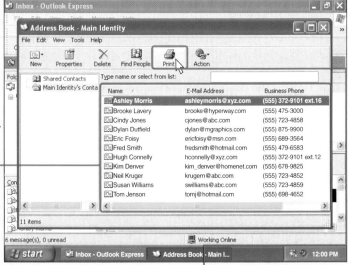

1 Click **Addresses** to display your address book.

■ The Address Book window appears.

■ This area displays the name, e-mail address and other information about each contact in your address book.

2 To print the information for every contact in your address book, click any contact in the list.

■ To print the information for only one contact, click the contact.

3 Click **Print** to print the information in your address book.

■ The Print dialog box appears.

Print a Group! To print the address book information for a group of contacts, you must select the contacts in your address book. To select a group of contacts in a continuous list, click the first contact you want to select and then press and hold down the Shift key as you click the last contact. To select random contacts, click one contact and then press and hold down the Ctrl key as you click each additional contact.

Change It! To change or add information for a contact in your address book, double-click the contact's name in the Address Book window. In the Properties dialog box that appears, click the appropriate tab and then make the changes or add the new information for the contact.

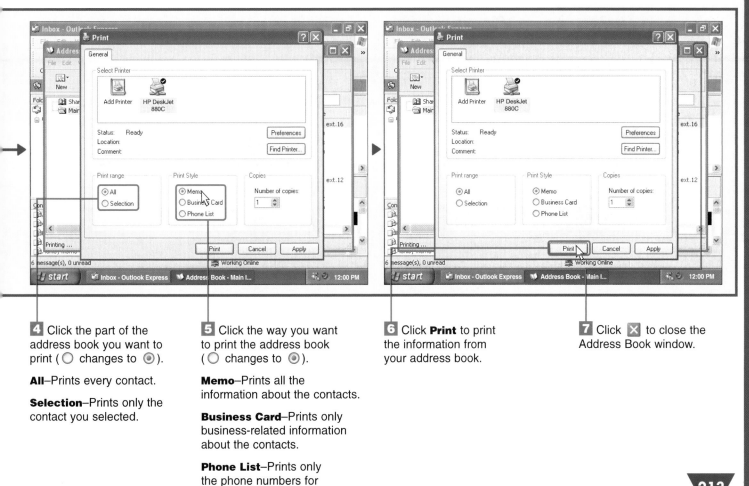

4 Click the part of the address book you want to print (⃝ changes to ⦿).

All–Prints every contact.

Selection–Prints only the contact you selected.

5 Click the way you want to print the address book (⃝ changes to ⦿).

Memo–Prints all the information about the contacts.

Business Card–Prints only business-related information about the contacts.

Phone List–Prints only the phone numbers for the contacts.

6 Click **Print** to print the information from your address book.

7 Click ✕ to close the Address Book window.

You can have Outlook Express automatically remove the messages stored in the Deleted Items folder each time you exit the program. Emptying the Deleted Items folder saves space on your computer and keeps the folder from becoming cluttered with old messages. The Deleted Items folder stores all the messages you have chosen to delete from other e-mail folders in Outlook Express.

You should keep in mind that the messages emptied from the Deleted Items folder will be permanently removed from your computer and will not be available the next time you open Outlook Express.

This means if you choose to automatically empty the folder, you will need to be careful to delete only messages you are sure you will not want to review again.

If you no longer want Outlook Express to delete messages stored in the Deleted Items folder when you exit the program, repeat the steps below to turn the option off. When the option is turned off, you can remove messages from the Deleted Items folder by deleting the messages manually.

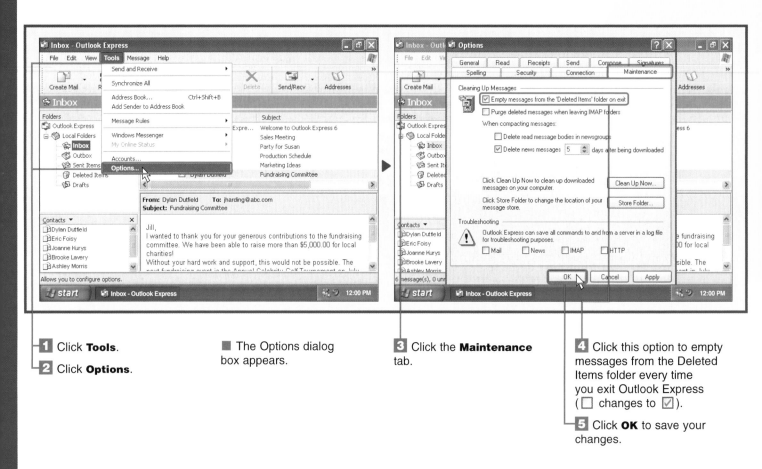

1 Click **Tools**.

2 Click **Options**.

■ The Options dialog box appears.

3 Click the **Maintenance** tab.

4 Click this option to empty messages from the Deleted Items folder every time you exit Outlook Express (☐ changes to ☑).

5 Click **OK** to save your changes.

You can stop Windows Messenger from starting automatically each time you turn on your computer. This prevents people from knowing when you are online and being able to send you instant messages, which can be useful if you want to start each day without any interruptions.

When you stop Windows Messenger from starting automatically, the Windows Messenger icon (👤) will no longer appear on the taskbar each time you turn on your computer.

When you want to be able to use Windows Messenger to send and receive instant messages, you will need to start the Windows Messenger program manually. Once you start the Windows Messenger program, the program will remain on until you turn off your computer.

If you once again want Windows Messenger to start automatically each time you turn on your computer, you can repeat the steps below to have the program start automatically.

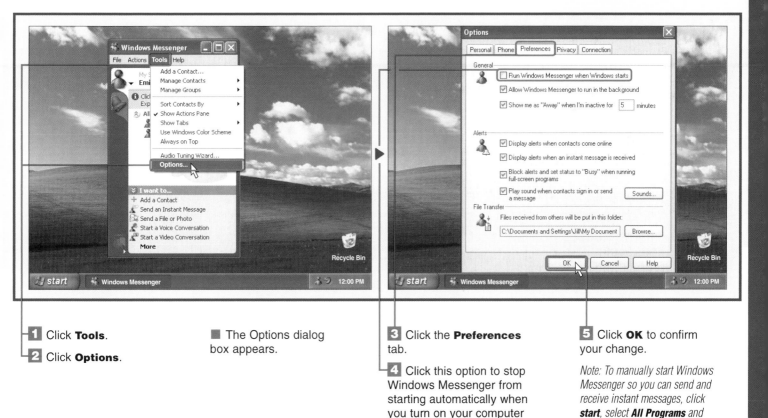

1 Click **Tools**.

2 Click **Options**.

■ The Options dialog box appears.

3 Click the **Preferences** tab.

4 Click this option to stop Windows Messenger from starting automatically when you turn on your computer (☑ changes to ☐).

5 Click **OK** to confirm your change.

*Note: To manually start Windows Messenger so you can send and receive instant messages, click **start**, select **All Programs** and then click **Windows Messenger**.*

Windows Messenger allows you to see and talk to another person over the Internet. Having a voice or video conversation over the Internet helps you avoid long-distance telephone charges.

To have a voice conversation with another person over the Internet using Windows Messenger, both computers must have sound capabilities and a microphone. To have a voice and video conversation, you must also have a video or web camera installed on your computer.

If the other person has a video or web camera installed, you will see video from the other person's camera during the conversation.

If your computer is protected by a firewall, you may not be able to use Windows Messenger to see or talk with another person.

The first time you start a voice or video conversation in Windows Messenger, the Audio and Video Tuning Wizard appears, helping you verify that your equipment is working properly.

TALK TO ANOTHER PERSON OVER THE INTERNET

1 Right-click the name of the person you want to talk to. A menu appears.

2 Click **Start a Voice Conversation**.

■ Windows Messenger sends the other person an invitation to start a voice conversation with you.

■ This message appears when the other person accepts the invitation. You can use your microphone to talk to the other person.

3 To adjust the speaker volume, drag this slider (▯) to the left or right.

4 To adjust the volume of your microphone, drag this slider (▯) to the left or right.

5 When you want to end the conversation, click **Stop Talking**.

Stop Rolling! You can stop your camera from sending video of yourself to the other person without ending the conversation. Below the video area, click Options and then select Stop Sending Video. Unless the other person stops sending video as well, you will continue to receive video from the other person's camera. You can repeat these steps to start sending video of yourself to the other person again.

Turn It Off! You can stop the small image of the video sent by your camera from appearing in your video area. Click Options below the video area and then select Show My Video as Picture-in-Picture to turn off the option. You can repeat these steps to turn on the Picture-in-Picture option again.

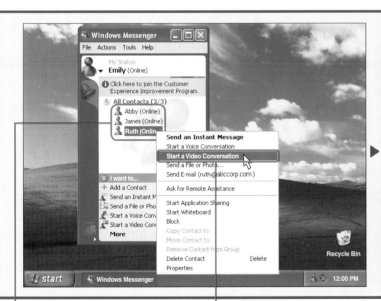

SEE EACH OTHER WHILE YOU TALK

1 Right-click the name of the person you want to talk to and see. A menu appears.

2 Click **Start a Video Conversation**.

■ Windows Messenger sends the other person an invitation to start a video and voice conversation with you.

■ This message appears when the other person accepts the invitation. You can use your microphone to talk to the other person.

■ This area displays the video sent by the other person's camera and a smaller image of the video sent by your camera.

3 When you want to end the conversation, click **Stop Camera**.

You can block a person from sending you instant messages in Windows Messenger. By default, anyone who knows the e-mail address you use with Windows Messenger can contact you. However, you can choose to block strangers or even a person in your contact list.

If you are in the contact list of a person you blocked, your status will always be shown as "Not Online" in their contact list. The person will not know you have blocked them from contacting you.

You can block a person when they add you to their contact list. You can choose to have Windows display a dialog box on your screen when someone adds you to their contact list. The dialog box will ask if you want to allow or block the person from contacting you.

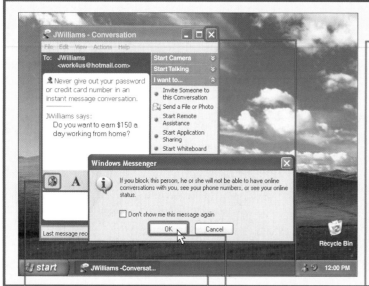

1 When you receive an instant message from a person you do not want to receive messages from, click 🔘 .

■ A dialog box appears, stating that if you block the person, the person will not be able to send you instant messages or view your online status.

2 Click **OK** to block the person.

3 Click 🗙 to close the Conversation window.

WORK WITH YOUR BLOCK LIST

1 In the Windows Messenger window, click **Tools**.

2 Click **Options**.

■ The Options dialog box appears.

Did You Know? You can see a list of all the people who have added you to their Windows Messenger contact list. In the Windows Messenger window, click Tools and then select Options. Click the Privacy tab and then click the View button. A list of people who have added you to their contact list appears. When you finish reviewing the list, click Close. Then click OK to close the Options dialog box.

Try This! If you are busy, you can let other people know that you are not available to exchange instant messages. In the Windows Messenger window, click your name. From the menu that appears, choose the option that best describes your status. Selecting Appear Offline prevents people from contacting you.

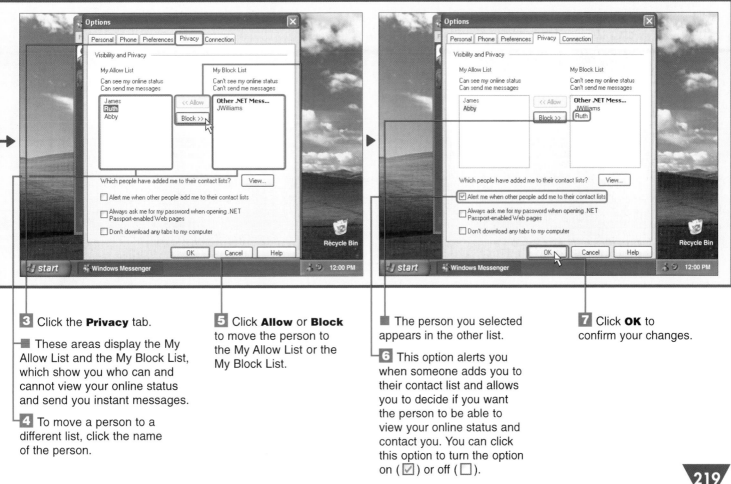

3 Click the **Privacy** tab.

■ These areas display the My Allow List and the My Block List, which show you who can and cannot view your online status and send you instant messages.

4 To move a person to a different list, click the name of the person.

5 Click **Allow** or **Block** to move the person to the My Allow List or the My Block List.

■ The person you selected appears in the other list.

6 This option alerts you when someone adds you to their contact list and allows you to decide if you want the person to be able to view your online status and contact you. You can click this option to turn the option on (☑) or off (☐).

7 Click **OK** to confirm your changes.

You can send a fax directly from your computer to a person across the city or around the world. Sending a fax from your computer saves you the time of having to print and then fax a document using a fax machine. The Windows fax feature is also useful when you do not have access to a fax machine.

You must have a fax device, such as a fax modem, installed on your computer to send and receive faxes.

The Send Fax Wizard allows you to fax a message on a cover page you specify. The wizard asks you for the information needed to send the fax, such as the name and fax number of the person you want to receive the fax.

The first time you use the fax feature, the Fax Configuration Wizard appears, allowing you to set up your computer to send and receive faxes. To set up your computer, click Next and then follow the instructions in the wizard. You must be logged on to Windows as a computer administrator to set up the fax component and specify options for sending and receiving faxes.

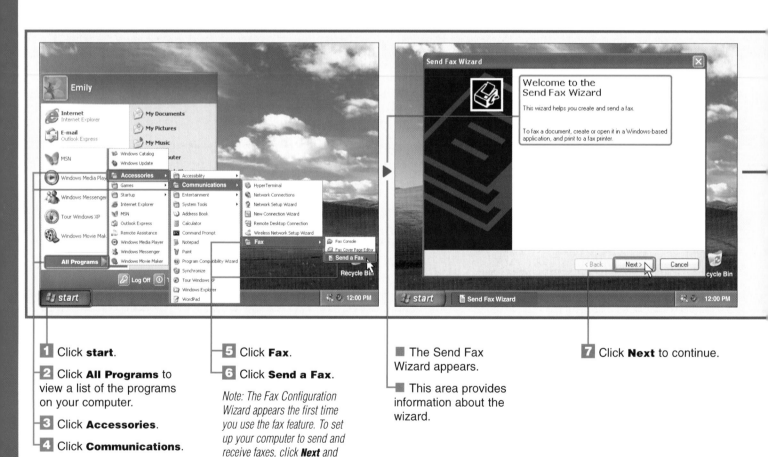

1 Click **start**.

2 Click **All Programs** to view a list of the programs on your computer.

3 Click **Accessories**.

4 Click **Communications**.

5 Click **Fax**.

6 Click **Send a Fax**.

*Note: The Fax Configuration Wizard appears the first time you use the fax feature. To set up your computer to send and receive faxes, click **Next** and then follow the instructions in the wizard.*

■ The Send Fax Wizard appears.

■ This area provides information about the wizard.

7 Click **Next** to continue.

Important! You must add the Fax Services component to your computer to be able to send and receive faxes. Only a computer administrator can add a component. Click start, select Control Panel, choose Add or Remove Programs and then click Add/Remove Windows Components. Click the box beside Fax Services (☐ changes to ☑) and then click Next. Insert the Windows XP CD-ROM disc when prompted and click OK. Then click Finish to close the Windows Components Wizard.

Change It! To change your computer's fax settings at any time, perform steps 1 to 5 below and then click Fax Console. In the Fax Console window, click the Tools menu and then click Configure Fax to start the Fax Configuration Wizard. Follow the instructions in the wizard to adjust your fax settings.

CONTINUED ▶

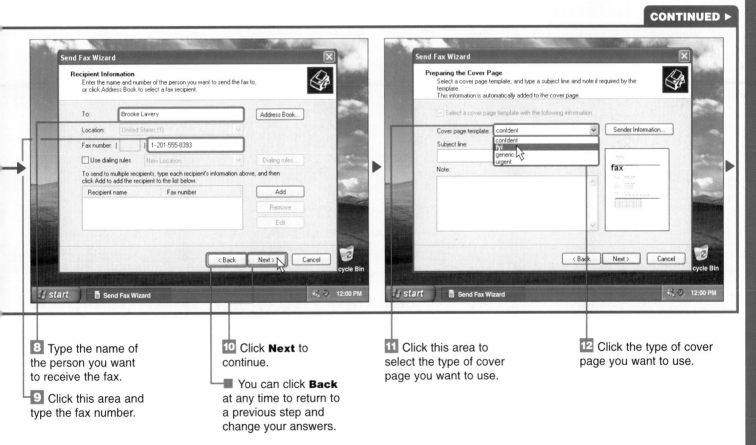

8 Type the name of the person you want to receive the fax.

9 Click this area and type the fax number.

10 Click **Next** to continue.

■ You can click **Back** at any time to return to a previous step and change your answers.

11 Click this area to select the type of cover page you want to use.

12 Click the type of cover page you want to use.

When sending a fax, you can include a subject for the fax, as well as a note to the person who will receive the fax.

Windows allows you to specify when you want to send the fax. You can send the fax immediately, when long-distance rates are lower or at a specific time within the next 24 hours. If you do not send the fax immediately, make sure your computer is turned on when the fax will be sent.

You can also specify a priority for your fax. If you are sending multiple faxes, higher priority faxes will be sent first.

While you are sending a fax, the Fax Monitor dialog box appears, displaying the status of the fax and the time that has elapsed since Windows started sending the fax. The Fax Monitor icon ( ) also appears on the taskbar.

After you send a fax, Windows stores a copy of the fax in the Sent Items folder in the Fax Console. Faxes you have chosen to send later are stored in the Outbox folder in the Fax Console.

CONTINUED ▶

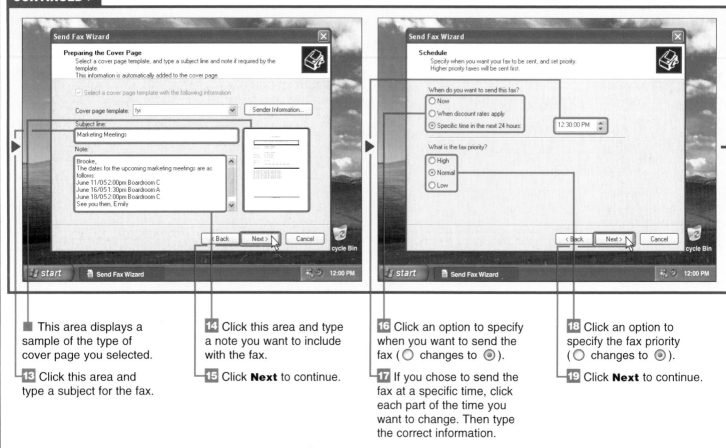

■ This area displays a sample of the type of cover page you selected.

13 Click this area and type a subject for the fax.

14 Click this area and type a note you want to include with the fax.

15 Click **Next** to continue.

16 Click an option to specify when you want to send the fax (○ changes to ◉).

17 If you chose to send the fax at a specific time, click each part of the time you want to change. Then type the correct information.

18 Click an option to specify the fax priority (○ changes to ◉).

19 Click **Next** to continue.

Apply It! You can usually fax a document directly from a program using the program's Print feature. In the program's window, select the File menu and click Print. In the Print dialog box, select the fax device as the printer you want to send the document to and then click the Print button. The Send Fax Wizard will start so you can continue sending the fax.

Preview It! The Send Fax Wizard allows you to see a preview of your fax before you send it. To preview the fax, click the Preview Fax button before performing step 20 below. Windows will display a preview of the fax in the Windows Picture and Fax Viewer window.

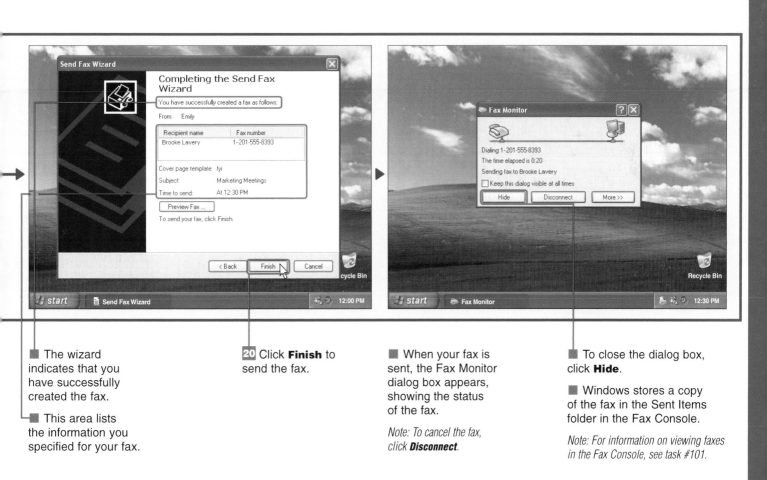

■ The wizard indicates that you have successfully created the fax.

■ This area lists the information you specified for your fax.

20 Click **Finish** to send the fax.

■ When your fax is sent, the Fax Monitor dialog box appears, showing the status of the fax.

*Note: To cancel the fax, click **Disconnect**.*

■ To close the dialog box, click **Hide**.

■ Windows stores a copy of the fax in the Sent Items folder in the Fax Console.

Note: For information on viewing faxes in the Fax Console, see task #101.

#101 | View faxes on your computer

You can use the Fax Console to view faxes you have sent as well as faxes you have created that have not yet been sent. If your computer is set up to receive faxes, you can also view faxes you have received. For information on changing your computer's fax settings to allow you to receive faxes, see the tip area on page 221.

The Fax Console has four folders that store your faxes. The Incoming folder temporarily stores faxes as you receive them. The Inbox folder stores faxes you have received. The Outbox folder stores faxes waiting to be sent and the Sent Items folder stores faxes you have sent.

When you double-click a fax stored in a folder in the Fax Console, Windows displays the fax in the Windows Picture and Fax Viewer window. Keep in mind that you cannot view or modify a fax using a word processing program.

You can easily delete a fax from the Fax Console by simply clicking the fax and pressing the Delete key. Then click Yes to confirm the deletion.

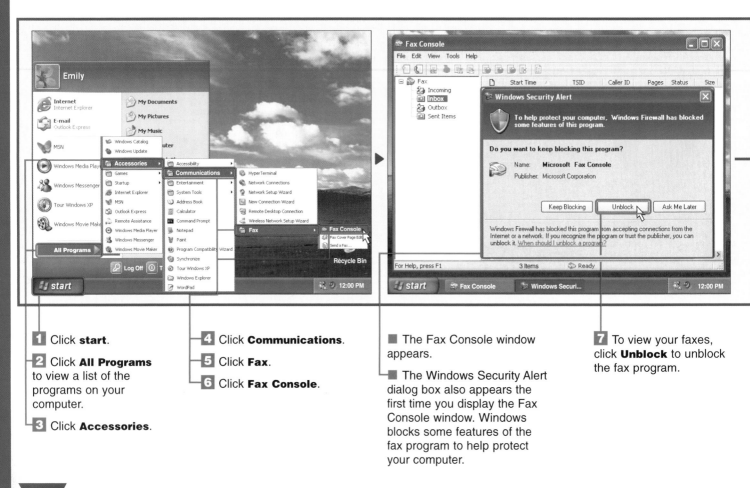

1 Click **start**.

2 Click **All Programs** to view a list of the programs on your computer.

3 Click **Accessories**.

4 Click **Communications**.

5 Click **Fax**.

6 Click **Fax Console**.

■ The Fax Console window appears.

■ The Windows Security Alert dialog box also appears the first time you display the Fax Console window. Windows blocks some features of the fax program to help protect your computer.

7 To view your faxes, click **Unblock** to unblock the fax program.

Rotate It! You can rotate a fax in the Windows Picture
and Fax Viewer window to change the way the
fax appears on your screen. Click ▨ to rotate
the fax 90 degrees clockwise or click ▨ to
rotate the fax 90 degrees counterclockwise.

More Options! The Windows Picture and Fax Viewer
window provides other options you
can use to work with a fax you are
viewing. You can click ✎ to highlight
a section of the fax or click Ⓐ or ▢
to add a note to the fax. You can also
click ▨ to print the fax or click ▨
to save the fax to a new location on
your computer.

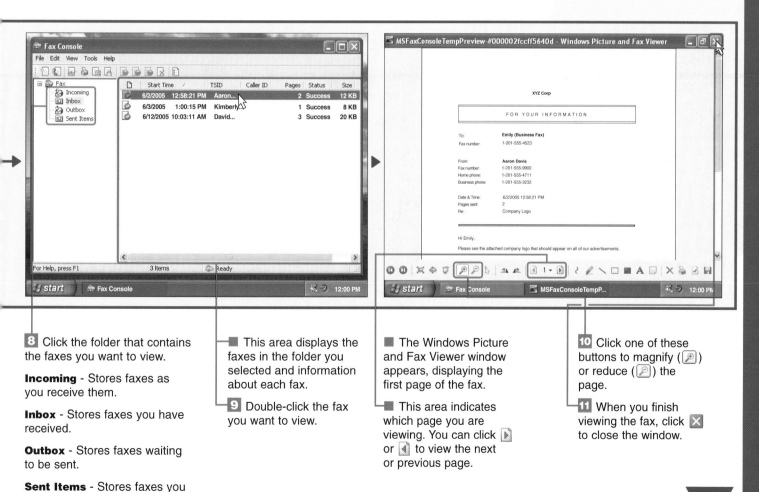

8 Click the folder that contains
the faxes you want to view.

Incoming - Stores faxes as
you receive them.

Inbox - Stores faxes you have
received.

Outbox - Stores faxes waiting
to be sent.

Sent Items - Stores faxes you
have sent.

■ This area displays the
faxes in the folder you
selected and information
about each fax.

9 Double-click the fax
you want to view.

■ The Windows Picture
and Fax Viewer window
appears, displaying the
first page of the fax.

■ This area indicates
which page you are
viewing. You can click ▶
or ◀ to view the next
or previous page.

10 Click one of these
buttons to magnify (⊕)
or reduce (⊖) the
page.

11 When you finish
viewing the fax, click ✕
to close the window.

225

Index

Index

Index

Index

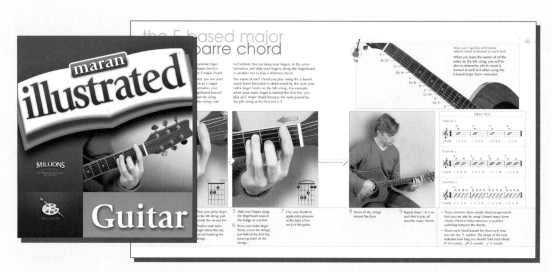

PIANO

MARAN ILLUSTRATED™ Piano is an information-packed resource for people who want to learn to play the piano, as well as current musicians looking to hone their skills. Combining full-color photographs and easy-to-follow instructions, this guide covers everything from the basics of piano playing to more advanced techniques. Not only does MARAN ILLUSTRATED™ Piano show you how to read music, play scales and chords and improvise while playing with other musicians, it also provides you with helpful information for purchasing and caring for your piano. You will also learn what to look for when you buy a piano or piano accessories, how to find the best location for your piano and how to clean your piano.

ISBN: 1-894182-13-8

Price: $24.99 US; $33.95 CDN

Page count: 304

DOG TRAINING

MARAN ILLUSTRATED™ Dog Training is an excellent guide for both current dog owners and people considering making a dog part of their family. Using clear, step-by-step instructions accompanied by over 400 full-color photographs, MARAN ILLUSTRATED™ Dog Training is perfect for any visual learner who prefers seeing what to do rather than reading lengthy explanations.

Beginning with insights into popular dog breeds and puppy development, this book emphasizes positive training methods to guide you through socializing, housetraining and teaching your dog many commands. You will also learn how to work with problem behaviors, such as destructive chewing, excessive barking and separation anxiety.

ISBN: 1-894182-16-2

Price: $19.99 US; $26.95 CDN

Page count: 256

KNITTING & CROCHETING

MARAN ILLUSTRATED™ Knitting & Crocheting contains a wealth of information about these two increasingly popular crafts. Whether you are just starting out or you are an experienced knitter or crocheter interested in picking up new tips and techniques, this information-packed resource will take you from the basics, such as how to hold the knitting needles or crochet hook and create different types of stitches, to more advanced skills, such as how to add decorative touches to your projects and fix mistakes. The easy-to-follow information is communicated through clear, step-by-step instructions and accompanied by over 600 full-color photographs—perfect for any visual learner.

This book also includes numerous easy-to-follow patterns for all kinds of items, from simple crocheted scarves to cozy knitted baby outfits.

ISBN: 1-894182-14-6
Price: $24.99 US; $33.95 CDN
Page count: 304

WEIGHT TRAINING

MARAN ILLUSTRATED™ Weight Training is an information-packed guide that covers all the basics of weight training, as well as more advanced techniques and exercises.

MARAN ILLUSTRATED™ Weight Training contains more than 500 full-color photographs of exercises for every major muscle group, along with clear, step-by-step instructions for performing the exercises. Useful tips provide additional information and advice to help enhance your weight training experience.

MARAN ILLUSTRATED™ Weight Training provides all the information you need to start weight training or to refresh your technique if you have been weight training for some time.

ISBN: 1-894182-10-3
Price: $24.99 US; $33.95 CDN
Page count: 320